DIVE INTO HISTORY

VOLUME 1:
WARSHIPS

HENRY C. KEATTS and GEORGE C. FARR

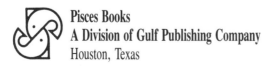

Pisces Books
A Division of Gulf Publishing Company
Houston, Texas

DIVE INTO HISTORY™

VOLUME 1:

WARSHIPS

Library of Congress Cataloging-in-Publication Data
Keatts, Henry.
  Warships / Henry C. Keatts and George C. Farr.
    p.   cm. — (Dive into history ; v. 1)
  Includes bibliographical references and index.
  ISBN 1-55992-039-4
  1. United States—History, Naval.   2. Warships—Atlantic Coast
(U.S.)—History.   3. Shipwrecks—Atlantic Coast (U.S.)—History.
4. Scuba diving—Atlantic Coast (U.S.)   5. Warships—Florida—Florida
Keys—History.   6. Shipwrecks—Florida—Florida Keys—History.
7. Scuba diving—Florida—Florida Keys.   I. Farr, George. II. Title.
III . Series.
E182.K27   1990
359′.00973—dc20   90-7428
                                                                CIP

CONTENTS

Preface, vi

Acknowledgments, vii

INTRODUCTION — EVOLUTION OF THE WARSHIP

The Development of the Sailing Warship 2, Armored Warships 3, Battleships 3, Cruisers 6, Destroyers 8

SAILING SHIPS

Chapter 1: **H.M.S.** *Cerberus* — **Scuttled Defender** **11**

Battle of Rhode Island 13, Defense Strategy 14, Self Destruct 16, Naval Action 17, British Triumph 18, Salvage 19

Chapter 2: **H.M.S.** *Culloden* — **Pilot Blunder** **23**

War Service 24, Nature Intervenes 25, Fortunes of War 26, French Threat 27, Disaster 29, Salvage 31, Search 32, Success 35, Pre-empted Claim 37, Preservation 38, Diving H.M.S. *Culloden* 40

Chapter 3: **U.S.S.** *Ohio* — **Power, Grace, and Speed** **43**

Colonial Navy 44, A Country Is Born 45, New Navy 46, Ships-of-the-Line 47, U.S.S. *Ohio* Is Launched 48, End of a Naval Career 53, Rediscovery of U.S.S. *Ohio* 55, Diving U.S.S. *Ohio* 56

Chapter 4: U.S.S. *New Hampshire* — The Last
Ship-of-the-Line 59

Salvage 63, Diving U.S.S. *New Hampshire* 64

Chapter 5: U.S.S. *Alligator* — Pirate Hunter 67

Diving U.S.S. *Alligator* 72

CRUISERS

Chapter 6: U.S.S. *Yankee* — Converted Liner 74

"Remember the *Maine!*" 75, Spanish-American War 76, Diving
U.S.S. *Yankee* 78

Chapter 7: U.S.S. *Schurz* — German-American Warship 81

Diving U.S.S. *Schurz* 88

Chapter 8: U.S.S. *San Diego* — Mined or Torpedoed? 91

The Sinking 95, Mine or Torpedo? 97, Liberty Bonds 100, Salvage
101, Diving U.S.S. *San Diego* 103

Chapter 9: U.S.S. *Wilkes-Barre* — Lethal Lady 108

Iwo Jima 112, Okinawa 113, Diving U.S.S. *Wilkes-Barre* 129

DESTROYERS, CUTTERS, AND PATROL VESSELS

Chapter 10: U.S.S. *Jacob Jones* — Double Jeopardy 132

Diving U.S.S. *Jacob Jones* 137

Chapter 11: U.S.S. *Sturtevant* — Sunk by a U.S. Mine 139

Salvage 141

Chapter 12: H.M.C.S. *St. Francis* — Lend-Lease
Four-Stacker 143

Convoy Escorts 144

Chapter 13: U.S.S. *Turner*—Disarming Error 149

Convoy Duty 150, Disaster 151

Chapter 14: **Revenue Cutter *Mohawk* — Cadet at Fault** **158**

Collision 158, Diving *Mohawk* 161

Chapter 15: **U.S.C.G. Cutters *Duane* and *Bibb* — An Honorable Artificial Reef** **163**

World War II 166, Artificial Reef 172, Diving *Duane* and *Bibb* 174

Chapter 16: **U.S.S. *Moonstone* — Luxurious Sub-Chaser** **176**

Diving U.S.S. *Moonstone* 178

THE DISCOVERED & UNDISCOVERED

Chapter 17: **A Summary of Warship Wrecks** **180**

Sailing Vessels: H.M.S. *Winchester* 180, H.M.S. *Feversham* and *Ferret* 181, *Le Chameau* 181, H.M.S. *Astrea* 181, *Celebre, Entreppenant, Capricieux* 181, H.M.S. *Augusta* and *Merlin* 182, H.M.S. *Tribune* 186, H.M.S. *DeBraak* 187, *General Arnold* 189, H.M.S. *Zebra* 190, *Warren* and *Defence* 190, H.M.S. *Amaranth* 201, U.S.S. *Huron* 201, H.M.S. *Somerset* 202, H.M.S. *Phoenix* 203

Battleships: U.S.S. *Texas* 203, U.S.S. *Massachusetts* 206

Destroyers, Cutters, and Assorted Vessels: H.M.C.S. *Assiniboine* 208, *Alexander* 208, *Albert Gallatin* 208, U.S.S. *Grouse* 210, U.S.S. *Strength* 213, U.S.S. *Tarantula* 213, U.S.S. *PC-11* and *-1203* 214, H.M.S. *Senateur Duhamel, Bedfordshire*, and *Pentland Firth* 214, U.S.S. *Rankin* 215

Chapter 18: **Warships Awaiting Discovery** **217**

Canada 217, Maine 220, Massachusetts 221, Rhode Island 221, New York 223, New Jersey 227, Delaware 228, Maryland 228, Virginia 228, North Carolina 230, South Carolina 233, Georgia 233, Florida 234

Bibliography **236**

Index **241**

PREFACE

Shipwrecks emit their siren song to sport divers, those intrepid amateur historians, photographers, salvagers, and artifact hunters who eagerly travel long distances at great expense to forego comfort and risk death in a brief dive to the site of a historic shipwreck. But expense, discomfort, and danger are a small price to pay for the opportunity to spend moments with sunken relics—to dive into history.

This first volume of the *Dive into History* series provides historical background on warships that date back as far as the American Revolution. Ships from the great age of sail, cruisers, destroyers, cutters, and patrol craft provide a glimpse at 200 years of American history. The era is one of momentous transition from sail to nuclear propulsion, wooden to armored hulls and primitive cannon to modern armament. That is the environment into which the curious scuba diver probes in search of historic naval artifacts that link the present to the past.

The floor of the Atlantic Ocean off the Eastern Seaboard of the United States is littered with the remains of many U.S. Navy vessels. Each has its own appeal, but as a group they share a special attraction as seaborne defenders of the principles of freedom and democracy that have been cornerstones of the United States since its inception. The warships selected for inclusion in this volume are primarily American, but several British ships of the Revolutionary period are also included. Others equally interesting have been excluded because they lie in depths greater than 250 feet, well beyond the limits of an amateur scuba diver. (Civil War warships will be covered in a future volume.)

This book is not an academic treatise, but one imperative has been rigidly observed in its preparation. Historical accuracy has been pursued to the fullest possible extent. If incorrect data, misinterpretation, undue emphasis, or lack of information exist, we would welcome input from our readers. It would be fruitless, even damaging to perpetuate a misleading historical representation. Additional information forwarded to Professor Henry Keatts, Suffolk Community College, Riverhead, N.Y. 11901 will receive appreciative attention and confirming research for inclusion in further editions of this work.

Henry C. Keatts
George C. Farr

ACKNOWLEDGMENTS

Without the contributions and cooperation of the following individuals and organizations, this book would not have been possible:

Frank Benoit
Steve Bielenda
Mel Brenner
Bill Campbell
Bill Carter
Bob Cembrola
Dave Clancy
Chip Cooper
Carlton Davidson

Billy Deans
Michael deCamp
Tim Firmie
Aaron Hirsch
Peter Hess
Jon Hulburt
Larry Listing
Mason Logie
Mike Moore

Bill Palmer
William P. Quinn
Tom Roach
Bill Scheibel
Brian Skerry
Brad Sheard
Mrs. Paul Sherman
Corky & Geo Toth
David Warsen

Hawaii State Archives
Historical Maritime Group of
    New England
Library of Congress
Mariners' Museum
National Archives
National Maritime Museum
Naval Historical Center

Old Print Shop
Peabody Museum of Salem
Portsmouth (N.H.) Naval Shipyard
Suffolk County Historical
    Society
U.S. Coast Guard
U.S. Naval Institute
WZ-Bilddienst

Special thanks are due to Viking Diving Division for use of their excellent diving suits and Poseidon regulators.

Locations of Shipwrecks

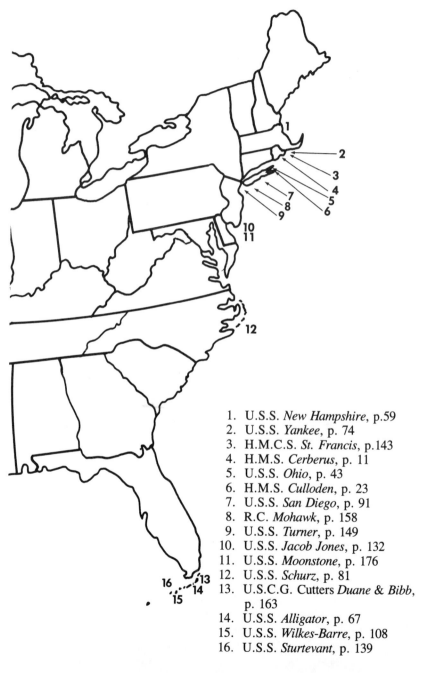

1. U.S.S. *New Hampshire*, p.59
2. U.S.S. *Yankee*, p. 74
3. H.M.C.S. *St. Francis*, p.143
4. H.M.S. *Cerberus*, p. 11
5. U.S.S. *Ohio*, p. 43
6. H.M.S. *Culloden*, p. 23
7. U.S.S. *San Diego*, p. 91
8. R.C. *Mohawk*, p. 158
9. U.S.S. *Turner*, p. 149
10. U.S.S. *Jacob Jones*, p. 132
11. U.S.S. *Moonstone*, p. 176
12. U.S.S. *Schurz*, p. 81
13. U.S.C.G. Cutters *Duane & Bibb*, p. 163
14. U.S.S. *Alligator*, p. 67
15. U.S.S. *Wilkes-Barre*, p. 108
16. U.S.S. *Sturtevant*, p. 139

Evolution of the Warship

An observer from outer space would be thwarted searching for the blue planet Earth in the expanse of the universe. Even the small star that holds it in orbit is a mere speck in the outer fringe of the galaxy we call the Milky Way. However, when the planet can be brought into view, it is clear that it is blue because seven-eighths of its surface is covered with seas, oceans, rivers, and lakes. The land portion is populated by a host of plants, trees, insects, birds, and animals dominated by two-legged creatures called man. Man rates higher in intelligence than other forms of life on the little globe, although that is not always apparent in his acts of self-destruction. His self-indulgence is ruining the atmosphere, polluting the seas, stripping the forests, poisoning the soil, and destroying those of his fellow men who disagree with him by a practice called war.

It is easy to speculate that the separation by water of one land mass from another stirred early man's interest in crossing from one side to the other. If the distance was short enough he could swim. If not, straddling a bobbing tree trunk would lead to lashing several together, then hollowing them out for crew, passengers, and cargo. Propulsion, first by current and paddling, was improved on with rigid, flat blades forced through the water by occupants of the craft. When someone realized that the wind could be harnessed to do the job better, skins of animals, woven sheets, or the like mounted on sticks above the boat allowed the wind to push it without manual effort. That worked so long as the wind blew toward the destination. Boatmen either rowed their way back or waited for a favorable change of wind

1

direction. As boats became larger and faster over the centuries, transportation and trade over the water increased.

The growth of water-borne commerce spawned attacks by predators and enemies, forcing merchants to arm their vessels for defense and nations to develop vessels for warfare. The earliest warships are credited to the Egyptians and Cretans, who built galleys propelled by 20 oars. The early Egyptian navy was based near Memphis and served primarily to transport the army, its supplies, and tribute from foreign lands. But the walls of Ramses III's (1190-1158 B.C.) mortuary temple record a great naval battle with the Sea Peoples. The Phoenicians added a second bank of oars to the galleys. Triremes, featuring three banks of oars were introduced in about 700 B.C. by the Greeks and Phoenicians. The trireme was the standard warship of the Mediterranean for the next 200 years.

The problem of sailing against the wind continued to plague mariners until Norwegian ships added a steering oar that was operated with a tiller off the right stern side of their boats. That "steer-board" came to be known as "starboard," the term that still refers to the right side of any vessel.

Several important changes occurred in ship design between about A.D. 1200 and the advent of the great age of sail that extended from 1460 until 1860. The Norwegian steering oar was replaced by the stern rudder for direction control. Its unknown inventor is believed to have been a shipwright in one of the lowland European countries on the North Sea, possibly Holland. The stern rudder was secured to the stern post on which it was pivoted laterally to change the course of the vessel. With it perverse winds could be harnessed to improve ship performance. That objective led to deeper hulls, hull shape changes, and vastly improved rigging. Masts were added and sails were changed in size, shape, and location on the vessel.

Viking warships changed to cope with an inherent defensive weakness; their low midships freeboard made them susceptible to easy boarding by the enemy. Housings called "castles" were raised on the bow and stern to provide the Vikings with final retreats for defense against boarding invaders. The structure in the bow was the "forecastle," later abbreviated to fo'c'sle, the forward part of the vessel designated for crew's quarters. That high bow and high stern profile influenced ship design until 1860. The Spanish galleon is a familiar example of that contour.

The Development of Sailing Warships

Heavy cast iron cannon were added to warships to increase their destructive power. The ships became larger, and the tactics of naval warfare changed. The greatest damage could be inflicted from a ship by standing off and delivering broadsides against an enemy. In a fleet engagement British warships of like firepower formed a battle line, stem to stern, windward of the enemy for maneuverability and freedom from the drifting smoke of cannon fire. The combined broadside of such a formation concentrated the maximum volume of fire on the foe. Warships of the British Royal Navy with 20 guns or more were rated on a scale based on their armament. Those of 64 or more guns were designated "ships-of-the-line" or "line-of-battle ships," from which the term battleship was derived. They were the ships of war large enough to have a place in the line of battle. They had earlier been referred to as "capital ships," a term that still refers to larger warships.

The British rating system changed between 1677 and 1792 from including only "ships-of-the-line" to six rates with 33 variations of number and size of guns. First- and second-rate ships were those of 90 to 110 guns (battleships); third-rate carried 64 to 80 guns (cruisers); fourth- or common-rate carried 50 to 74 guns (also cruisers); fifth-rate ships, with 32 to 40 guns (frigates), were used as commerce raiders; and sixth-rate ships, with 16 to 22 guns (sloops), served as couriers and escorts. The crews ranged from 195 sailors on a 125-foot sixth-rate sloop to 720 on a 490-foot first-rate "ship-of-the-line."

Armored Warships

The first departure from wooden warships was the French Navy's *Gloire* in 1860, which had a belt of armor plate around the hull and was powered by steam. The day she was launched marked the end of wooden warships powered by sail. Two years later two fully armed, low profile warships, *Monitor* and *Merrimac* sounded the death knell for the great age of sail in their 1862 confrontation at Hampton Roads, Virginia during the American Civil War.

Battleships

By the end of the 19th century armor-plated, steam-driven warships featuring 12- and 13-inch long-range guns dominated the navies of the world. The effectiveness of armor plate posed a challenge that was countered by armor-piercing shells. The age of the armor-plated, big-gun battleship hurling armor-piercing shells arrived with the defeat of the Russians in the Russo-Japanese War of 1904-05. In a precursor to the sneak attack on Pearl Harbor 37 years later, Japanese torpedo boats struck the Russian fleet in Port Arthur without warning on February 8, 1904. On May 27, 1905 the Russian Baltic fleet of 30 warships reached Tsushima Strait, between Japan and Korea after a 10,000-mile voyage around the Cape of Good Hope. The

The 1862 confrontation between the armored, steam-powered Monitor *and* Merrimac *sounded the death knell for the Great Age of Sail. (Courtesy of the Naval Historical Center.)*

Japanese fleet under Admiral Togo Haihachiro intercepted the Russians in the world's first fleet action between ironclad warships. The next day only 6 of the 30 Russian warships had escaped from the heavier-gunned Japanese force that had hurled armor-piercing shells from long-range, high-caliber guns in an overwhelming demonstration of power.

The ensuing naval race ushered in a period referred to as the "Dreadnaught Era." Size, speed, and armament advances by one country signalled other naval powers to build even larger, faster, and more heavily armed goliaths. By the beginning of World War I, the British had 28 battleships and 9 battlecruisers; Germany had 22 battleships and 5 battlecruisers; and the United States had 12 battleships, 45 destroyers, and a few small submarines.

World War I

Most World War I battleships were protected by up to 16 inches of armor. The added weight of that protection made the ponderous warships slow and more difficult to maneuver. In order to achieve a faster warship with the firepower of a battleship, the British adopted a concept that had been suggested in 1896 by a French ship builder, Emile Bertin. Sir John Fisher, First Sea Lord of the British Admiralty had three battlecruisers laid down (construction began) in 1906. They had all the firepower of a battleship, but only seven inches of armor protected their gun turrets and other vital areas including ammunition magazines.

The Battle of Jutland was a massive sea engagement that pitted the German High Seas Fleet under Vice Admiral Rheinhard Scheer, commander-in-chief of the German Navy, against the British Grand Fleet commanded by Admiral Sir John Jellicoe. On May 31, 1916 the folly of Fisher's sacrifice of armor for speed was demonstrated by 11-inch armor-piercing German shells. The British lost three of their battlecruisers that might have survived with heavier armor. They also lost three heavy cruisers and eight destroyers. German losses were one battleship, one battlecruiser, four light cruisers, and five destroyers. Of even greater significance, the failure of the more powerful British fleet to destroy the German force was attributed to the lack of "eyes" (today's radar and air reconnaissance) to guide Admiral Jellicoe, aboard the powerful blind battleship *Iron Duke,* to the fleeing enemy as daylight waned. That disadvantage prompted him to call off pursuit until the following morning rather than risk the loss of his battleships to German torpedoes or mines.

After Jutland, the world's naval powers concluded that battleships were too vulnerable to mines and torpedoes, were "fair-weather" ships that were effective only against targets that were in view of the bridge, and were too costly to build and maintain. The 1922 Washington Naval Conference agreed to limit battleships to 35,000 tons and 16-inch guns. U.S. Army General William "Billy" Mitchell was convinced that battleships were also vulnerable to air attack. He conducted tests in 1921 and 1923 to prove that conviction. His airmen sank three old battleships, a destroyer, and a light cruiser. Critics objected that the targets were undefended against the bombing attacks and that the sinking of the ex-German battleship *Ostriesland* in 1921 was accomplished by 2 near-misses after 16 direct bomb hits had failed. Advocates of the battleship also pointed to the failure of a test of aerial bombs against the U.S. battleship *Washington* in 1924. The bombs were placed underwater at distances of 60 and 30 feet from *Washington's* hull, then detonated from the surface. Work parties, forerunners of the Underwater Explosive Research Division (see Chapter 9), went on board to check hull damage. *Washington* was sunk later by broadsides from the battleship *Texas.* In August 1989, after extensive research, Gary Gentile located the wreck keel up in 280 feet of water, off the coast of Virginia.

Mitchell's findings made little impression on the navies of the world, and a new flurry of battleship construction followed. By September 1939, the British had added five of 44,000 tons, Germany two of 52,000 tons, the

United States four of 58,000 tons, and two mammoth 72,000-ton battleships with 18-inch guns had been added to the Japanese Navy.

Mitchell's proof of the battleship's vulnerability to air attack had not escaped the attention of everyone in authority. By the early 1930's the American and Japanese navies were building aircraft carriers. When World War II opened, the U.S. Navy had seven large fleet carriers and Japan had ten. Cruisers and destroyers provided defensive screening for the carriers from air, sea or underwater attack. Hit-and-run torpedo boats and large, fleet-class submarines provided powerful and elusive attack capabilities for additional protection of the floating airfields from enemy attack.

World War II

There were no large-scale naval engagements in the European theater during World War II. However, battleships were lost in individual actions that destroyed the Royal Navy's *Hood* and Germany's *Bismarck, Graf Spee, Tirpitz, Gniesenau,* and *Scharnhorst.* In the Far East, two British battleships, *Prince of Wales* and *Repulse* fell victim to Japanese planes in the China Sea a few days after the attack on Pearl Harbor. They were the first battleships to fulfill Billy Mitchell's warning, because they were sunk by aerial attack while alert, underway, and under anti-aircraft protection.

Leyte Gulf in October 1944 marked the final battleship action of the war. Although there were 12 American battleships in the largest concentration of U.S. naval power ever assembled, it was hundreds of planes operating from aircraft carriers that destroyed the Japanese Navy as a fighting force. The awesome toll of Japanese losses was three battleships, including the mammoth 72,000-ton *Mushashi*, four carriers, ten cruisers, and nine destroyers.

Cruisers

"Cruiser" is the most ambiguous designation in naval parlance. For hundreds of years it has referred to warships that might have been called "frigate," "gunboat," "destroyer," or "battleship." They were the frigates of the great age of sail, too small in armament to qualify for the line of battle, but the eyes of the fleet in any major action. They reported enemy movements to the admiral, whose own visibility was hampered by smoke or weather conditions. They also provided protection against attacks by light craft on the cumbersome ships-of-the-line that took as much as a half hour to come about. The most important characteristic of a cruiser throughout history has been the high speed that made it ideal for escort duty, raiding, pursuit, and escape from a superior enemy.

For years the U.S. cruiser Wampanoag *(name later changed to* Florida*) was the fastest ship in the world. (Photo courtesy of the Naval Historical Center.)*

During the Civil War, the cruiser was a swift, unarmored warship that carried sixteen 10-inch or 11-inch smooth-bore guns. The large cruiser *Wampanoag,* designed to run down Southern commerce raiders, was for years the fastest ship in the world. In 1866, the British laid down their cruiser *Inconstant,* the first to be built partly of iron, with wood sheathing, and coppered. By the late 1800's "cruiser" had come to signify a specific type of warship between the battleship and the destroyer. It was protected by light armor and carried smaller guns than the steam battleship of the era, but it retained speed and range advantages for scouting and "showing-the-flag" at remote stations throughout the world.

The development of today's cruiser started in the 1870's, initially with the armored cruiser, then the protected cruiser with steel decks but no side armor. Later, a belt of side armor was added to the armored cruiser. Early in the 20th century, the battlecruiser came into being. It had the size and firepower of a battleship but with lighter armor for higher speed. The unarmored, high-speed light cruiser fitted with turbine engines followed. Cruisers grew larger and more heavily armed, but always with the inevitable compromise of armor for speed and firepower.

In World War I, cruisers were used to scout, protect convoys, raid enemy convoys, operate in groups against strong enemy concentrations, and designed to be fast enough to escape from a superior enemy force. The Washington Naval Conference of the 1920's established two sub-classifications: heavy cruisers with batteries of 8-inch guns and light cruisers with

6-inch guns. During World War II, the anti-aircraft cruiser was developed, equipped with a large battery of anti-aircraft guns. Its effective screening of giant aircraft carriers against Japanese air attack played a vital role in the success of the U.S. Navy in the Pacific.

The cruiser of the great age of sail was any warship that was sent off on an independent mission—not a specific type of ship. Since then it has developed into a variety of design configurations, but with the two basic requirements that have always characterized the cruiser: high speed and great endurance. They are now armed with the most modern missiles and guidance systems, and remain one of the key ships of the U.S. Navy.

Destroyers

The destroyer was a versatile, all-purpose warship in World War II, far removed from the single-purpose craft that was developed in the 1890's for the sole objective of destroying torpedo boats. In less than 30 years those small, high-speed vessels had proven the vulnerability of capital ships to their hit-and-run torpedo attacks. The destroyer was to contain that threat with higher speed and heavier armament.

The torpedo boat emerged from two Civil War successes, one by Lt. George E. Dixon of the Confederate Navy early in 1862, the other by the Union's Lt. William B. Cushing on October 27, 1864. Dixon sank U.S.S. *Housatonic* in Charleston Harbor with a torpedo on the end of a spar attached to the bow of the world's first successful submarine, C.S.S. *Hunley*. Cushing adopted Dixon's idea by attaching his own spar torpedo to the bow of a small motor launch to sink the Confederacy's massive ironclad, *Albermarle*. In neither instance was the torpedo self-propelled. It was more mine than torpedo, but it was the forerunner of the self-propelled torpedo that was developed in 1868 by Robert Whitehead, a British engineer. Whitehead had collaborated with Captain Luppis of the Austrian Navy who is credited with the invention. Whitehead used compressed air and later added two counter-rotating screws to hold the torpedo on course.

The first torpedo boat with a torpedo launching tube was Britain's *Miranda*, a light river launch that was modified for the purpose. In 1874, the U.S. Navy entered the torpedo boat era by attaching a Whitehead torpedo tube to the bow of a modified steam motor launch. That was followed two years later with the small, swift U.S.S. *Lightning*, a 58-foot wooden vessel that was designed primarily as a torpedo boat. Ten years later, France, Germany, and Russia had a total of 375 torpedo boats and scores of others were in the navies of lesser nations. The United States still had only one, the original *Lightning*. The U.S. Navy recognized the need, and by 1898 a

The first U.S. destroyer, Bainbridge *(DD-1), was capable of 29 knots, an amazing speed in 1898. (Photo courtesy of the Naval Historical Center.)*

total of 35 modern, steel torpedo boats were either commissioned or under construction.

The tiny torpedo boat proved to be a fast and formidable foe that defied existing defensive measures in its threat to capital ships. Clearly, a new type of vessel was needed, one that was fast and powerful enough to search out, overtake, and destroy enemy torpedo boats before they could reach their targets.

The first torpedo boat destroyer was launched by the British in 1893. The United States followed on May 4, 1898 with authorization to construct 16 coal-burning torpedo boat destroyers, 248 feet 8 inches long and displacing 420 tons. Their narrow beam of 23 feet 7 inches provided high speed and their 6-foot 6-inch draft allowed them shallow water pursuit of the elusive torpedo boat. They were armed with two 3-inch guns, five 6-pounders, and two stern torpedo tubes. Two reciprocating engines drove the new warships at 29 knots, an amazing speed in 1898. The crew consisted of 4 officers and 69 enlisted men. The new warships were the *Bainbridge*-class destroyers that saw duty through World War I, their four stacks billowing thick sooty smoke by day and brilliant sparks of burning soot by night.

Between 1906 and 1910, new classes of destroyers joined the U.S. Navy. The *Smith* and *Paulding* classes were three- or four-funnel craft with steam turbines. The *Paulding*-class was the first of the Navy's oil-fired destroyers. During World War I, the destroyer changed from a small, special-purpose craft to a warship that integrated itself into the fleet by its versatility. It had been conceived to cope with the challenges of the torpedo boat, but it was readily adapted for dealing with submarines and proved its worth in routine patrols and escort duty.

When World War I ended, economy dictated fleet size reductions and the U.S. Navy was left with a surplus of inefficient destroyers whose needed upgrading was denied because of budget restrictions. The Washington Naval Treaty established limits and ratios on the types of warships allowed to each country, which put Japan at a disadvantage. Their ratio was 3:5 in relation to the U.S. and British navies. In 1923, Japan ordered five enormous destroyers of a new type, *Fubuki*-class, which achieved a balance of power without violating the numerical constraints of the treaty. The new destroyers established a new standard for future construction—300 feet long, 1,750 tons displacement, 50,000 horsepower geared turbines, and a theoretical top speed of 38 knots. Armament included twin 5-inch guns. It took ten years for the U.S. Navy to respond with eight large *Porter*-class destroyers comparable to the *Fubuki*-class. The U.S. *Mahan*-class followed, with three banks of quadruple 21-inch torpedo tubes.

Extensive armament upgrading during World War II added to the power of new classes of destroyers, particularly against air attack. They remained fast, but that speed had to be paid for in light armor. Destroyer plating was no more than ⅛-inch (3 mm) thick. That made them subject to heavy damage from any hit. They worked hard in trying conditions, bucking gales of the Atlantic and typhoons of the Pacific. The ravages of enemy fire and the destructive forces of nature took a heavy toll on them during the war. The Allies lost 324 destroyers, 99 of them U.S. Navy. The Axis lost 293 of their destroyers.

Between 1959 and 1964, 131 U.S. Navy destroyers were overhauled and updated under the Fleet Rehabilitation and Modernization (FRAM) program. Wiring was replaced, anti-submarine armament improved and boilers and machinery overhauled. The hull life of the more modern destroyers was extended eight to ten years, older destroyers at least five years. In addition, the more modern ones were equipped with a helicopter landing pad under the Drone Anti-submarine Helicopter (DASH) program. That concept failed when experience proved that it was impractical to try and land a remote-controlled drone helicopter on the pitching deck of a destroyer.

The history of the destroyer is less than 100 years old. In that time it has grown from a frail single-purpose craft into an enormous multipurpose warship. Its role in the future is unpredictable, but its heritage in the annals of naval warfare is one of speed, endurance, and heroic performance.

After 2,500 years of wooden warships that ended abruptly in the 19th century, the mighty battleship that dominated the naval scene for 50 years was succeeded by the aircraft carrier. Those lofty floating superstructures, in turn, may be displaced by long-range underwater warships in determining the balance of power in the navies of tomorrow.

SAILING SHIPS

Chapter 1

H.M.S. *Cerberus*— Scuttled Defender

Location: Narragansett Bay, Rhode Island
Approximate depth of water: 10 to 20 feet
Visibility: *Cerberus* good, *Orpheus* bad
Current: light
Access: boat

The American Revolution may have been won as early as 1763, 12 years before it began. That was when the Treaty of Paris ended Great Britain's Seven Year War with France and Spain. The punitive terms of the treaty elevated the victor from an island kingdom to a worldwide empire. New territories in the Mediterranean, India, Africa, and the Far East became hers—but that was not enough for Britain. In the Western Hemisphere, Canada, Granada, Tobago, Dominica, and St. Vincent were taken from France; Spain ceded Florida.

The penalty for losing was severe, and the losers were not quick to forget. Their dreams of retaliation made both countries ready allies for the struggling colonists when help was needed. Britain's navy had dominated the first three years of the war, from the outset at Lexington and Concord until France signed The Treaty of Alliance with the American Commissioner on February 6, 1778.

On March 13, after announcement of the alliance, the British recalled their ambassador from France. France made her move a month later; the Compte d'Estaing, Henri Theodat, sailed for America with 16 French warships and 4,000 troops. Events moved slowly; two more months passed before war was declared on June 14, 1778; one year later, Spain added her support. The intervention of those two countries managed to divert Britain's land and sea forces from the task of subduing her rebellious colonists.

Eventually, it was another French fleet that prevented Britain's Admiral Graves from delivering essential supplies to General Cornwallis, an action that forced Cornwallis to surrender in October 1781, ending hostilities. The 1783 Treaty of Paris that formally ended the war granted the United States what it had been fighting for—recognition as a sovereign nation.

The D'Estaing fleet that was headed for America in 1778 intended to neutralize a British squadron under Admiral Lord Richard Howe by keeping it blockaded at its reported location in Delaware Bay. Howe had seven ships—five 64-gun, one 50-gun, and an armed supply ship. Keeping them out of action would impede the Royal Navy's ability to transport and supply large bodies of troops where they were most needed. That problem had plagued Washington's troops since the war began. The vast superiority of the French squadron in number and firepower assured it of almost certain success. Howe's seven ships would face one 90-gun ship-of-the-line, one 80, six 74's, three 64's, and one 50 in addition to six frigates.

The confrontation was thwarted by the leisurely Atlantic crossing by the French. D'Estaing's insistence on holding practice maneuvers en route delayed his arrival off the Delaware Capes until July 6—a voyage of 85 days. He just missed the British; they had left for New York only one week earlier. The French followed, and arrived off Sandy Hook on July 11, only to lose the chase because several of their larger vessels had drafts of up to 25 feet and would have to cross a sand bar with a normal depth of 23 feet.

Disappointed at the lost opportunity, George Washington wrote:

> Had a passage of even ordinary length taken place, Lord Howe with the British ships of war and all the transports in the River Delaware must inevitably have fallen.

The aide Washington dispatched to confer with d'Estaing was even more disappointed to learn that Paris had put a time limit on the help the French fleet could devote to their new allies. France was now engaged in a world war, and the warships had to leave for the Caribbean to guard against British action in the West Indies. It was agreed, however, that there was time for

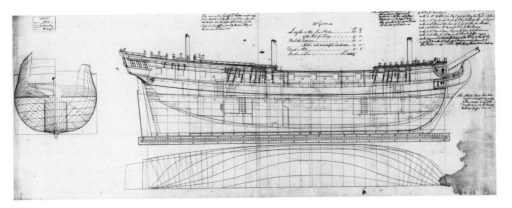

A line drawing of the 28-gun British frigate Coventry, *sister ship of* Cerberus. *(Courtesy of The National Maritime Museum, Greenwich, England.)*

one action in the New York area—an attack on the strategic harbor at Newport, Rhode Island. That target had been occupied by the British since December 1776, and was garrisoned with 3,000 troops under the command of General Sir Robert Pigot.

Battle of Rhode Island

Washington and d'Estaing mapped out a pincer strategy—d'Estaing would land his 4,000 French troops, while General John Sullivan attacked from Providence with 10,000 American volunteers, militia, and Continental regimental troops.

Newport's naval defense consisted of five British frigates, a sloop, and two galleys. They were prepared to do battle with the few ships the Colonists might risk in an attack on their base, but not the sight that greeted them on the morning of July 28, 1778. Sixteen large, heavily armed French warships sailed over the horizon heading for Rhode Island. Without reinforcement, Newport was lost, and Admiral Howe had already declined to do battle with d'Estaing's fleet.

When the French arrived off Rhode Island, four British frigates, *Cerberus* (28 guns) and *Orpheus, Lark,* and *Juno* (32 guns each) were deployed north of Newport, in Middle Channel. (Newport is on the western shore of Aquidneck Island; it is separated from Conanicut Island to the west by Middle Channel, a body of water that connects Narragansett Bay to Rhode Island Sound. Narragansett Inlet, a parallel route to the Sound, is west of Conanicut Island. It converges with Middle Channel at the island's northern tip, Conanicut Point.) The 16-gun sloop *King Fisher* and two galleys, *Alarm*

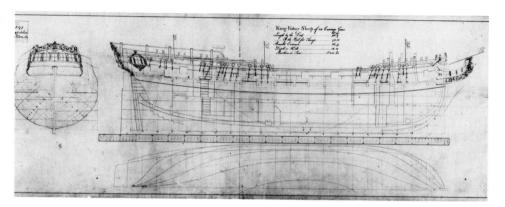

A line drawing of the 16-gun British sloop-of-war King Fisher. *(Courtesy of The National Maritime Museum, Greenwich, England.)*

and *Spitfire,* were stationed in the Sakonnet River, east of Aquidneck Island, as protection against a flank attack on Newport. The first move by the French was to anchor two 36-gun frigates, *L'Aimable* and *L'Alemene,* and the brigantine *Stanley* at the mouth of the Sakonnet. Reacting to that threat, *King Fisher* and the two galleys retreated above the Fogland shore battery for protection.

The next morning, July 30, two French 64-gun ships, *Sagittaire* and *Fantasque,* ran up Narragansett Passage and anchored off the north end of Conanicut Island. That move blocked passage from Middle Channel; it also posed a threat to the island. The British objective was to defend Newport, not to be diverted by small battles for peripheral positions. Troops were withdrawn from both Conanicut Island and the Domplins after supplies were removed and their batteries were destroyed.

That afternoon the French frigates and brigantine in the Sakonnet made their move against *King Fisher* and the two British galleys whose guns, ammunition, and provisions had already been landed to reinforce the shore battery. The sloop and two galleys were set afire at about 2 p.m. to prevent their capture (see Chapter 20).

Defense Strategy

The British defense strategy was to use its small naval force to reinforce critical shore batteries. After unloading guns, ammunition, and supplies, the ships would be destroyed if necessary to prevent their capture. *King Fisher* and the two galleys had followed those orders.

The sloop *Falcon* had left Newport with dispatches to Admiral Howe on July 27; unfavorable winds forced her return to port the same day. Her guns and supplies, and *Flora's*, were unloaded there to strengthen the defense of Inner Harbor. *Juno* was ordered to Coddington Cove, just north of Newport where her armament and provisions were landed; *Orpheus* and *Cerberus* were positioned behind Dyers Island to support the local battery with their guns and supplies.

General Pigot decided to concentrate Newport's defenses at Inner Harbor. The frigates were ordered to retrieve all the guns, ammunition, and supplies they had unloaded. *Orpheus* and *Lark* joined *Flora* in the harbor on August 1, while *Cerberus* remained on guard between Pest Island and Blue Rocks. The crews of *King Fisher* and the two galleys were assigned to strengthen

A 1777 map of Rhode Island and the surrounding area. (Courtesy of the U.S. Naval History Division.)

shore batteries. Ten transports at dockside were prepared for dismasting and scuttling if needed.

By August 3, dispatches from Admiral Howe reversed General Pigot's disposition of the British ships, and three frigates returned to Middle Channel. *Cerberus* and *Orpheus* returned to Dyers Island; *Lark* took up a position off Arnolds Point. Five transports were sunk between Goat Island and Blue Rocks to block the French from that passage. Their masts were cut off seven feet above the deck so they would project just above the water, as a visible deterrent to the French. Five others were dispatched to be sunk later between Goat and Rose Islands.

On Wednesday, August 5, the frigates in Middle Channel received new orders from General Pigot to reinforce Inner Harbor against imminent attack by the French fleet. It was too late. At 5 a.m., as the British ships prepared to head for Newport, Admiral Suffren cut them off by bringing the two French 64's and a third two-decker that had joined them the day before around the north end of Conanicut Island. Captain Symons, of *Cerberus,* entered in his log:

> . . . loosed the topsails, which as soon as we did the two French ships in the Narragansett got under weigh: cutt (sic) the cable & made sail . . .
>
> Tacked and stood toward Rhode Island in hopes the enemy ships would not attempt to pass between the Halfway Rock and the south end of Prudence (Island) . . .

The French men-of-war continued on course, passing between Halfway Rock and Prudence Island with no problem, to which Symons noted:

> . . . it was therefore impossible to stand to the westward again without endangering the ship & people falling into enemy hands . . .

Self Destruct

Strict Admiralty orders held each captain responsible for ensuring that his ship not fall into the hands of the enemy. *Cerberus* was intentionally run onto shore, and Symons ordered his crew of 200 into boats, leaving a small party on board to destroy the vessel. The larger French ships hauled up to avoid bottoming in the shallow water. Their crews watched as *Cerberus'* masts were cut away and five fires were set aboard the British frigate. Captain Symons and his crew watched from the brow of a nearby hill abreast of the wreck as their ship was destroyed by fire and explosion, only three hours after the French ships made their move.

The end came for *Cerberus* at the hands of her own crew. A full year had passed since her career almost ended by enemy action while she lay west of New London, Connecticut, on August 13, 1777. An inventive Yankee, David Bushnell, was convinced that an underwater mine or torpedo could easily sink a ship-of-the-line. He developed an underwater mine and a unique one-man delivery system, *Turtle*, a small, egg-shaped, wooden submarine operated by hand and foot. It held air for 30 minutes of operation. The ingenious device failed only because illness, human error, unfavorable tides, and current combined to defeat three attempts to sink British warships.

Bushnell, determined to prove the effectiveness of his underwater explosive device, selected *Cerberus* as the target that would prove its value. Under cover of night, he towed one of his mines behind a whaleboat, planning to cut it loose so the current would carry it against the hull of the frigate. His luck was still bad; he missed the objective in the darkness. Captain John Symons' journal reports that at 10 p.m. Bushnell's mine was pulled aboard the tender of a schooner Symons had earlier destroyed. The mine had missed the target, but its power was demonstrated. The tender sank, and three of the four men aboard were killed. *Cerberus* was spared from destruction for one more year. Then she would be the victim of self-inflicted punishment, not enemy action.

The frigates *Orpheus, Lark,* and *Juno* (see Chapter 20) were also sunk by their crews, within a few miles of one another. During his court martial (mandatory for any vessel loss), Captain Charles Hudson, of *Orpheus,* testified:

> Time did not allow the removal of the crew's hammocks or personal belongings, prior to the ship's destruction . . .

In blunt testimony to their priorities, the crews spared no effort to save stores of rum that were aboard, but they had no time for guns or personal belongings; nor did the crews of the other British frigates *Orpheus, Lark,* and *Juno,* each carrying 220 men. Added to the 200 aboard *Cerberus,* 860 men lost most of their personal possessions, and they still remain scattered on the bottom.

Naval Action

At about 4 p.m. on August 8, the French fleet entered Middle Channel under heavy fire from shore batteries at Brenton Point, Goat Island, and the north end of town. When the French ran past the batteries, defenders scuttled the sloop *Falcon* off the southeast end of Goat Island and the 32-gun frigate *Flora* between that island and Newport's Long Wharf. The rest of the British transports were also scuttled to block the enemy for as long as possible. The

The French squadron in the foreground had just been fired upon by Lord Howe's British fleet when an impending storm forced the combatants to halt fighting and maneuver for their own safety. (Courtesy of the Library of Congress.)

French anchored close to shore between Goat and Conanicut Islands, and landed troops on Conanicut Island all morning.

All seemed lost for the British. Suddenly, on Sunday, August 9, Admiral Howe arrived off Newport with dramatic timing. His reinforced fleet included eight ships-of-the-line, twelve frigates, three fire ships, two small ships, and four galleys. Admiral d'Estaing deferred his attack on Newport until he could dispose of the new threat. He recalled his land forces, and sailed out to confront Howe.

The seasoned opponents maneuvered for advantage until a furious gale struck on the night of August 11. The tempest tore into the warships of both fleets for two days of crippling damage that ended all thoughts of combat. The British returned to New York for repairs, while d'Estaing's battered ships limped back to join the American land forces around Newport.

British Triumph

While the British and French fleets had been sparring with each other, then struggling to survive the storm, General Sullivan's troops launched an ill-advised attack on Newport's fortified positions. Without the French fleet and their troops to contend with, the British decisively repelled the American assault. Upset at the unilateral action and military failure of the Americans, d'Estaing withdrew his ships to Boston for badly needed refitting; then he ignored the American cause and headed for the West Indies to defend French interests there.

Without French support, the confidence of American volunteers and militia waned; they deserted in droves. Newport remained in British hands for another year. In October 1779, the British left Newport, claiming that it held no further strategic value. Colonial forces quickly took their place, and the port became a valued naval base for the French when they returned.

The tempest demasted the French warship Languedoc *and heavy seas destroyed her rudder, leaving her at the mercy of the British 50-gun* Renown. *The French rigged two small sails from the ship's launch to steady their vessel.* Renown's *first broadside riddled the crippled enemy ship before it was saved by timely arrival of the French fleet. (Courtesy of the Library of Congress.)*

Salvage

The successful defense of Newport had cost the British five frigates, two sloops, two galleys and ten transports—all at their own hands. *Flora*, scuttled to deter the French from entering Newport Harbor, was later salvaged. The 32-gun frigate had originally served in the French Navy as *Vestale* until her capture by the British *Unicorn* on January 8, 1761, when she was renamed *Flora*. After her recovery by the Americans in 1784, she was turned over to France to serve the French Navy again as the privateer *Flore*. Her long, confusing history of switched allegiances ended when Britain's *Phaeton* recaptured her on September 7, 1798. Instead of returning to the British fleet, the aged warship was sold for scrap. She was too old for sea duty.

The British never attempted to salvage the four burned frigates, and the Americans either had no interest, or couldn't find them after the war ended. It was 1970 before Al Davis, a research associate at the University of Rhode Island, launched a search for the lost wrecks. His interest was stimulated by an old chart from a local library. It provided him with the approximate locations of the vessels.

Davis concentrated his efforts on *Cerberus* and *Lark* because the bottom where the chart indicated them to be is harder than where *Orpheus* and *Juno* went down. Three years of diving almost every suitable weekend produced only a few random artifacts, but no sign of the wrecks. Still, there was enough to encourage him to continue his search.

Davis enlisted the help of his father who found the log of H.M.S. *Cerberus* at the Greenwich Maritime Museum in England. It provided the key to locating the frigate: a description of her crew standing on the brow of a hill

Cerberus *cannon after removal of marine encrustations. (Photo courtesy of Bob Cembrola.)*

abreast of the ship, watching it burn. Davis and his buddy diver, Russ Walker, found that "brow of a hill" almost ¾ of a mile south of the position indicated on the chart they had originally used. Two days of diving located the remains of *Cerberus* in less than 20 feet of water, her heavy cannon strewn around her remains. Two weeks later, *Lark* was located, she too in the midst of her large cannon.

Initial funding to excavate the wrecks was provided by a grant to U.R.I. from the National Science Foundation, and work began. *Cerberus* was chosen to work on first because she was in shallow water, nearer to shore. One summer was spent recovering her artifacts, with an occasional dive on *Lark.* The silt bottom was strewn with seaweed-covered rocks, timbers and pieces of wood, ballast stones, large cannon, and heaps of cannon grapeshot. Three cannon, a pewter teapot, old bottles, hand grenades, shoes, coins, ballast bars, cannon balls, and a musket plate were raised and treated for preservation. Precautions were intensified when one cannon rusted before it could be properly coated. Another cannon was permanently loaned to the National Maritime Museum, the source of the ship's log that helped Davis to locate the frigate.

Orpheus, largest of the frigates, was found after only two hours of search, using additional research findings from the London Public Records Office. The wreck, like the two others, was surrounded by cannon, each weighing almost 3,000 pounds. Her oak timbers, protected by seven feet of bottom sediment, were remarkably well preserved.

Davis used the site for a field course, "Introduction to Marine Archaeology," with six students enrolled. The now-abandoned grid structure of

Insignia of the Royal Grenadiers (soldiers who carried and threw grenades from the rigging of a warship) recovered from Orpheus. *(Photo courtesy of Bob Cembrola.)*

Hand grenades recovered from Orpheus. *The grenades were small, hollow, iron spheres filled with gunpowder and ignited by hand. (Photo courtesy of Bob Cembrola.)*

steel pipe that they used is still in place, but is overgrown and slowly rusting away. During the two years that *Orpheus* was stationed in Newport, livestock had been taken aboard to supplement naval stores. The skeletons of cattle, pigs, and fowl that went down with the frigate were well preserved over the

A cluster of grape shot (above) and an array of bottles (below), both from Orpheus. *The bottles are well preserved because* Orpheus *lies in soft silt.* Cerberus *went down on a rock-strewn bottom. Her remains were not so well protected. (Photos courtesy of Bob Cembrola U.R.I.-R.I.H.P.C.)*

years by layers of silt. They provided the student archaeologists with an underwater treasury of bones for study and classification.

Al Davis had not yet located *Juno* when he learned that money had run out, and no further funding would be available from any source. When his pleas for financial assistance to recover the historic artifacts for public enjoyment and education were ignored, Davis abandoned the project for a career in ocean engineering. Ultimately, the underwater relics of the American Revolution that still remain at the site will be lost. The location has been added to the National Register of Historic Places to protect the artifacts that are still buried there from intruders—but not from nature.

Chapter 2

H.M.S. *Culloden*— Pilot Blunder

Location: Culloden Point, Montauk, New York
Approximate depth of water: 20 feet
Visibility: varies—flood tide is best
Current: on occasion a light to moderate current
Access: beach or boat

April 17, 1746 marked the bloody Battle of Culloden—the critical conflict for the throne of England between the royal army of the House of Hanover and the forces of Bonnie Prince Charles, claimant of the throne for the House of Stuart. That claim was forever silenced by the resounding defeat of Charles and his supporters on the Scottish moors of Culloden and Dunmossie, five miles east of Inverness at the head of Loch Ness.

The decisive victory so impressed the British that the following year a new warship was named for the battle site. That first H.M.S. *Culloden* sailed under the British flag for 27 years until she went out of commission in 1770. Six years later, a new *Culloden* was launched at Deptford on May 18, 1776—only seven weeks before the American colonies declared their independence. The bow of the new 74-gun ship-of-the-line was adorned with a figurehead of Britain's reigning monarch, King George III. The warship, symbol of England's victory over the insurgents of Scotland, was destined to be lost in His Majesty's defeat by ill-equipped but dedicated rebels who

The British ship-of-the-line Culloden. *(Courtesy of Suffolk County Historical Society.)*

had been stung to rebellion by the continuing infringement of their liberties. Thus, *Culloden* forged a historic link between two divergent societies, one dominated by royal decree, the other freed from such domination.

Culloden's specifications were impressive:

Length of gundeck........170 feet
Beam.......................47 feet 2 inches
Depth of hold.............19 feet 11 inches
Tonnage....................1,650

Armament	Number	Pounds
Gun deck	28	32
Upper deck	28	18
Quarter deck	14	9
Forecastle	4	9

War Service

The new 74-gun ship-of-the-line carried 650 officers and crew under Captain George Balfour who remained in command for the life of the vessel. She spent her first year intercepting French and Spanish ships supplying the rebellious American Colonists. Her first American encounter occurred during the winter of 1777, the capture of a small colonial merchant vessel bound for Bordeaux with a cargo of deerskins, tobacco, rice, and indigo.

French sympathies for the American cause led to an open alliance between the two, and war between England and France. A French fleet of 16 warships sailed from Toulon on April 13, 1778. Its three-fold mission was to deliver the first French minister to the United States to his new assignment, to intercept a British squadron under Admiral Richard Howe, and to keep it blockaded in Delaware Bay. The British countered with a powerful fleet of 14 ships that sailed from England under Vice-Admiral John Byron, grandfather of the illustrious poet. *Culloden* was one of Byron's ships.

Nature Intervenes

The Atlantic crossing was a disaster for Byron's fleet. It was battered by torrential storms and gale-force winds. Six ships were lost, and the eight that limped into Sandy Hook, New Jersey needed major repairs before they were fit for action. Although ten years would pass before the birth of his poet grandson, Admiral Byron's emotions as he surveyed his decimated fleet were captured in Lord Byron's epic poem, *The Isles of Greece:*

> A king sat on the rocky brow
>   Which looks o'er sea-born Salamis;
> And ships by thousands lay below,
>   And men in nations; all were his!
> He counted them at break of day—
>   And when the sun set, where were they?

Byron's objective, the French fleet, was still to be dealt with, but it lay safely anchored in Boston harbor as the English left the protection of Sandy Hook to fulfill their mission. En route to Boston, a fierce Atlantic gale struck the northeast, and Admiral Byron's ships were again buffeted and battered by nature. That repeat performance, so soon after his disastrous Atlantic crossing, earned Byron the nickname, "Foul Weather Jack."

Culloden, only two years old, was dismasted and swept to sea, a target for total destruction if another Atlantic storm should strike. Fortunately, the weather held, and she managed to limp home to Milford Haven, England by December 1778 for refitting after six months of furious battle—against neither the French nor the Americans, but the forces of nature. The humiliating return voyage did provide some compensation, however. The damaged warship managed to recapture the former British brig *Sandy,* lost to the French earlier in the year. A short, uneventful tour of duty in the Caribbean followed; then she returned to the English Channel with other ships-of-the-line to protect England against possible invasion by the French.

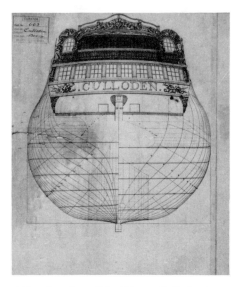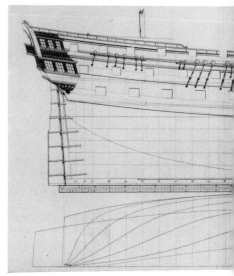

A line drawing of the 74-gun Culloden's *stern. (Courtesy of The National Maritime Museum, Greenwich, England.)*

Fortunes of War

On December 27, 1779, *Culloden* sailed for the West Indies, this time part of a large fleet commanded by Admiral George Brydges Rodney. England's woes had been compounded early in 1779 when Spain joined forces with the American rebels and the French. Gibraltar was under threat, and Rodney's fleet was to reprovision the garrison on the way to the West Indies. A Spanish fleet of 21 men-of-war escorting 15 provision-laden merchant vessels was encountered off Cape Finisterre on January 8, 1780. Seven Spanish warships, 1,295 seamen and all 15 merchant ships were taken. The enemy flagship *Guipuscoano* (64 guns), only six months old, was recommissioned into the British navy by Admiral Rodney, as H.M.S. *Prince William.*

A Spanish squadron was reported cruising off Cape St. Vincent with 14 ships-of-the-line. Rodney's 21 warships, including *Culloden* and several frigates, engaged and defeated the enemy on January 16, capturing 11 ships-of-the-line. In addition to the total loss of their fleet, the Spanish Navy suffered heavy casualties compared to British losses of only 32 men killed and 102 wounded.

The victory left Rodney with a remarkable record of 18 warships and 15 merchant vessels to his credit for the still-young war cruise. Five of the

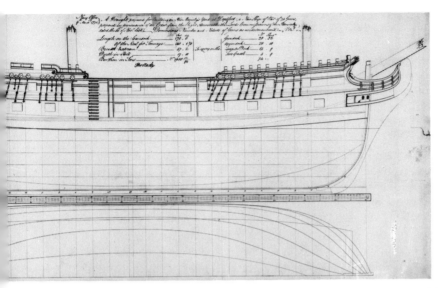

A line drawing of Culloden*'s bow. (Courtesy of The National Maritime Museum, Greenwich, England.)*

prizes were dispatched to England under the escort of *Culloden* and 14 other British warships. En route, another enemy ship was captured from a small French convoy. The victorious returning squadron arrived at Portsmouth, England on March 9, with the early fruits of Admiral Rodney's continuing mission.

Meanwhile, the French had inflicted serious damage to Rodney's Caribbean fleet in a major sea battle that might have turned out differently if Rodney had not sent the 15 warships back to England. His request for reinforcements brought *Culloden* back again to American waters. She left Portsmouth on June 3, and cruised the Caribbean under Admiral Rodney for the rest of the summer.

French Threat

The French were also active in the American Colonies, where they created a major problem for British interests by establishing a strong base at Newport, Rhode Island. Their seven ships-of-the-line and 6,000 troops posed a constant threat to Admiral Marriot Arbuthnot, Great Britain's commander-in-chief of North America. He lacked the naval power to cope with the situation and requested naval reinforcements from Admiral Rodney's Caribbean fleet. The positive response was far more than

Arbuthnot expected, or wanted. Admiral Rodney, himself, was in command when the reinforcements arrived on September 13, 1780. Rodney outranked Arbuthnot, and he assumed overall command. Protests were dismissed by Rodney with, "I am convinced no man has His Majesty's service more at heart than yourself," continuing, perhaps with tongue in cheek, "It was not inclination which brought me . . . it was the duty I owed my King and my country."

As relations between the two admirals worsened, the British cause suffered. Arbuthnot accused Rodney of "partial interferring with the American War." Rodney, in turn, was enraged by Arbuthnot's disregard of his orders, which he reported to the Admiralty as "unprecedented" actions.

That was the political situation when *Culloden,* with three other ships of the same class, *Centaur, Shrewsbury,* and *Russel,* sighted the American ship *Washington* on October 18. They were cruising "between the South End of Nantucker (sic) Shoals and Montock (sic) Point," and chased the enemy vessel for six hours before she was captured and claimed for the Crown. The prize, a 20-gun privateer with a crew of 120, was overwhelmed by the firepower of the four British 74's.

The ruffled feelings between the two admirals were sorely aggravated when the prize money of 3,000 pounds was awarded to Rodney as senior officer. Arbuthnot's responsibility for the squadron's actions and Rodney's absence in New York at the time were ignored.

British naval dominance left the cause of the Colonists heavily dependent on the French fleet. General Washington wrote to France:

Next to a loan of money, a constant naval superiority on these coasts is the object most interesting. This would instantly reduce the enemy to a difficult defensive . . . removing all prospect of extending their acquisitions. . . .

The selection of Newport as the French base moved Arbuthnot to locate his own headquarters at Gardiner's Bay on Gardiner's Island, New York—close enough to keep track of the French fleet. From there, a spyglass could bring the enemy ships into view on a clear day. Besides, Gardiner's Bay was a perfect haven—with a diameter of 6 miles and a depth of 3.5 to 7 fathoms—more than adequate to maneuver the largest warships. Plum Gut, between Plum Island and Gardiner's Island, provided harbor entry for the largest ships in the fleet.

Arbuthnot's headquarters were set up in the island's manor house. The overseer's house, "T'Other House," as it was known, was established as the base hospital. Several reminders of the British presence remain—a checkerboard carved into the upstairs floor of the hospital and the gravesites of several British seamen. The admiral enjoyed a good social relationship with the Gardiner family. He and his higher ranking officers exchanged visits with the Gardiners, entertaining aboard his flagship, *Royal Oak,* and being entertained at Abraham Gardiner's mansion on Main Street, East Hampton, Long Island.

Arbuthnot had cause to celebrate when Admiral Rodney left New York for the Leeward Islands on November 19th, leaving *Culloden* behind to serve in Arbuthnot's fleet. As soon as Rodney left, Arbuthnot headed for New York to replace Rodney's appointments with his own men. That task accomplished, he returned to Gardiner's Island.

Disaster

On January 20, 1781, the British received word that several French warships at Newport were about to run the British blockade. *Culloden, America,* and *Bedford* were ordered to intercept them if such an attempt was made. They rendezvoused in Block Island Sound on the 22nd. The next night, a heavy winter storm struck the area, packing the kind of violence the *Culloden* crew had good cause to remember. She was severely battered, as she had been three years earlier. Gale force winds lashed the three ships with sleet and snow that blinded half-frozen lookouts.

The British ships headed for the open sea to ride out the storm, *Culloden* following *Bedford*'s lights. *Bedford* came about at 12:30 a.m., a change of course that confused Third Lieutenant John Cannon, on watch aboard *Culloden.* He informed Balfour, and the captain decided to maintain *Culloden*'s course on the premise that neither he nor the captain of *Bedford* could be certain of his position. There could be no danger; every half hour, a crewman was taking soundings with a 20-fathom hand lead without finding bottom.

Fourth Lieutenant Ralph Grey relieved Cannon at 4 a.m., and was instructed to maintain course while the pilot was in the captain's cabin discussing the situation with Balfour. Without warning, pounding surf and coastline loomed directly ahead. Balfour raced on deck and ordered the anchors cut free to keep the vessel offshore. But before the crew could comply, *Culloden* shuddered violently; her copper-clad bottom had run fast aground. Shortly after, her rudder broke in two and was lost. The shore, barely visible through darkness and foul weather, led the pilot to conclude that the ship had grounded on Block Island. Dawn revealed that it was really Welles Point (known today as Culloden Point), near the northeastern edge of Fort Pond Bay—not far from Montauk Point, Long Island.

Lieutenant Grey's log entry reads:

> . . . at 8 a.m. we backed her head off shore, then filled and endeavored to run her off, but her bow came around to the westward and lay fast . . . at 10 the gale increased, also the sea, she laboured and strained much.

Captain Balfour was determined to save his command, if at all possible. He ordered the top and main masts cut away and kept men on the pumps continuously. The water being pumped out was filled with sand and gravel, indicating that the heavy seas had probably split the seams of the ship. The storm ended with *Culloden* still fast into the sand. "We made every effort to get her off at high water," wrote Lieutenant Grey. But every effort was not enough because planking on the starboard bow gave, allowing water to pour into the ship. By 10 a.m., nine feet of seawater had accumulated below decks.

The hopeless situation prompted Balfour to order everything possible transferred to shore. Powder, gunner's stores, blocks, sails, carpenter's stores, pitch, and tar were stacked under tents for protection. Even water-soaked bread was laid out to dry. Later in the day, Balfour sent a boat to Gardiner's Island to report the disaster.

Bedford had come close to following *Culloden*'s fatal example—driven toward shore until her forward progress was halted by releasing her anchors. Finally, her masts were cut away to reduce the effect of the heavy winds.

America fared better than either of her sister ships. During the storm, several hull planks were loosened, but she reached the open Atlantic afloat and still capable of maneuvering on her own. Even so, the storm carried her down the Atlantic coast to the Virginia Capes; the return voyage took almost two weeks.

The French ships that were reported to be running the blockade fared even better. They had returned to their protected harbor the day before the storm. By that action, they gained a total victory over the British who suffered a major defeat—by Mother Nature.

The transport *William* and the brig *Adventure* were ordered from Gardiner's Bay to salvage *Culloden*'s stores and guns, and to ensure that nothing useful would fall into enemy hands. Even Arbuthnot's flagship, *Royal Oak,* moved materials to Gardiner's Bay and to the dismasted *Bedford* for jury rigging her with *Culloden*'s masts and rigging. By February 5, *Bedford* was again ready for sea duty.

Blocks and tackle removed at least 46 cannon, gun carriages, and anchors from *Culloden.* Several days of heavy labor were required to remove the ship's King George bowsprit. Intermittent strong gales, driving snow and pounding breakers delayed salvage completion until March 1. The 28 obsolete 32-pound iron cannon—not worth salvaging—were spiked, and the ravaged hull was set afire. Saddened British seamen watched their proud ship-of-the-line burn to the water line in less than four hours.

The French had considered attacking the British base on Gardiner's Island after the storm. They had suffered less naval damage than the enemy, but they were uncertain how much of an advantage that provided them. Arbuthnot wrote to Lieutenant General Sir Henry Clinton, K.B., British Army Commander in North America, that on February 3rd, "a French officer landed from New London in a whale boat on Plumb (sic) Island and made a minute enquiry of our forces." If there had been such a plan, it was abandoned; instead, the French sent two frigates out in search of a British naval force off the coast of Virginia.

Arbuthnot conducted a preliminary investigation of the *Culloden* disaster. His finding was that the pilot believed his ship had already cleared Montauk Point, and could safely bear due south. On March 28, 1781, a court martial was held in Lynnhaven Bay, Virginia. Admiral Graves, presiding as judge advocate, merely reprimanded the pilot for using the wrong sounding lead; Admiralty regulations called for a heavier (50-lb) deep sea sounding lead every half hour instead of the hand lead. In what seems like an unusually compassionate verdict, Captain Balfour, his officers, and his men were honorably acquitted. Balfour's record remained so unblemished that he was promoted to rear admiral in 1787.

Salvage

After the British left the *Culloden* remains, Joseph Woodbridge of Groton, Connecticut salvaged 16 of her 32-pound iron cannon. He offered them to General George Washington on July 24, 1781, adding that he could recover 14 more guns and a quantity of shot. The Continental government, always short of funds, probably could not afford the offer.

Two dedicated sport divers, Frederick P. Schmitt and Donald E. Schmid, later conducted extensive research that resulted in a factual booklet, *H.M.S. Culloden*, but it sheds no further light on the Woodbridge offer, nor does it provide any trace of the salvaged cannon.

Another salvage attempt, headed by the caretaker of Gardiner's Island in 1796, removed iron fittings, copper bolts, sheathing and the remaining rigging. An article in the *Long Island Star*, July 26, 1815, describes the only other early salvage operation. Captain Samuel Jeffers, of Sag Harbor, Long Island used a diving bell to retrieve twelve tons of pig iron and a 32-pound cannon. That was the last disturbance of the wreck for 158 years. During that time, Welles Point has become known as Culloden Point. The location, mostly covered with underbrush, is now Culloden Shores, a development with only a few scattered homes. *Culloden* lives on in the identity of the historic site.

Mrs. Jeannette Edwards Rattray wrote a 1955 book, *Ship Ashore,* that renewed interest in many all-but-forgotten shipwrecks around Long Island. She has commented on *Culloden*:

> As soon as the book was out, local fishermen told me they had never seen a vestige of the ship supposed to have gone down there. But Emerson Taber, who used to set his lobster pots in Gardiner's Bay, told me that a good deal of the *Culloden*'s skeleton was still visible when the tide was right. I went to look. Sure enough, the ship's ribs were sticking up four to six feet from the sand . . . .

In June 1958, Frederick P. Schmitt was absorbed by Mrs. Rattray's account. He and a fellow sport diver, Donald E. Schmid, interviewed Mrs. Rattray in East Hampton, N.Y. She mentioned that the ribs of the old vessel were still visible when the tide was right.

Search

Schmitt and Schmid were so intrigued by the possibility of locating *Culloden* that they formed one of the area's first scuba diving clubs, the Club Sous-Marin of Long Island, for undersea research and exploration. Late in June they launched an intensive, three-year search for the wreck. A large rib, about 60 feet long, was found on their first trip to the area. The huge, hard oak timber still held wrought iron fasteners and oaken pegs. They thought it might be the wreckage mentioned by Mrs. Rattray. The location was right, but before the artifact could be authenticated it was set afire by picnickers. Two weeks later, one of the divers, Don Hegeman, discovered a large oak beam, water-logged and rotting, about 30 feet long and one foot thick with a wrought iron pin in one end. It was half buried in sand under three feet of water west of Culloden Point.

Schmitt and Schmid obtained a copy of *Culloden*'s log and a complete set of her construction plans from the National Maritime Museum at Greenwich, England. Through the fall and winter of 1958, they spent weekends at the New York Public Library researching British naval history, but found nothing new on her location. The Public Record Office, in London, was more productive. A microfilm copy of *Culloden's* officers' court martial transcript revealed that the ship had run aground in sand and gravel, not rocks. Thus, the wreck must be buried in the sand—and most of the area around Culloden Point is rocky.

The best instrument to locate a wreck under sand is a sensitive metal detector, but such a costly device was beyond the limited resources of the new diving club. They finally abandoned the search after hundreds of hours of diving, but their carefully researched material has survived. It exists in Schmitt and Schmid's *H.M.S. Culloden,* published by the Mystic (Conn.) Historical Association. Frederick Schmitt's ties to the sea remained strong; he became curator of the Cold Spring Harbor (N.Y.) Whaling Museum.

Mrs. Rattray recalled that in 1971 Club Sous-Marin divers had brought pieces of timber with old nails in them to her for authentication. Expensive scientific testing, too costly for the divers, was needed to determine the age of the artifacts, so they were turned over to the East Hampton Town Marine Museum, where they are now part of the *Culloden* exhibit.

A new personality entered the search for *Culloden* when Carlton Davidson, a Long Island diver from East Moriches, New York, read *H.M.S. Culloden* in 1970. He was so intrigued by the history of the lost shipwreck that he devoted the next three years to research and hundreds of hours underwater to pinpoint *Culloden*'s location. He has been credited as the first to locate the main part of the wreck, including its hull and five cannon, one of which he donated to the town of East Hampton. That generous gesture, unfortunately, led to bitter harassment of Davidson by many, including the state of New York. The period of Davidson's travail has been referred to as "The Second Battle of the *Culloden.*"

Davidson gained two important clues—both from the book by Schmitt and Schmid. The first was that *Culloden* had stranded in sand and gravel, not a rocky area. The second clue was that not all 74 cannon had been salvaged. A search for old nautical charts revealed that American charts only go back to about 1848, and charts obtained from England failed to show any local areas of sand or gravel.

Davidson's continuing research led him to the Suffolk County Center, Riverhead, N.Y., where he learned that a 1661 map involved in a lawsuit might include his area of interest. A local justice, Judge Tasker, showed him the map, which included updating with the new designation, Culloden Point, in place of the original Welles Point name. A large sand shoal was clearly outlined off the Point.

Davidson and two friends searched the sandy area with a small metal detector during the summer of 1970 and intermittently over several years. Their task was made more difficult than it should have been by their primitive metal detector, a hand-held model that can locate lost coins just below the sand, but is unsuited for the kind of search they were conducting.

Meanwhile, others looking for the wreck were getting results. Two scuba divers, David Warsen of Hampton Bays and Bob Miller of Aquebogue, were credited by Mrs. Rattray, as the first to produce positive identification of *Culloden* wreckage. An August 5, 1971 *East Hampton Star* article reported that she had met with Warsen, an insurance man, and Miller, a painter, to hear their story, and view their relics.

The two divers had made only three visits to *Culloden*, for a total of only nine hours since March. At first, they found only big pieces of timber six or eight feet under the water. In mid-May, Warsen uncovered a large bronze object. As he fanned its edge, the name Culoden (sic) appeared. He exposed enough of the find to reveal its outlines, then spent two days at the Smithsonian Institution in Washington, where he identified it as a gudgeon, a pivot attached to the sternpost of a ship to receive the rudder pintle, or pivot pin.

Frederick Schmitt's book *H.M.S. Culloden* states: "Soon after she had struck, the rudder broke in two and was lost." The solid brass, 300-pound, 6½-foot-long gudgeon Warsen had found was broken off, and so was the 40-pound pintle, a big metal pin, about three inches across, attached to a piece of the rudder. The two had also recovered a piece of the ship's rudder with a broken bronze pin attached. That pin was a pintle.

The divers explained to Mrs. Rattray how they had raised the heavy gudgeon from the bottom. They had immersed a 55-gallon drum, open on the bottom, and inserted air into it through the regulator hose of a scuba tank. The air displaced water and the buoyant barrel became a lift bag capable of raising about 400 pounds.

Three brass pintles, one still attached to a piece of the rudder (at the foot of Robert Miller, left). The pintles and the broken gudgeon in the foreground were recovered by Miller and David Warsen, right. Mrs. Jeanette E. Ratray (deceased), an authority on Long Island shipwrecks, holds a copy of her book Ship Ashore. *(Photo courtesy of David Warsen.)*

A 300-pound brass gudgeon recovered by David Warsen and Robert Miller, with the ship's name misspelled when it was cast at the foundry. A broken pintle-pin protrudes through the gudgeon socket. (Courtesy of David Warsen.)

Other artifacts found by Warsen and Miller were copper sheathing with a wide-headed nail, timbers, bits of heavy crockery, and a 1,000-pound anchor. Although it is difficult to date a ship's hardware, some of the pieces were marked with the King's broad arrows, typical of British warships of the era.

Success

Davidson continued his own search, teaming up with Miller and Paul Knight, a fellow member of Miller's 20-man diving club, the Suffolk Sub-mariners, headquartered in Riverhead, Long Island. The trio launched an intensive scuba and metal detector search that continued for two years. They divided the sandy area into a grid of ten-, five-, and one-foot squares, using a buoy for reference.

Davidson was underwater with a friend, George Olish, on August 12, 1973, when his primitive metal detector located an iron cannon, 14 inches under sand. He uncovered the find, to reveal the cascabel (a round projection behind the breech) and part of the breech. Davidson's first reaction was that

Carlton Davidson, on the right, and the controversial Culloden *cannon. (Photo courtesy of C. Davidson.)*

it was a cannon ball, but as more sand was removed he realized that his long search had been rewarded.

Two weeks probing with steel rods produced three more cannon from beneath the hull. After they had been spiked, then dropped overboard by the British, they were covered as the wreckage settled over them. Heartened, Davidson paid $450 of vacation savings to rent a barge-mounted crane from the Preston company of Greenport, L.I., New York.

By September 29, Davidson and Knight had cleared sand from around one of the imbedded cannon by forcing air through a 3½-inch fire hose. They encircled it with wood strips in a wire sling, to avoid damaging the surface of the historic relic. They struggled for four hours before they raised it to the deck of the rented barge. Instead of the 15-ton crane Davidson had ordered, the one that was delivered was rated for only three tons. The 6,328-pound prize was finally hauled aboard by traveling the boom—seven weeks after it was uncovered. It was the first cannon retrieved from the wreck since Samuel Jeffers raised a 32-pounder on July 14, 1815, 158 years earlier.

A fifth cannon was discovered as the sand was cleared away from one of the original four. Anticipating the ultimate recovery of all five, Davidson announced his intention to donate the first to the East Hampton Town Marine Museum in an interview with a reporter from the *East Hampton Star.* He transported the 6,328-pound, 10½-foot relic to his home and submerged it in a long wooden box of fresh water. The National Maritime Museum of England recommends such treatment for any salt-water artifact (especially cast iron) before any steps toward permanent conservation are started. Further, such a large object requires such soaking for at least two years.

Pre-empted Claim

On October 2, 1973, only four days after Davidson recovered his cannon, New York State officials claimed it as property of the State Education Department and the State Office of General Services. The claim was based on a law giving the state title to any treasure found within its borders—including all artifacts found in waters within the three-mile limit. The state had no immediate plans for the item, but a spokesman said that the cannon was such a good find that it was being considered as the centerpiece for an American Bicentennial celebration. However, the chief curator of the New York State Education Department, John Still, had no idea of how the relic should be cured.

Davidson was told by the Department of Education that he was guilty of a misdemeanor, punishable by up to one year in prison for diving without a joint permit from that department and the State Office of General Services. Davidson felt that he had covered the subject before he retrieved the cannon by discussing his plans with another state official, New York Assembly Minority Leader, Perry B. Duryea, Jr., who had informed him that no permit was necessary. He even advised Davidson that public funding might be available to preserve the cannon.

Davidson applied for a permit to work the wreck site, intentionally omitting what he considered proprietary information—the location and depth of the wreck. The state denied his application, and instead granted Dr. Henry Moeller, New York Ocean Science Laboratory, a permit to study, map, photograph, and ultimately perform archaeological excavation of the *Culloden* site. The state's decision was based on the opinion of officials that Dr. Moeller's laboratory had better research equipment and facilities, and was close to the site.

Barred from diving the wreck, Davidson complained of being followed by state police—presumably to ensure that he did not violate the restriction. Frederick Schmitt, co-author of *H.M.S. Culloden*, observed that Davidson was being generally harassed. "They really got tough with him," he declared, adding that Davidson had "received letters with carbon copies to the state police. . . ." In Schmitt's opinion, Davidson's sole objective was to bring up his artifact and see it on display—but he stumbled into a hornet's nest. Moeller claimed, on the contrary, that

Davidson had taken the cannon for himself, intending to keep it as his own backyard ornament, adding that the offer to present it to the museum in Amagansett was made only under pressure.

The press added to Davidson's woes by accusing him of worsening the cannon's deterioration by leaving it untended in his backyard for more than a year. That was typical of the false rumors that were circulated, such as Davidson charging admission to view the cannon. On the contrary, anyone willing to spend time viewing the artifact was welcome to do so, at no charge. Hundreds of school children trooped through the Davidson backyard on field trips to view some of their country's early history—with no charge to them or their schools.

Dr. Moeller called on the United States Military Academy's Scuba Diving Club to help search for *Culloden*'s remains. Twenty-four cadets and six officers spent the weekend of September 28, 1974, searching for remnants of the ship and its equipment. They worked a grid pattern of the bottom that had been laid out by Dr. Moeller and two student assistants, Christine Gustafson and John Allgauer. Temporary buoys were set to mark findings, and locations were marked on a chart. Working in small teams, and swimming an arm's length apart, divers scoured the area in visibility that was at times only 4 or 5 feet. The cadets used their own metal detector, but as one noted, "This whole area is metallic...like the oxide in the rocks. . . ."

One year later, over the weekend of September 6, 1975, another contingent of West Point cadets joined the effort. A system of "double transits" was used by the team of 25 divers to establish permanent markers around the search area. It was also planned that they would participate in an air lift to raise part of *Culloden*'s hull. That was thwarted by the failure of an air compressor on the research boat *Swordfish*.

After the wreck was located Dr. Moeller worked the site with students of his underwater archaeology class at the New York Ocean Science Laboratory from the summer of 1976 through the summer of 1979. They air lifted part of the wreck, and recovered a multitude of artifacts—wood, ballast rock, fire bricks, leather, hemp, glass, pottery shards, cannon balls, a hand grenade, lead shot, pewter spoons, buckles, buttons, copper sheathing, nails and barrel hoops. Their identification, classification, and preservation are a continuing program at the East Hampton Town Marine Museum.

Preservation

Davidson knew he must find a chemical process to stop corrosion of *Culloden*'s valuable cannon. While he kept it in fresh water, he obtained a book, *History Under The Sea* by Mendel Peterson, from the Smithsonian Institution. He learned that the *Culloden* cannon had been made in Scotland by Graham and Sons. The National Maritime Museum in England provided information that the Defense Standards Laboratories in Victoria, Australia, had preserved similar iron cannon. The Australians responded to Davidson with a publication, *Report 508, Restoration of Cannon and Other Relics from H.M.B. Endeavor,* by C. Pearson. *Endeavor,* from which the cannon had been jettisoned, was the ship in which Captain James Cook toured the world during the 18th century to chart the transit of Venus.

Davidson had all the information he needed to preserve his cannon—but no funds to do so. He hadn't anticipated the problem of preservation when he announced his intention of donating it to the local museum. He searched for any museum that would accept the historic relic—and assure its required treatment, even contacting President Nixon, with no success.

Mrs. Betty Kuss of East Hampton, New York provided the solution. She arranged through East Hampton Councilwoman Mary Fallon (later town supervisor) for the town to accept the cannon on permanent loan from Davidson—even though New York State was still pressing its claim of ownership. Its preservation was to be included in the arrangement. The conditions under which Davidson concluded his loan agreement with the town on September 20, 1974 provided that:

1. The cannon be properly restored and preserved, and exhibited for the people of East Hampton,
2. Carlton Davidson be invited to participate in the restoration, and
3. If the restoration was not completed in time for the Bicentennial celebration, the cannon would be returned to Davidson, in order that he might continue work on its preservation.

Scientists from the Ocean Science Laboratory supervised the preservation process with Davidson assisting. Restoration of the cannon and its display became a community-wide Bicentennial project. The exhibit was designed by the director of the Town Marine Museum, Ralph Carpentier. George A. Schutte provided the facilities of his antique-restoration shop to construct an authentic replica of the cannon's gun carriage. Its oaken timbers were stripped from a barn that had served as George Washington's headquarters in Tarrytown, N.Y. Sid Cullum and Associates forged the iron work, and the cannon was mounted on a section of typical 18th century gun decking built by local carpentry students.

Funds for the restoration were raised by the East Hampton Historical Society, the Town Baymen's Association, and the Town Bicentennial Committee, chaired by Councilwoman Mary Fallon. The restoration and its display proved to be East Hampton's most impressive and enduring Bicentennial project. The exhibit was opened to the public at the East Hampton Town Marine Museum, Bluff Road, Amagansett, N.Y., on July 11, 1976.

Diving H.M.S. *Culloden*

The remains of *Culloden* lie almost entirely imbedded in the sand shoal to the east of Culloden Point. The site is readily accessible to sport divers, about 150 feet from shore in approximately 20 feet of water. Protected from the ocean, there is no surge, and visibility is not usually a problem. However, on occasion there is a slight current.

From year to year, winter storms expose parts of the wreckage or artifacts, such as the cascabel of a sand-covered cannon, cannon balls, timbers, and planking. They may be observed and photographed, but not removed. The site has been placed under New York State protection, with severe restrictions against the unauthorized removal of artifacts.

Hundreds of *Culloden*'s relics have survived recovery from the sea and their transfer to the East Hampton Town Marine Museum, where

Culloden *cannon on display in the East Hampton Town Marine Museum. Restoration work was only partially successful. Exterior sections had separated and repairs were made with auto body putty (note the lighter colored area on the right). (Photo by H. Keatts.)*

An East Hampton Town Marine Museum display of the wreck location during mapping, sketching, and excavation of the site by Dr. Moeller. (Photo by H. Keatts.)

Elizabeth B. O'Donnel supervised their preservation. They are now displayed at the Marine Museum.

In addition to the gudgeon and pintles recovered by Dave Warsen and Bob Miller, another gudgeon was found by two boys from Lindenhurst, N.Y. The youths were guests at a Montauk motel between the entrance to Lake Montauk and Fort Pond Bay when they found the relic. Unaware of its historic value, they planned to sell it for its value as scrap metal. Fortunately, the motel keeper realized that it might have come from the *Culloden* wreck. He informed Ralph Carpentier, director of the museum, of the find, and Carpentier contacted Frank Joseph, father of one of the boys. Mr. Joseph agreed to retrieve the relic and turn it over to the museum, but by that time it had been cut into three pieces—so it could be handled easily by two boys. That is how it is now exhibited, with an explanation of how it came to be in that condition.

The days of H.M.S. *Culloden* as a fighting ship in the cause of King George III ended more than 200 years ago. Her revival as an object of historical interest has generated a remarkable reaction in contemporary

Above: Wood timbers are covered and uncovered by the shifting sand. Note the piece of copper sheathing with a sheathing nail protruding, in front of the timbers (right center). (Photo by H. Keatts.)

Left: One of the many Culloden *artifacts recovered by Dr. Henry Moeller, and now on display at the East Hampton Town Museum. (Photo by H. Keatts.)*

Americans—an entire spectrum of human impulses, emotions, and behavior. The lure of a lost wreck, self-sacrifice, intensity of the search, persistence, competition, excitement of the find, sharing, frustration, depression, hope, community-wide cooperation and patriotic fervor were all stimulated by the historic remains of a proud warship of the British Navy, one that grounded on the coast of Long Island in January, 1781, H.M.S. *Culloden.*

Chapter 3

U.S.S. *Ohio* —
Power, Grace, and Speed

Location: Greenport, New York
Approximate depth of water: 10 to 20 feet
Visibility: usually poor—flood tide is best
Current: light
Access: beach or boat

The Statue of Liberty vies with the stars and stripes as the symbol of Americanism. Known throughout the world as a shrine of freedom, that "Green Lady" has extended her welcome at the entrance to New York Harbor since 1886. The citizens of France, in an unprecedented demonstration of international friendship, presented the statue as a gift to commemorate 100 years of United States independence. The magnificent gesture might better have been reversed. The coast of France should be adorned with a memorial—an American one dedicated to the decisive role of the French Navy in this country's successful Revolution.

The impoverished Colonists stood impotent against the impressive sea power of Great Britain. They were defiant and determined—but they had no navy. The British advantage of sea-borne commerce threatened early defeat for the insurgents until France intervened in 1778. The move was not without self-interest; the cautious French had been waiting for the right moment to enter the conflict and settle their own score with the British. The formidable French fleet filled the void for the Colonists. It provided time for the new country to develop some semblance of a navy, to gradually improve it—and ultimately, to survive as an independent nation.

Colonial Navy

As early as 1775, with the war barely in progress, the Continental Congress recognized the urgent need for Colonial naval resistance to British sea power. Funds were scarce, the few Colonial privateers were woefully inadequate, and the Americans were on their own—as they would be until French intervention three years later. The quickest action was to convert commercial vessels to warships. A naval committee appointed by the Continental Congress immediately purchased 16 vessels—2 large square-rigged ships, 6 brigantines, 3 schooners, and 5 sloops. They were refitted, but they were armed inadequately, and their crews were poorly trained. Still, they served a useful purpose as commerce raiders, capturing sorely needed supplies and munitions for the war effort.

The war was still in its first year, but Congress recognized the need for action; authorization was granted to construct 13 frigates, each to carry 24 to 32 guns. By the time they were completed, all large ports and entrances to important waterways had been captured or blockaded by the British—keeping six of the warships out of action. The seven that eluded the blockade sailed under the Continental flag until all were either captured or destroyed. One, *Randolph* (32 guns), was blown up in action on March 17, 1778 by the British 64-gun *Yarmouth*. Only four of *Randolph*'s seamen survived. A second frigate, *Warren,* was burned in 1779 to prevent her capture.

The other five frigates ended up in British hands; four were commissioned into the Royal Navy, a tribute to the quality of Colonial design and construction. One, the 32-gun *Hancock,* was so highly regarded that the British described her as the ''finest and fastest frigate in the world.'' She was captured by the 44-gun *Rainbow,* July 8, 1777, renamed *Iris,* and became a favorite chase vessel for British naval officers, who built their personal fortunes through the capture of prizes.

Iris captured the American frigate *Trumbull* for the British Navy in 1781. Later that year, she suffered the same indignity—captured by a French squadron, then transferred into the French Navy. French naval support of the American cause had plagued the British for the past three years, and would continue for two more. *Iris* survived the war, but in 1793 the 12-year French Navy veteran was destroyed when the British captured the port of Toulon. She had been serving as a powder hulk—last survivor of the 13 Continental frigates.

A Country Is Born

The Declaration of Independence introduced a new country to the world in 1776. It would require a substantial navy—not only to survive the war, but also to protect future commerce and what was even then an extensive coastline. In December 1776, before the 13 Continental frigates were completed, orders were placed for additional warships to bolster the fledgling navy. Three of the new ships were to carry 74 guns, but only one, *America,* was completed—and she never served under the American flag. Instead, she was presented to France in 1782 in appreciation of that nation's role in the war, and to replace a 74-gun French ship that had been lost at Boston Harbor in the rebel cause. That first American attempt at building a 74-gun ship proved to be a disaster. The French found that *America* lacked qualities that a vessel of her class should have. Four years after the presentation, the ship was found to be rotten and was broken up—a short career.

Military spending faced stern opposition after the Revolution. The new government was so desperately short of funds that fiscal-minded leaders found a ready audience for their proposal to eliminate the small navy. Two of the young nation's most prominent patriots expressed shocked opposition to such ill-conceived action. George Washington cautioned that if the nation wanted its neutral flag to be respected, an organized naval force must be ready to protect it from insult or aggression. In his words:

This may even prevent the necessity of going to war by discouraging belligerent powers from committing such violations of the rights of the neutral party as may, first or last, leave no other option.

Alexander Hamilton asserted:

With a navy, a price would be set, not only on our friendship, but upon our neutrality.

The sage advice of those eminent leaders went unheeded, overwhelmed by arguments for austerity; the Navy's last vessel was sold in 1785. The decision to terminate the short-lived navy was founded on the hope of trusting but naive individuals that goodwill and amity of the world powers would prevail. They managed to persuade the country that an American Navy and its attendant cost were an unneeded luxury. International contempt, indignities, and humiliation followed.

The French Revolution of 1789 led to Franco-British hostilities that continued until 1802. The navies of both belligerents freely preyed on American merchant ships, ignoring claims of neutrality. American vessels were attacked and captured, even within their own waters; cargoes were confiscated, and crews were impressed into foreign service. It took such events to prove the wisdom of Washington's and Hamilton's words of caution.

New Navy

The United States was left with no option but to build a navy capable of protecting the country's interests on the high seas. Congress acted on March 27, 1794, authorizing the construction of 6 frigates, each carrying 24 to 50 guns—the nucleus of the new United States Navy. Two, *Constellation* and *Constitution,* built in the 1790's, are still afloat as historic relics.

Constellation, commanded by Thomas Truxton, promptly led in victories over French warships in the western Atlantic and Caribbean during the quasi-war with France. Both were instrumental in freeing American shipping from the yoke of the Barbary pirates, *Constitution* playing a somewhat larger role.

The notorious free-booters had preyed on unprotected American merchant vessels without reprisal—capturing them and enslaving their crews. The small squadron of United States warships gained worldwide recognition by bringing the pirates to terms. In Tripoli, the American consul commented:

> It must be mortifying to some of the neighboring European powers to see that the Barbary States have been taught their first lesson of humiliation from the Western World.

During the administration of John Adams, Congress passed an act creating the Navy Department. Benjamin Stoddert was appointed the first Secretary of the Navy on May 18, 1798. He recommended enlarging the navy to at least 12 ships of 74 guns, 12 frigates, and 20 or 30 smaller vessels. Congress responded February 25, 1799, with authorization to build six 74-gun ships and six sloops-of-war. But a navy is built by appropriation, not authorization, and funds were appropriated only for the sloops.

Financial problems and public apathy continued to hamper naval build-up until British squadrons committed the major sea provocations that led to the War of 1812. Britain confronted the United States with more than 100 first-class warships while the Americans could muster only slightly more than a dozen fighting vessels, other than gunboats. In *The History of the American Sailing Navy,* Howard I. Chapelle wrote:

There was widespread doubt that Americans could possibly cope with the British Navy at sea. . . . There was no reserve of trained naval seamen, and naval funds were lacking. One thing alone the navy possessed, a fine officers' corps, well disciplined and trained, spirited, and aggressive.

Chapelle's book includes the following commentary on the early success of the small American Navy:

The defeat of three fine British frigates by American ships in the first months of the war, not only created confidence and tremendous pride on the part of the American public, but also horrified the British public and established American prestige in Europe.

Of greater importance, continued Chapelle:

. . . the American public was now convinced of the necessity of a navy, and, on the whole, very proud of what it had accomplished in the war.

One important achievement was to highlight the country's need to bolster its Navy's meager fleet with larger warships. Congress was convinced; the Act of January 2, 1813 ordered construction to begin on the U.S. Navy's first ships-of-the-line.

Ships-of-the-Line

These magnificent warships were the battleships of the age of sail, with armament that qualified them for position in the first line of a sea battle. They carried from 64 to more than 120 heavy guns, floating fortresses that were a nation's most tangible symbol of seapower throughout the 1700's— until they were outdated by steam power and iron hulls in the mid 1800's. The square-rigged, three-masted vessels bristled with guns from two or three enclosed decks and from the upper spar deck. The Naval History Division of the Navy Department, in *American Ships Of The Line*, pays tribute to those heavily armed goliaths:

In the days of sail, this great ship of the battleline sailed nobly for generations as the backbone of fleets. It was the mighty, mobile fortress that could hit the hardest blows and take the most punishment—for in war one must expect to suffer as well as to harm. It was matchless in grace, speed, and beauty. Then when iron and steam replaced wood and sail, the successor that evolved for the sailing ship of the battleline came to be called battleship.

On April 29, 1816, Congress authorized construction of nine more ships-of-the-line, each no fewer than 74 guns. One million dollars a year funding for the next eight years was specified to ensure that they would be built. Construction was to be in government yards rather than private shipyards because of the uncertainty of the eight-year funding. The newly formed Board of Navy Commissioners knew that delayed appropriations might keep a ship on the stocks for years. No private builder would accept such an unpredictable program—except on a high rental basis. The Navy's concern proved to be well founded; as early as 1818, seven 74's were on the stocks officially, but construction was underway on only three, *Ohio, Delaware,* and *North Carolina.* The other four, *Vermont, New York, Alabama* (renamed *New Hampshire),* and *Virginia* were at a virtual standstill.

Predictably, economy dictated the completion schedules of the new ships. The powerful 74's would be held in readiness, and were to be launched only as required to protect the nation. Two never reached the water; *New York* was still on the stocks when the Civil War broke out, and was burned when the Norfolk Navy Yard was destroyed; *Virginia* was broken up in 1874, still incomplete at the Boston Navy Yard—58 years after her authorization by Congress.

Delaware was launched in 1820 at the Norfolk Navy Yard, *North Carolina* in 1821 at Philadelphia, and *Vermont* in 1848 at Boston. *Vermont* was the last ship-of-the-line built for the United States Navy, although *Alabama* was still to be launched.

Alabama was almost completed by 1825, but she remained on the stocks for an additional 39 years, until she was needed for Civil War service, having been "under construction" for 45 years. She was re-named *New Hampshire,* a name more suitable for federal service during the war with the Confederate States. The obsolete sailing vessel was fitted for wartime use as an administrative receiving ship, not a line-of-battle ship. Her first assignment after commissioning on May 13, 1864 was to relieve *Vermont* as receiving ship at Port Royal, South Carolina. By then, obsolescence had indeed caught up with the once mighty ships-of-the-line.

U.S.S. *Ohio*

Ohio was first of the 74's to be launched, two and a half years after her keel was laid in November, 1817 at the New York Navy Yard (later Brooklyn Navy Yard). However, after her launching on May 20, 1820, she spent the next 18 years in ordinary, a term that means "moth-balled," with only a skeleton crew aboard. An English naval officer who visited *Ohio* in 1826 while she lay in ordinary at New York observed, "A more splendid ship I never beheld." Still, the overriding interest of economy kept the beautiful warship languishing at anchor for another eleven years.

Currier & Ives lithograph of U.S.S. Ohio. *(Courtesy of Kenneth M. Newman, Old Print Shop, New York.)*

Ohio, like the other six ships-of-the-line of her class, was based upon the design of the Washington Navy Yard's naval architect, William Doughty. However, she was built in New York by another naval architect, Henry Eckford, with his own substantial modifications that put *Ohio* into a class of her own for size, speed, firepower, and sailing quality. Eckford's design was slightly larger and considerably deeper than Doughty's. Consequently, the decks of *Ohio* rode higher above the water, permitting effective use of lower deck guns, even in rough seas. The specifications of Eckford's final product were impressive:

Spar deck length	208 feet
Between perpendiculars	196 feet 3 inches
Molded beam	53 feet 10 inches
Depth in hold	14 feet
Displacement	2,757 tons
Draft	26 feet
Sail	18,000 yards

Ohio carried a complement of 820, including marines. The ship's armament varied from one command to another—usually 84 guns. Her modest cost of $547,889.00 permitted very little ornamental work—only a light gallery at the stern and an impressive figurehead of Hercules with a British lion skin and club on the bow. The figurehead was produced by Wood and Sharpe, New York City woodcarvers. Expense-minded critics could hardly have considered the $1,500.00 bow decoration essential to defense, but there it remained.

In 1837, Captain L. Kearney sailed the 18-year-old ship-of-the-line to the Boston Navy Yard for fitting out. She was commissioned on October 11, 1838, and placed under command of Captain Joseph Smith. On October 17, she sailed back to New York to be armed. In the 22 years since Congress authorized their construction, much consideration had been devoted to arming the 74-gun warships. From Mr. Chappelle's book, *The History of the American Sailing Navy:*

> The War of 1812 had confirmed, it was thought, the early proposition of giving all ships the heaviest armament possible in a given rate. Single-ship actions in the war had shown pretty clearly the advantages of ships so built and armed, and it was decided that all American naval vessels should be superior in size and armament to their European counterparts; hence any American ship not capable of greatly exceeding her rate in gun power was deemed a failure.

Naval architect Doughty left no question concerning his design objectives in the new ships-of-the-line:

> Instead of the ships of our navy possessing inferior properties to those of the same classes of other nations, it is desirable, and indeed of considerable importance, that they should excel in all their principal qualifications . . . .

Mr. Chapelle continued:

> At the end of the War of 1812, the arming of naval ships with guns of a single weight of shot was popular, since the use of one size of ball simplified supplying the ships, with no danger of part of the ship's batteries being made useless for want of shot. In compliance with the American policy of employing the heaviest broadside fire possible, American ships armed in this manner usually carried 32-pdrs. Liners had long guns on the lower deck, medium guns on the gun deck, and carronades on the spar deck.

The emphasis on 32-pounders (weight of the ball that was fired) placed unacceptable constraints on the firepower of American ships. They were unable to carry the larger 42-pounders. That limitation was corrected by sacrificing the logistical advantage of single size shot. Some ships-of-the-line were rearmed with a mix of 32's and 42's. Like the others of her class, *Ohio* was designed for maximum firepower. She was nominally a 74, but carried anywhere from 84 to 104 guns, depending on the decision of her various captains.

The Bureau of Ordnance Gun Register lists *Ohio*'s armament in 1845 as 90 guns:

Spar deck—	two	32-pounder cannon
	twenty-four	42-pounder carronades
		(short iron cannon)
Main deck—	thirty-two	32-pounder cannon
Lower deck—	thirty-two	42-pounder cannon

The heavily armed ships-of-the-line posed major design problems for marine architects. They carried large numbers of heavy guns, ammunition, stores, and crew. They also had to stand up under fire. That combination

U.S.S. Ohio, *although rated as a 74, carried 84 to 104 cannon, depending upon the whim of her captain. Note the Hercules figurehead on the bow. (Photo from the collection of H. Keatts.)*

called for massive dimensions and heavy armor. Yet, speed and maneuverability were essential to maintain tactical superiority over enemy naval forces, and could not be sacrificed for size, armor, or armament. *Ohio* was a prime example of that refusal to compromise.

Commodore Isaac Hull, a veteran rich in naval experience, selected *Ohio* as his flagship in 1838. The commodore's most famous command was "Old Ironsides," 26 years earlier, at the outbreak of the War of 1812. His standards of performance were high, and he expected much of his new flagship. *Ohio* did not disappoint him. She set sail on December 6, 1838, still under the command of Captain Joseph Smith, to join the U.S. Navy Mediterranean Squadron at Gibraltar. The massive warship confirmed the commodore's confidence as she overcame rough Atlantic seas for an average speed of 12 knots. During her career, *Ohio* was acknowledged to be the Navy's fastest ship-of-the-line. In 1850, she averaged almost 14 knots while logging 335 knots in 24 hours, heading for home from Cape Horn.

For over two years, *Ohio* patrolled the Mediterranean, leading a U.S. Navy squadron to display the flag and provide protection for American commerce. She returned to Boston on July 17, 1841 to spend the next five years in administrative service as a receiving ship, also known as a floating naval depot.

War with Mexico broke out, and *Ohio* sailed to Vera Cruz under the command of Captain Silas H. Stringham in March 1847. She contributed to the fall of that city—not in a naval engagement, but by landing a contingent of seamen and marines equipped with ten of her guns to participate in the assault.

The large ship-of-the-line drew too much water for effective operation along the shallow coast of the Gulf of Mexico. She left Mexico on May 9, 1847, for return to New York, where the new U.S. Minister to Brazil, D. Todd, was waiting for transportation to his new post. He left for Rio de Janiero aboard *Ohio* on June 26, 1847. The impressive warship remained at that Brazilian port as a symbol of naval power after safely delivering the diplomat. That military presence most assuredly attracted Brazilian notice during negotiations between the two governments.

Ohio left Rio on December 7, 1847, sailing south around Cape Horn to reinforce the U.S. Navy Pacific Squadron commanded by Commodore Thomas Gatsbey Jones. She served as the commodore's flagship for the duration of the Mexican War.

When hostilities ended, the gold rush that followed the acquisition of California by the United States generated a boom economy on the West Coast. *Ohio* was called on to provide protection for commerce during that chaotic period. She policed the newly acquired California Territory when the Navy's major problem was to deter U.S. Navy crewmen from deserting

Two "old salts" alongside the ship's bell on the forecastle. The photo was taken in the 1870's. (Courtesy of the Naval Historical Center.)

to look for gold in the California mountains. One officer was badly mauled during an aborted attempt by two would-be deserters. A drumhead court martial found the two guilty and sentenced them to be strung from *Ohio*'s yardarms. The bodies remained there as a grim warning to others who might otherwise have been tempted by gold.

Commodore Cornelius K. Stribling relieved Commodore Jones on August 19, 1848. By that time, ships-of-the-line had become too costly to operate. Most of the Navy's large warships were already being retired to "in ordinary" status, where they slowly deteriorated. But the career of U.S.S. *Ohio* was far from over. Commodore Cornelius K. Stribling retained the 28-year-old 74 as the flagship of his Pacific Squadron for another year, visiting Hawaii and Samoa.

In 1849, the ship-of-the-line returned to Boston, where she was decommissioned on May 3, 1850 and again went into ordinary. A year later, she was recommissioned, and served as a receiving ship for the next 24 years.

End of a Naval Career

In 1875, *Ohio* was once again placed in ordinary, until her 63-year career ended on September 27, 1883, when she was sold to Israel L. Snow of Rockland, Maine for $17,000.00. Snow later sold her to Greenport, Long Island, New York shipyard owners for $20,000. Two tugs, *Luther C. Ward* and *Germania,* towed *Ohio* out of her berth in the Boston Navy Yard's "rotten row" on October 28, 1883. Four days later, they delivered her to Greenport Harbor.

Local residents, viewing the old warship in tow, recalled the days when no ship-of-the-line could compare with her for speed and handling. There was the "norther" she rode out off Vera Cruz, when some 80 merchant sailing ships parted their cables and went ashore. Then, caught in a terrible gale in San Francisco Harbor, she was the only one of 37 vessels to escape.

Ohio was moored alongside Main Street Wharf to accommodate the thousands of sightseers who streamed aboard and walked the decks of the old ship-of-the-line for a small fee. But it was for her copper and bronze fastenings, not display, that the warship had been purchased. Dismantling was interrupted in April 1884 by a violent storm that broke the vessel loose of her moorings and stranded her near Fanning Point, at the end of Fourth Street in Greenport. She was burned to reduce her obstruction to shipping, but much of the hulk resisted the flames.

Metal fastenings and other salvage were gathered at the site, sometimes with the help of dynamite cartridges that were exploded to facilitate break up of the wreck. On the morning of July 26, 1884, Robert N. Corey of

The old ship-of-the-line at her pier in Greenport, N.Y. after being sold for scrap. (Photo courtesy of the Naval Historical Center.)

Carole Keatts beside Ohio's *Hercules figurehead, now located at the Village Green, Stony Brook, N.Y. (Photo by H. Keatts.)*

Greenport, a professional wrecker, exploded one of the cartridges in timbers containing prized bronze spikes and pins. He lit the fuse, ran approximately 80 paces, and turned away from the blast. A horrified observer later reported watching a 15-inch iron bolt, blown in a high arc above its restraining timbers, plunge into Corey's skull with piledriver impact. Mr. Corey died three hours later.

The $1,500 heroic figurehead of Hercules was removed from its place on the bow and sold at auction for $10. Later, it was resold to the owners of Canoe Place Inn, Hampton Bays, New York for $15. In 1951, Hercules was transferred to the Village Green, at Stony Brook, New York where it is prominently displayed with *Ohio*'s anchor—vestiges of one of the most magnificent warships of the 19th century U.S. Navy.

Rediscovery of U.S.S. *Ohio*

Almost a century passed before extensive research by the Peconic Bay branch of the British Sub Aqua Club discovered the wreckage of *Ohio*, late in 1973. Those local scuba divers, determined to protect the location of the wreck from predatory abuses, passed the following resolution:

If and when a member of our unit is asked to be a guest speaker at any social, educational or private meeting he or she must first advise the membership and ask permission. All information our club has to artifacts and/or wrecks found shall be classified as secret information.

The club's objective was to raise the hull for use as the central theme of a marine museum that was being planned. The location of the wreck remained a secret until the Mobil Oil Company of Greenport applied for a permit to add clusters of pilings, called dolphins, in their mooring area to improve safety in the unloading of oil barges. The Sub Aqua group contested the permit request because the new dolphins would penetrate the wreck site. Their determination to preserve the historic relic had forced them to divulge its general location. Ultimately, the dolphins were installed without appreciable damage to the wreck.

Local newspapers carried the story of the dialogue between the Corps of Engineers, Mobil Oil and local divers, attracting the attention of other scuba divers. Stephen Bielenda, a YMCA scuba-diving program director, salvage diver, and captain of a charter boat for scuba divers, launched his own search for *Ohio* with several scuba-diving friends. They located it, and dove to the wreck that the British Sub Aqua group had tried so hard to protect.

When Bielenda and his friends returned to shore, they were confronted by Greenport Village police, who informed them that the dive site was off-limits to them; it was open only to members of the Sub Aqua Club. Bielenda argued that no village law prohibited him from diving in the area and it would be discriminatory to permit only the local diving club to dive the site. The Village Board countered with a proposed ordinance, "Preservation of Historic Landmarks," to provide for preservation of *Ohio*. That effort was abandoned when it was learned that the wreck lies within the province of the Army Corps of Engineers, outside municipal boundaries.

Diving U.S.S. *Ohio*

Some dives pose a challenge because of visibility, currents, surge, depth, conditions on a wreck, or the time one must spend on a charter boat for too little down time. *Ohio* offers a pleasant relief from such problems. It rests close to shore, in Greenport Harbor on the North Fork of Long Island, less than 100 miles east of New York City. The Mobil Oil Company dolphins that led to disclosure of the wreck site have since been removed, and are no longer marking the location. With very little wreckage usually exposed, the wreck can be difficult to find.

Diving from shore is favored by local divers; they can wade halfway to the spot where the old ship-of-the-line lies less than 100 yards off shore, in

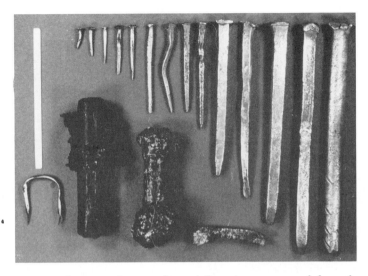

An assortment of copper, iron, and wood fastenings recovered from the wreck. (Photo by H. Keatts.)

only 20 feet of water. Once there, the real work begins. Only painstaking, patient efforts will reap rewards—a piece of sheathing, a fastening or a bottle. The artifacts may be brass, copper, iron, wood or glass, but catch bags may also collect clams or an occasional lobster.

The wreck has settled into the bottom, and only a couple of ribs and a few planks are exposed. Many brass fastenings have been found close to shore—in only four to six feet of water. Visibility is usually poor, and it worsens when sediment is disturbed by a diver's fins or probing the bottom for the tell-tale green of oxidized brass. Diving at the end of a flood tide increases the chances of improved visibility for two reasons. Water from Block Island Sound is clearer than that from Peconic Bay, and with the water still moving, sediment raised by probing or fanning the bottom will be carried away, out of the diver's search area.

At a depth of 20 feet, only the amount of air carried determines the duration of a diver's stay on the bottom. While there, the throbbing engines of the Greenport-Shelter Island ferry interrupt on a regular schedule. It is difficult to ignore them, but after the initial distraction, they provide a background accompaniment for the dive. Schooners and smaller sailing craft pass silently overhead, but for that reason, they may be more dangerous to a surfacing diver than the high pitched whine that warns of a speeding outboard. Until 1985, the Mobil Oil Company dolphins in the wreck site provided relative safety from passing boats for divers surfacing alongside

Not much of the U.S.S. Ohio *remains above the sand bottom. In the poor visibility that generally prevails, even scattered planks and beams such as these are hard to find. (Photos by Mike Casalino.)*

them. Now that they are gone, divers must exercise extreme caution to avoid boat traffic when surfacing. There are two recommendations for diving *Ohio.* The first is to observe the state law that divers must tow a float with a dive flag attached. The second is to carry a compass to guide the diver back to shallow water, away from the dangers of the main boat channel.

The dive is not as challenging as some others, the wreck is far from picturesque and the potential for artifacts is uncertain. Other, less tangible rewards attract amateur underwater historians; to them, the old hulk is a memorial—the forerunner of today's battleship. They know that the few scattered timbers and copper nails now exposed once sailed in glory as the pride of an emerging United States Navy, the grand old ship-of-the-line, U.S.S. *Ohio.*

Chapter 4

U.S.S. *New Hampshire—* The Last Ship-of-the-Line

Location: Graves Island, Manchester, Massachusetts
Approximate depth of water: 10 to 40 feet
Visibility: usually good
Current: unusual, but there can be a surge in shallow water
Access: boat

The last surviving American ship-of-the-line was lost to the sea in July 1922. Congress had authorized her construction 106 years before.

While *Ohio* basked in the glory of her years as the pride of the U.S. Navy, her sister ship *Alabama* remained, still on stocks, waiting to be launched for her first commission. It took the Civil War to bring her into service. The warship was renamed *New Hampshire,* which was considered more appropriate for service against the Confederacy. She was launched April 23, 1864, and commissioned May 13, 1864. The three-masted, square-rigged ship was fitted for wartime service as a receiving ship (a floating naval depot), not as a line of battle ship-of-the-line. Although her hull was pierced for 102 guns, *New Hampshire*'s original armament was only four 100-pounder Parrott rifled guns and six 9-inch Dahlgren smooth-bore guns. Her 203-foot 9-inch length, 51-foot 5-inch beam, and 2,633 tons certainly classified her as a ship-of-the-line, but she was to serve as a non-combatant for more than 57 years. Her first commander, Commodore

New Hampshire*'s hull was pierced for 102 guns, but she only carried 10 when she was launched. (Photo courtesy of the Peabody Museum of Salem.)*

Aboard New Hampshire *off Charleston, S.C. during the Civil War. A "powder monkey" stands alongside a 100-pounder Parrott rifled gun. (Photo courtesy of the Library of Congress.)*

The warship was used as a receiving ship for many years following the Civil War. (Photo courtesy of the National Archives.)

Henry K. Thatcher sailed her to Port Royal, South Carolina, to relieve her sister ship *Vermont,* and serve as a supply and hospital ship for the remainder of the war.

Beginning June 8, 1866, she served as a receiving ship at Norfolk, Virginia for ten years. On May 10, 1876 she returned to Port Royal, still a receiving ship. In 1881, she sailed to Norfolk for more of the same duty until ordered to Newport, Rhode Island, under Commodore Stephen B. Luce. The obsolete wooden warship served the next ten years as flagship of an innovative Apprentice Training Squadron—still a non-combatant, but her old timbers were building men for the future Navy.

In 1891, she was towed from Newport to New London, Connecticut, for another year as a receiving ship. She was decommissioned on June 5, 1892 and placed into ordinary. One year later, *New Hampshire* was loaned to the New York State Naval Militia as a training ship and armory. Nearly a thousand officers and men who trained aboard her served in the Spanish-American War.

On November 30, 1904, *New Hampshire* was renamed *Granite State* to make her name available for a steam-powered, steel-hulled battleship to be laid down May 1, 1905. Time had really caught up with the ships-of-the-line. On April 25, 1913 her career almost ended with a fire that spread rapidly through the forecastle and superstructure. Almost certain destruction was averted by timely flooding of the ship's magazines. Some of the crew were treated for smoke inhalation, but there were no serious injuries. After repairs, she continued her service as a training ship. As a consequence of that duty, the country entered World War I with trained State Naval Militia immediately available to the U.S. Navy. They were mustered in as National Naval Volunteers. Secretary of the Navy Josephus Daniels, in *Our Navy at War,* stated:

> Never again will men dare ridicule the volunteer, the reservist, the man who in a national crisis lays aside civilian duty to become a soldier or sailor—they fought well. They died well. They have left in deeds and words a record that will be an inspiration to unborn generations.

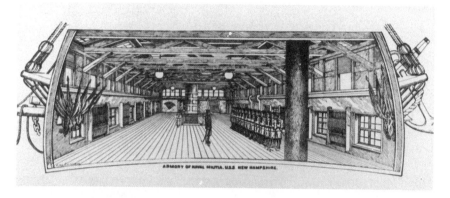

The old ship-of-the-line was converted into an armory for the naval militia in 1892. (Courtesy of the Naval Historical Center.)

The old vessel remained in service as a training ship, on the Hudson River until a second major fire struck on May 23, 1921. This time, the vessel did not fare as well as eight years earlier. A large pool of fuel oil had collected on the surface from a leaking six-inch Standard Oil pipeline under the river. At 3 p.m. three sailors in a captain's gig came through the oil slick, approaching the pier to which *Granite State* was moored. The gig's motor back-fired several times, shooting sparks and flame from the exhaust, igniting the fuel oil.

The sailors escaped, but not the old warship or the three-story naval office and storehouse on the Ninety-sixth Street pier. President Harding had landed at the pier that morning, but he was not near at the time and his yacht *Mayflower* was safely at anchor several hundred yards offshore while the fire took its toll.

Fire stations ashore could not be used to save the ship because of low water pressure. Firemen and two fireboats were assisted by the ship's crew and those from other naval vessels in a valiant but unrewarding effort to save the ship. Only her mooring chains kept her from capsizing as she listed sharply to port and settled into the muddy river bottom, a smoldering hulk. The damage was estimated at $250,000, but there was never a thought of repair—her original cost was $304,533.85.

The Mulholland Machinery Corporation of New York bought the remains for $5,000 at auction in August 1921. After the sale, a brief military ceremony ended with a bugler sounding taps to signal the end of the career for the United States Navy's last 74-gun ship-of-the-line, *Alabama/New Hampshire/Granite State*.

Salvage

The new owners calculated that the hull contained $70,000.00 in salvageable materials. Like *Ohio,* she was copper fastened, and her hull of valuable hardwood was covered with 100 tons of copper sheathing. Rumor had it that somewhere in her keel she had three gold spikes. Her two anchors weighed five tons each, and she carried 100 tons of chain.

Divers sealed gun ports and patched holes in the hull with three layers of canvas before the ship was raised with pontoons. After five months to complete the operation, *Granite State* was taken in tow in July 1922, bound for Eastport, Maine for removal of her copper fastenings. A July 27, 1922 newspaper account detailed the final phase of her undistinguished career:

> The old warrior limped out of New York in tow of the ocean tug *Perth Amboy.* On the hulk were Joseph Mulholland, representing the firm of owners, George Pilska, and Nathaniel Aronsson. The *Granite State* was at one end of a cable 175 fathoms in length, which was made fast to an anchor jammed in her bow, in the absence of proper towing bitts. At 10:30 o'clock yesterday morning Captain Tapley of the tug saw smoke rising from the bow of the hulk and supposed the men on board were cooking . . . .

But it was not cooking that raised the smoke. The old ship was fighting her third battle with fire. Flames spread rapidly, and the original tow line parted from the flaming bow. Mulholland and Aronsson left the burning vessel in a rowboat. The tug dropped back to pick them up as the third man, George Pilska remained aboard to assist the tug's crew in trying to secure a second line. Searing flames defeated the effort, and Pilska was removed to the tug.

New Hampshire *burned and sank in New York Harbor in 1921. The hulk was raised and under tow when she sank in Massachusetts Bay. Note the four canvas patches on her stern. (Photo courtesy of the Naval Historical Center.)*

The burning ship drifted, until she stranded on the granite shore, off the southwest corner of Graves Island in Massachusetts Bay. The next morning local residents descended on the fire-ravaged hulk and appropriated vast quantities of her valuable metals. The wreck settled, abandoned and almost forgotten for years while storms battered the hull against the rocks until broken ribs and timbers slowly disappeared into the sand.

Diving U.S.S. *New Hampshire*

Born *Alabama,* lived *New Hampshire,* died *Granite State,* the shipwreck is best known by the name she carried through her years of glory. Thirty years passed before divers rediscovered the wreck of *New Hampshire;* since, salvagers have ravaged it three times. On each occasion they retrieved huge oak timbers with copper spikes and drift pins still attached. Those fastenings, an anchor, and many cannon balls that had been carried as ballast were sold for their metal content. What a pity it was to lose those historical artifacts.

The fastenings are believed to have been forged at the Paul Revere Foundry. Revere received a contract for a large quantity of copper spikes, drift pins, sheathing, and sheathing nails from the Navy in 1816. The fittings are identical to those on the smaller *Constitution,* whose fittings were made by Revere.

Spikes used to hold planks in place measured six to twelve inches in length. Drift pins were substantially longer than spikes, and were used as rods to reinforce the ship's structural members. The term "drift pin" comes from beating them into pre-drilled holes, a process called drifting.

Copper sheathing protected the hulls of ships from shipworms (not really worms, but bivalves like clams). *Skin Diver* magazine, July 1976, explains why copper sheathing from this wreck is treasured:

> . . . The sheathing is of special note from both an industrial as well as historic standpoint. Prior to Paul Revere's impact on metalworking, sheathing and any sheet metals were forged by pounding, a procedure which took a great deal of time, yielded relatively small sheets, and provided only tolerable thickness uniformity. Revere's industrial genius had him create the world's first metal rolling machine and therewith the ability to produce great quantities of sheet metal, in large sizes, and uniform thickness . . . .

Every dive on *New Hampshire* becomes a new experience. Like *Ohio,* she can be best described as "wreckage," rather than a wreck. Her remains are scattered about the bottom in 10 to 40 feet of water, with her giant curved ribs rising out of the sand. Storms continue to cover and uncover those ribs and other pieces to provide an ever-changing underwater panorama.

Spikes and other fastenings are scattered in the sand and in the crevices of rocks close to the island. Rock crevices warrant careful search; they can

An assortment of copper fastenings recovered from the wreck. (Photo by Dave Clancy.)

A scabbard buckle, a key and a nameplate, relics recovered and photographed by Bill Carter.

be explored thoroughly after the seaweed attached to the rocks is pulled away. Working the sand along the edges of exposed beams is another worthwhile technique that frequently produces good results.

Some, but not all, spikes and drift pins from this wreck and from U.S.S. *Ohio* bear the legend ''US'' impressed into them. There is an unconfirmed belief that they came from Revere's foundry. Whether or not that is so, all of *New Hampshire*'s fastenings are highly prized as historical artifacts.

Accessibility is one of the truly attractive aspects of diving this wreck. The location, Graves Island, is just offshore from Graves Beach, Manchester, Massachusetts. One could walk from the beach to the island at low tide, but the shore adjacent to the island is privately owned and access to the wreck site must be made by boat. That poses no problem, particularly when seas are calm; the location is only about three and one half miles down the coast from the entrance to Gloucester Harbor.

Although visibility varies, it is usually sufficient to search for artifacts. The shallow depth makes the wreck site suitable, even for the novice diver. But, in rough seas, the turbulence can create treacherous conditions, because the wreckage is so near the island's rocky shore.

Unheralded in service, overshadowed by her more glamorous sister ships, U.S.S. *New Hampshire,* last of the ships-of-the-line, is known by many as New England's most famous shipwreck. In the year of this country's bicentennial the wreck site received what was probably *New Hampshire*'s greatest distinction: its acceptance into the National Register of Historic Places.

Chapter 5

U.S.S. *Alligator*— Pirate Hunter

Location: Alligator Light, Indian Key, Florida
Approximate depth of water: 10 to 15 feet
Visibility: excellent
Current: little or none
Access: boat

Piracy, it is claimed, is humanity's third oldest profession—after prostitution and medicine. Records of the early civilizations of the Middle East, the Cretans, the Vikings, and the Barbary corsairs of North Africa show that it has thrived wherever the potential for profit has exceeded the probability of punishment. Warring European countries, French, Dutch and British, refined piracy to their own purposes, commissioning the crews of privately owned ships as "privateers." Those quasi-legal naval auxiliaries were free to attack and loot enemy sea transports, under authorizations termed "letters of marque and reprisal," or simply "letters of marque." The major distinction between a privateer and a pirate was that a privateer could be (but often was not) conscientious and humane. He would steal. That was his mission, but he would not kill; the pirate would do both.

By dawn of the nineteenth century, piracy had flourished in the West Indies for two and a half centuries. Legendary brigands such as Francis Drake, Henry Morgan, and Blackbeard ruled the waves and bloodied the waters of the Caribbean—almost at will. Jean Laffite, the coolest and most defiant pirate the world has known, even involved the most prominent citizens of New Orleans in the smuggling of stolen goods from his base on the nearby island of Grand Terre, in Barataria Bay. He captured booty, moved it into the city, and had it sold there by respected merchants, to their mutual gain.

Captain David Porter took command of the U.S. Naval Station in New Orleans after the 1803 Louisiana Purchase put that clearinghouse for pirated goods under United States control. His efforts to take decisive action were thwarted by city authorities who were unwilling to interfere with pirate activities that were so closely linked to the elite of their community. However, he and his successor, Commodore Daniel C. Patterson, took strong measures against the ships and land bases of pirates in the New Orleans area. Despite their intensive efforts and temporary successes, pirate aggression continued, and even intensified.

Piracy was carried on along the entire shore of the Gulf of Mexico and the Caribbean, the islands of the Bahamas and the West Indies—even the southern Atlantic coast of the United States. During the year 1820, 27 American vessels were reported to have been seized and robbed, although the President had been authorized early in 1819 to employ a suitable naval force to protect commerce. The same act of Congress instructed naval commanders to seize vessels committing piratical violations and send them into port. It authorized merchantmen to oppose and capture such vessels, and provided for the trial and condemnation of the culprits, with death the penalty for piracy.

The commitment of the United States to suppress piracy in the Caribbean led to the construction of five small U.S. Navy schooners. They were suitable for the task and inexpensive to man and maintain. Four of the five were assigned to naval architect William Doughty of the Washington Navy Yard. The Navy's seven 74-gun ships-of-the-line, including *Ohio* and *New Hampshire,* were built to his basic design. His schooner design was a Baltimore Clipper, 86 feet between perpendiculars, 24 feet 9 inches molded beam, and 10 feet 3 inches depth of hold. *Alligator* was built at Boston Navy Yard, *Dolphin* at the Philadelphia Yard, *Shark* at the Washington Yard, and *Porpoise* at the Portsmouth Yard.

Local discretion was allowed in finishing the vessels, as was the case with the 74's designed by Doughty, leading to variations between them when they were completed. *Alligator,* for example, measured two inches less beam and one inch more depth of hold than Doughty had specified. The four schooners differed in cosmetic features such as moldings, channels, dead-eyes, stems and bow, reflecting the lack of detailed specifications because of the accelerated building program.

U.S.S. Alligator*'s plan of spars and sails. (Courtesy of the Naval Historical Center.)*

Alligator, the third U.S. Navy vessel to carry that name, was laid down on June 26, 1820, with Joshua Barker as master builder. Isaac Hull, commandant of the yard, was the Commodore Hull who 18 years later, selected U.S.S. *Ohio* as his flagship. The 198-ton, 12-gun *Alligator* was launched November 2, and was commissioned in March 1821 with Lt. Robert F. Stockton in command. A trial run on March 12 found her to be a "stiff and good sailer, making up to 8 knots on a wind under her lower sails alone."

Alligator embarked from Boston on April 3 on a two-fold mission—to capture ships engaged in the illegal slave trade and to select a site for setting up a colony of relocated slaves. She took on additional crew at New York, and sailed for Cape Verde, on the coast of Africa. Stockton was ordered to cruise as far south as the Equator, following the course regularly used by slave trading vessels. The schooner was to remain on the African coast as long as provisions permitted, then to sail home to a convenient port in the United States by way of the West Indies, again along routes used by slave traders.

A United States agent and Dr. Ayres, a member of the American Colonization Society, were picked up on the coast of Africa. Their mission was to find the best location for a colony of returned slaves. Lt. Stockton was instrumental in selecting and acquiring territory around Cape Mesurado for that purpose. Negotiations with the primary native chieftan, King Peter, were fraught with danger because his people were noted slavers themselves.

After initial discussions, King Peter withdrew 20 miles inland, challenging Stockton to follow him "if he dare." Stockton and Ayres accepted the challenge, and penetrated the swamps and jungle. They not only survived, but Lt. Stockton singlehandedly cowed the native leader and his 500 followers by his forceful personality. The result was that the parcel of coast around Cape Mesurado was made available, providing the nucleus from which the Republic of Liberia evolved.

Alligator's mission to capture slave trading ships was equally successful. By the time she returned to Boston in July, four slavers had been taken, including the schooners *Mathilde, L'Eliza*, and *Daphne*.

A second African cruise on October 4, 1821 provided the crew with an unusual encounter. On November 5, a strange sail was sighted ahead steering an intercepting course. It flew a distress flag and lay to, awaiting *Alligator*'s approach. As the American schooner came within range of the stranger's guns, the vessel hoisted a Portuguese flag and opened fire. *Alligator,* with her smaller guns, was forced to weather the bombardment, suffering several casualties in getting the enemy within range. Her first volley was accurate. It sent the aggressor's crew scurrying for shelter.

After absorbing 20 minutes of punishing broadsides, the enemy struck her colors. Records of the action identify the vessel by two slightly different names, *Mariano Foliero* and *Marianna Flora*. When her captain was ordered aboard the American schooner he claimed to be operating under a Portuguese letter of marque. Unimpressed by that claim of privateer status, Lt. Stockton put a prize crew aboard and sent the vessel back to the United States to be condemned by an Admiralty Court. If he was impressed at all, it was by the unprovoked attack on a U.S. Navy warship and the misguided premise that it could be justified by a contract with a friendly foreign nation. However, the Portuguese government interceded, and the Admiralty Court returned the vessel to her owners. The logic of that decision is difficult to appreciate.

Following those visits to the African coast, *Alligator* was ordered to the West Indies as part of the force under the command of Commodore Biddle who had been charged with the responsibility for suppressing piracy against the United States in those waters. On April 30, she took the Colombian privateer schooner *Cienega* off Nuevitas, Cuba. The chartered schooner *Jane*, with a shallower draft than *Alligator*, was placed under the command of Lt. Stockton. The crew consisted of 60 men from *Alligator* and *Grampus*. On May 1 the strike force burned one pirate schooner in the area of Sugar Key, Cuba, took another schooner and a sloop from the pirates, and recovered an English brig, the captain and mate of which had already been hanged by the freebooters.

Alligator *attacking three pirate schooners off Matanzas, Cuba in November 1822.*
(Courtesy of the Mariners' Museum, Newport News, Virginia.)

After a successful tour of duty, Lt. Stockton was replaced as commander of *Alligator* by thirty-two year old Lt. William H. Allen, who had gained distinction in battle during the War of 1812. Allen was esteemed by his superiors, and was held in high regard and affection by his subordinates. On November 8, he learned that two American merchantmen recently taken by pirates were lying in a bay about 40 miles east of his position, off Matanzas, Cuba. *Alligator* set sail for the bay at once.

At daybreak on November 9, Allen discovered not only the two merchantmen, but three others—and also three pirate schooners, with a total of more than a hundred men. Shallows barred access to the anchorage, so Allen and 40 sailors and marines took to the vessel's small boats. As the boats closed in, with Allen standing erect issuing orders, the pirates opened fire with guns and muskets. One of the musket balls grazed Allen's head but he remained erect, ordering the fire returned and the chase pressed. The pirates abandoned their ship as the Americans prepared to board. They fled to one of the schooners that had sailed to their aid, firing as she approached.

The pirate schooner began to sail off as soon as the fugitives were aboard, with the small boats of the American boarding party in pursuit. She was joined in flight by the third pirate ship. In the exchange of fire, the pirates suffered a heavy toll, but their return fire was effective. Several sailors and marines were hit, and a musket ball thudded into Allen's chest. Although he was mortally wounded, he maintained command until the pirates escaped, leaving behind their abandoned ship and the five merchant vessels.

Allen's death raised cries for vengeance from the American people. Congress responded by authorizing a new West Indies Squadron consisting of eight schooners, five barges and an old New York ferry boat, *Sea Gull*, to tow barges. The ferry was the first steam-powered vessel used by the U.S. Navy. The Squadron set up its base in Cayo Hueso with Captain David

Porter in command. The location was renamed Allentown in honor of *Alligator*'s fallen captain. Today, it is Key West. Porter's orders were to "get rid of the pirates." That feat was accomplished after a long, hard struggle, and Allen was avenged.

Nine days after Lt. Allen's death, with Lt. John M. Dale in command, *Alligator* sailed from Matanzas, escorting a convoy. Before dawn the following morning, she ran aground on Carysford Reef, Florida, four miles from Indian Key. Dale later reported to the Navy Department:

> . . . after remaining by her three days, using every exertion to get her off, but to no purpose, and expecting any moment that she would go to pieces, I was forced . . . to come to the resolution of abandoning her and making an encampment on one of the Keys.

However, that encampment would not be necessary. The crew of the American brig *Ann Maria*, bound for New York, saw *Alligator* stranded on the reef.

Lt. Dale ordered all armament and other government property transferred to *Ann Maria*. He wanted nothing left behind that might be put to use by the pirates of the area. Dale later wrote, "I shall ever sincerely lament the unfortunate affair." Then, on November 23, 1922, after a two-year career of illustrious service, U.S. Navy schooner *Alligator* was set afire and blew up.

The hazardous stretch of what was then Carysford Reef became known as Alligator Reef, a recognized threat to shipping. The *Florida Herald,* a St. Augustine newspaper, reported on June 2, 1846:

> . . . This is an extremely dangerous point of navigation which is not indicated by any light. The current of the Gulf Stream sweeps in directly upon this reef . . . and it is a very easy thing for even the most prudent navigator, with his lead line constantly going, to find himself on the rocks.

Carysford Reef had succeeded where the pirates had failed, ending the career of U.S.S. *Alligator*. Piracy was eventually subdued as a threat to American shipping, but the Florida Reefs continued to take their toll. From 1848 through 1858, wreckers salvaged 618 ships along the Florida Keys. However, not until November 25, 1873 was $185,000 expended to install Alligator Reef Light to provide protection for sea commerce.

Diving U.S.S. *Alligator*

The site of the wreck, four miles from Indian Key, can be located readily by sport divers. A prominent mound of coral encrusted ballast stones from

Above: The dark area in front of Alligator Light is a coral-encrusted mound of the schooner's ballast stones. (Photo by H. Keatts.)

Left: a diver exposes one of Alligator's *beams by fanning the sand after setting aside his metal detector. (Photo by H. Keatts.)*

the ship lie only a few feet below the surface on the seaward side of Alligator Light. They are easily recognized. The water is warm, clear, and shallow—ideal for exploring the area leisurely and thoroughly.

There is no structure rising above the bottom to identify the ship, but its timbers can be located by probing and fanning the sand around the ballast pile. Metal detectors are useful in locating bronze spikes and cannon balls encrusted in the coral or buried in the sand. Each is an historic artifact of the United States Navy's war on piracy.

Chapter 6

U.S.S. *Yankee*— Converted Liner

Location: Buzzards Bay, New Bedford, Massachusetts
Approximate depth of water: 55 feet
Visibility: bad
Current: moderate to strong
Access: boat

The closing years of the nineteenth century were a turning point in American history. They marked the end of an era of relative isolation and the beginning of a period during which the United States would emerge as a world power. The end of the Spanish-American War is generally accepted as the dividing line between the two epochs.

During the 1890's, many newspaper editors pounded the drum of Manifest Destiny. Captain Alfred Mahan, a prominent naval officer and writer, was one of the foremost proponents of expansion. He was a firm believer in a canal linking the Atlantic and Pacific Oceans, under complete American control. For geographic reasons, it would have to be in Central America and the United States would need Caribbean bases to protect it.

Another vocal expansionist was the young Henry Cabot Lodge of Massachusetts. He felt that Cuba should be taken by force from Spain, and the islands of the Pacific "snatched from the grasping hands of European nations." There were, however, vigorous opponents to expansion, President Grover Cleveland for one. Many New Englanders were strong in their denunciation of what they termed imperialism.

Captain Mahan believed America's best offense and defense was a strong navy. The stronger navy demanded by Mahan and other expansionists began to materialize during the 1890's.

The advocates of expansion needed a cause and found one in the Cuban insurrection of 1895. Spanish measures of repression were harsh and the atrocity stories, exaggerated in the columns of the "yellow" press, horrified America. Public opinion demanded a halt to Spanish hostilities.

"Remember the *Maine*"

On February 15, 1898 a tragic explosion destroyed the battleship *Maine* in Havana Harbor. The loss of the U.S. warship and 266 men was the breaking point. In April Congress passed four resolutions that amounted to a declaration of war, with the realization that the conflict would not be restricted to Cuba. It would also include Spain's Pacific possessions. Spain's Navy outnumbered the United States: 137 to 86. Although American warships were newer and better armed, more were needed, quickly.

The passenger liner *El Norte* was built in 1892 by the Newport News Shipbuilding and Drydock Company of Newport News, Virginia for the Southern Pacific Company. The liner's specifications were: length—406 feet; beam—48 feet 3 inches; and 6,888 tons. She was bought by the Navy Department on April 6, 1898 and renamed *Yankee*.

The liner was well-suited for conversion into an auxiliary cruiser. She could make 16 knots, fast for her time. More important, the ship was large enough to take heavy armament. *Yankee*'s iron hull was pierced for eight broadside hull casemates, each containing a 5-inch rapid-fire gun. Also, she was armed with two additional 5-inch guns, six 6-pounders, and two Colt Automatics. Accommodations were retained for a wartime crew of 15 officers and 267 men. The conversion from liner to cruiser was accomplished at the New York Navy Yard, with most of her crew reservists from the New York Naval Militia. Many had trained on the old ship-of-the-line *New Hampshire* (see Chapter 4).

Spanish-American War

Yankee was commissioned on April 14, 1898 and the following month left New York to patrol between Cape Cod and Cape Henlopen in search of Spanish merchant ships. On May 29, the auxiliary cruiser was ordered to Cuba and arrived off Santiago on June 3. *Yankee* engaged in a night action with Spanish torpedo boats the following night.

On June 6, the cruiser participated in the bombardment of Spanish fortifications at Santiago. The American fleet fired about 2,000 rounds. The Spanish batteries at Morro Castle and Fort Aguadores were hit frequently. Spanish losses were 3 killed and 40 wounded. Their response was feeble; *Massachusetts* was hit once, but *Yankee* and the other U.S. warships were unscathed. The following day, the *Yankee* and another warship engaged two Spanish gunboats at Guantanamo, driving them into the upper bay. On June 10, under a heavy protecting fire, *Yankee* and two other warships landed a force of 600 marines at Guantanamo Bay, the first organized United States force to land in Cuba. After fierce fighting they captured the important port. Three days later, while patrolling off Cienfuegos, *Yankee* had another encounter with two Spanish gunboats. Her heavy fire forced them to withdraw into the harbor.

The cruiser continued blockade duty until her dwindling supply of coal forced her to head for Key West. En route, *Yankee* destroyed five Spanish fishing vessels at the Isle of Pines.

The cruiser was ordered from Key West to New York and Norfolk to take on ammunition for the blockading fleet. She returned to Guantanamo in late July for the tedious and dangerous task of transferring her cargo of ammunition to various warships.

Spain sued for peace the following month, and *Yankee* returned to New York. She was decommissioned at the Philadelphia Navy Yard on March 16, 1899.

The "splendid little war," as Secretary of State John Hay termed it, netted the United States possession of Puerto Rico, Guam, and the Philippines, and a guardianship over Cuba.

Yankee was recommissioned as a training ship in May 1903. In December 1904, she was ordered to Panama to exchange marine garrisons in the Canal Zone. For the next year and a half she played a role in the United States' "Gunboat Diplomacy" in the Caribbean, moving from island to island in support of American forces and citizens.

In August 1906, *Yankee* returned to the United States. She participated in President Theodore Roosevelt's Naval Review held at Oyster Bay, New York in September. During the same month she was again taken out of commission, but two years later the cruiser was recommissioned for a

The auxiliary cruiser Yankee *participated in the Spanish-American War. Four of her 5-inch guns are visible in hull ports. (Photo courtesy of the Naval Historical Center.)*

Yankee *on May 2, 1898 at the New York Navy Yard. Note the 5-inch gun turret on the stern. (Photo courtesy of the Naval Historical Center.)*

The cruiser aground off Westport, Massachussets in 1908. (Photo from the collection of William P. Quinn.)

familiar duty—training. On August 19, 1908, *Yankee* embarked a class of Naval Academy midshipmen for exercises off Fishers Island, Boston, and New Bedford, Massachusetts. In Newport, on September 20, Rhode Island Naval Militia were added, increasing her complement to 600 officers and men. Three days later, in a dense fog, compounded by smoke from forest fires, the cruiser ran aground on Spindle Rock off Westport, Massachusetts.

The ship had grounded at high tide; her bow was seven to eight feet out of the water, and it was necessary to lighten her before she could be refloated. Divers tried to plug the many punctures in the cruiser's hull and her guns were removed. She was pulled off on December 4, but, while being towed to New Bedford, she sank in Buzzards Bay, about five miles south of that port.

Diving U.S.S. *Yankee*

Yankee sank in about 55 feet of water and was periodically salvaged until September 1920. Then, because it was considered a hazard to navigation, the cruiser was blown apart.

Water currents in the area range from moderate to strong. Visibility is usually as low as one to five feet. On rare occasions, however, it can be as much as 20 feet. Divers are cautioned to stay clear of the jagged edges

The cruiser submerged in Buzzards Bay. (Photo from the collection of William P. Quinn.)

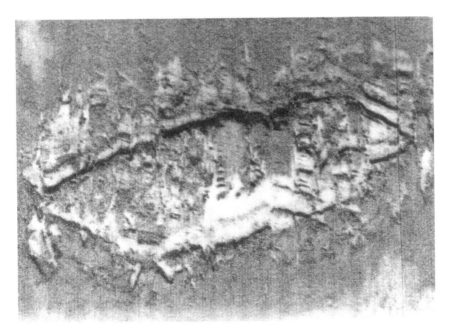

Side-scan sonar printout of Yankee *showing scattered wreckage. (Courtesy of the Historical Maritime Group of New England.)*

of metal wreckage that are particularly hazardous because visibility is usually so low.

Wreckage is flattened out on either side of the hull over a considerable distance. The main part of the hull, however, is distinguishable and can be followed from bow to stern when good visibility prevails. Some sections of the wreck extend six to ten feet off the bottom. The bow and stern are distinguishable only by the parts, the anchor hawser opening and the rudder posts. The wreck is loaded with portholes (she had about 180) and other artifacts typical of a navy vessel of the late 1900's. Solid brass railroad wheels used on gun turrets to pivot the guns, are occasionally recovered. To the amateur historian scuba diver, such a relic of the Spanish-American War is a priceless treasure.

This porthole recovered from the cruiser by Bob Cartier is one of the first examples of safety glass. Note the wire mesh inside the glass. (Photo by H. Keatts.)

An assortment of tools and parts of the cruiser recovered by Bill Carters.

Chapter 7

U.S.S. *Schurz*—
German-American Warship

Location: About 28 miles from Beaufort Inlet, North Carolina
Approximate depth of water: 110 feet
Visibility: good to excellent
Current: little or none
Access: boat

In late July 1914, the Imperial German Navy's antiquated gunboat *Geier* slowly made her way across the Pacific on a routine "flag-showing" cruise to the Kaiser's Far Eastern colonies. The "Great War" was brewing, and the powers of Europe were flexing their muscles in preparation. *Geier* was one of the last steam sailing ships built for Germany. She was not the most impressive symbol of naval strength, but lightly defended targets could be easy prey for her eight 4.1-inch guns (which fired 21-pound projectiles), five 1-pounders, two machine guns, and two 18-inch torpedo tubes.

The 20-year-old *Geier* was built at Wilhelmshaven, Germany in 1894 as an unprotected cruiser, then later reclassified as a gunboat. She had a ram bow, three masts (later converted to two), and one funnel. Her two, triple-expansion, coal-fired engines produced a speed of 16 knots; she was 295 feet in length, had a beam of 33 feet, and displaced 1,630 tons.

When war was declared, the German Admiralty flashed the news to all ships at sea, including *Geier* and her complement of 161, alone on

Geier early in her German Imperial Navy career. (Photo courtesy of the Naval Historical Center.)

the Pacific. Admiral von Spee's China Squadron was too distant to provide any support for the little gunboat. Her only hope was to drop from sight and avoid the French, British, and Japanese warships that were known to be active in the Pacific. Although she was not much of a threat to most warships, she could be deadly to merchant shipping, a threat her enemies wanted to eliminate.

For one month the British and their allies, including the Japanese, who opposed Germany during World War I, could find no trace of the German gunboat—she became a ghost ship. One intelligence report placed her off Singapore, but that sighting proved to be von Spee's armored cruiser *Gneisenau.* By the end of August, British intelligence had located all Germany's warships except two, the light cruiser *Koenigsberg* and the gunboat *Geier.* Then, on September 4, *Geier* made a sudden appearance at Kusaie in the Eastern Carolines, where *Southport,* an unarmed British freighter of 3,588 tons lay at anchor in the harbor. Her crew was not even aware that war had been declared when *Geier*'s captain sent a prize crew aboard to disable the freighter. That was accomplished by removing the engines' main and high-pressure eccentric gears, the intermediate stop valve, and many of the ship's store of maintenance tools. Then the gunboat left the area.

As the German warship disappeared over the horizon, the British seamen examined the damage and went to work on repairs. In 11 days they managed to restore the engines to limited working condition by fitting the eccentric gear from the astern low-pressure cylinder to the forward high-pressure cylinder, eliminating the middle cylinder. The result was some semblance of a compound engine that could move the ship forward, but she could not move astern. Despite that limitation, the freighter sailed for Australia on September 18, and arrived at Brisbane 12 days later.

Southport's delayed report of the incident launched an intensive search for *Geier* by an armada of Allied warships. The German gunboat managed to elude detection until empty coal bunkers and the need for maintenance drove her to seek asylum in the then-neutral port of Honolulu in mid-October. President Wilson had announced on August 4, 1914 that no one in the United States "shall take part, directly or indirectly, in the said wars, but shall maintain a strict and impartial neutrality." Under the rules of neutrality, the German gunboat would have been allowed sufficient time to make the necessary repairs to sail for the nearest friendly port. But when her presence was reported, two Japanese warships, the battleship *Hizen* and the armored cruiser *Asama* took up stations, patrolling Honolulu's 3-mile limit to intercept the gunboat if she should try to leave that sanctuary.

Geier remained in port for over two years—safe, but non-combatant. When the interned Germans realized that the United States would be drawn into the war, they sabotaged their ship's machinery and boilers, and set the gunboat on fire on February 4, 1917. U.S. naval detachments turned over most of *Geier*'s crew to the army for detention after that action. Subsequent inspection of the ship turned up machine guns and ammunition, in violation of orders to her commanding officer that all arms and munitions were to be turned over to U.S. naval authorities.

They had further violated U.S. sanctuary by telegraphing messages between German agents in America and Japan, collaborating with Count von Bernstoff, the German Ambassador to the United States, to get members of the crew back to Germany and circulating false plans of the United States to invade Canada. The diary kept by Karl Grasshof, the captain of *Geier*, was very informative on those violations.

Geier was taken to Pearl Harbor with her flag and pennant flying and a skeleton crew aboard in accordance with internment regulations. One week later, charges against the German officers and men were dismissed in federal court at the request of the U.S. District Attorney. Two months later war was declared against Germany, and the gunboat was seized by the U.S. Navy under an executive order dated May 22, 1917. Her name was changed to U.S.S. *Schurz* on June 9, 1917 to honor Carl Schurz, a renowned German-American statesman and reformer who had fled his country after the 1848 revolution.

The German cruiser's ornate bow and stern. The photographs were taken while the warship was interned in Honolulu Harbor. (Photos courtesy of the Hawaii State Archives.)

German sailors aboard Geier *in Honolulu Harbor. Their hatbands read: S.M.S.* Geier. *(Photo courtesy of the Hawaii State Archives.)*

The German gunboat burning at her slip in Honolulu Harbor. (Photo courtesy of the Hawaii State Archives.)

German sailors from Geier *being taken to detention. (Photo courtesy of the Hawaii State Archives.)*

The renamed warship was commissioned into the U.S. Navy on September 15, 1917, and her main battery of German guns was replaced by four 5-inch U.S. Navy guns. She had served Germany for almost 23 years; she would be in the service of her new masters for less than one.

Schurz, under command of Captain Arthur Crenshaw, departed Pearl Harbor on October 31, escorting a convoy of four submarines (*K-3*, *K-4*, *K-7*, and *K-8*) to San Diego, California. She performed escort duty for convoys along the west coast of Mexico and Central America until December 30, when she transited the Panama Canal. She operated off the coast of Honduras until January 11, 1918, then sailed for Key West, Florida. Until February 12, she operated out of Gulf ports, then was ordered to Charleston, South Carolina for overhaul.

Schurz was placed under the command of Commander W. B. Wells in April 1918, and was attached to the American Patrol Detachment, U.S. Atlantic Fleet, performing routine exercises and patrol duties. After Guantanamo Bay, the Canal Zone, and two days in New York, the gunboat left New York for Key West on June 19, as an escort to a convoy.

Two days later, at 4:44 a.m., the steel bow of the tanker *Florida* knifed into *Schurz*'s starboard side, although the gunboat had been running with masthead lights on, despite the threat of U-boat attack. The tanker, running without lights, sighted the gunboat at about 900 yards, turned on running lights, and blew four warning whistle blasts. *Schurz*'s crew responded by putting her rudder hard left and stopping both engines, actions that did nothing to prevent the collision.

The tanker struck the small warship abreast of the starboard bridge, crumpling that wing of the bridge and penetrating deep into the berth deck. Seaman 2nd Class Manuel Gouveia, Jr., the starboard bridge lookout, was hurled over the bridge onto the fire-room hatch by the impact and died instantly. He had performed his duty by reporting the impending collision, then he remained paralyzed as the onrushing bow knifed through his ship's hull like a sharp cleaver. His was the only death of the disaster.

Florida sheared through coal bunker #3 into the forward fire-room. Commander Wells was wounded in the chest and face when the bridge rail of his ship crumpled, but he retained command and ordered S.O.S. calls sent out. The severe chest injuries he suffered probably contributed to his early death a few years after the disaster. In addition to the single death, three officers and nine men of the 217 aboard were injured.

The order to abandon ship was given 16 minutes after the collision. Executive officer, Lieutenant Commander Glenn F. Howell, directed the operation, and it was conducted with perfect discipline. Sixteen years later Howell wrote to a fellow officer:

> One interesting feature of the collision between the ships was the fact that the *Florida* rammed her bow so far into the *Schurz* that she cut through a coal bunker and actually touched a steaming boiler. Both ships were stopped at the instant of collision, but during the crumpling up of the bridge of the *Schurz*, the engine telegraphs were wrecked, giving a backing signal as this occurred. The inrushing water chased the firemen up the ladder, but they were uninjured, and the boiler did not explode. The ship remained afloat for three hours after the collision, though her obvious condition made abandonment necessary immediately.

Lifeboats from Saramacca *pick up survivors from* Schurz, *which lost only one seaman in its collision with the tanker* Florida. *The tanker, with a gaping hole in her bow, can be seen in the background. The captions of early reproductions of this photograph mistakenly identified the ship as* Schurz. *(Photo courtesy of the Naval Historical Center.)*

Florida took 180 of her victim's officers and men on board. Thirty minutes later the American steamship *Saramacca* arrived in response to the gunboat's distress calls. Her boats picked up the remaining survivors from a life raft. Meanwhile, *Florida,* with a gaping hole in her bow, was in danger of sinking in the high seas. Her oil cargo was pumped overboard to lighten her; the resulting slick helped to calm the seas during the rescue operations. The tanker's condition worsened, and her captain signaled *Saramacca* at 5:30 a.m. that the gunboat's survivors should be transferred at once. Boats of the three ships were used to accomplish the transfer without incident or injury.

A crew of volunteers was formed to return to the warship and beach her in the lee of Cape Lookout (almost 30 miles distant). However, the gunboat took a sudden list to port at 7:50 a.m. before the volunteers could come on board. She slowly sank by the bow as the stern rose to a perpendicular position. At 7:58 a.m. U.S.S. *Schurz* (née *Geier*) disappeared into 110 feet of water at 34° 09′N, 75° 47′W. Her survivors arrived in New York three days later.

Five officers and seven crewmen were cited by the secretary of the navy for their coolness and courage during the disaster—actions that were responsible for the survival of all but the lookout who was killed at the time of the collision and the extremely low injury rate.

A Naval Court of Inquiry determined that the collision was due to a navigational error by *Florida*'s captain.

Diving U.S.S. *Schurz*

The wreck remained undisturbed for more than 50 years until the early 1970's, when George Purifoy and fellow divers from Morehead City discovered its location. Since then, Purifoy has taken hundreds of divers to the site on his boats *Olympus I* and *II.* They are attracted by water temperatures in the mid-70's and 80's, little or no current, and extremely good visibility of 30 to 150 feet. At times, the 110-foot deep wreck is visible from the surface.

Schurz, often referred to as the "World War I wreck," lies 27.7 miles from Beaufort Inlet, a long boat trip. However, divers will find her one of the best sources of artifacts off the coast of North Carolina, well worth the time and discomfort. Both German and U.S. naval artifacts can be retrieved. Many marker plaques bear English inscriptions on one side and German on the other. Some of the artifacts that are known to have been recovered are two of her four telegraphs, two compasses, portholes with brass covers weighing more than 60 pounds, and brass cleats weighing as much as 50 pounds. Many clips of small caliber (rifle) ammunition and 5-inch shells are scattered about the site.

Divers search for artifacts amidst Schurz*'s scattered wreckage. (Photos by Brad Sheard.)*

Much of the wreckage is scattered. Large steel hull plates are strewn along the bottom. In some areas, however, the hull extends ten feet off the bottom. Jagged metal and hard coral abound; they can be hazardous to a careless diver.

Fish swim around two of the warship's boilers (above) and scattered wreckage (below). (Photos by Brad Sheard.)

A colorful variety of sea anemones, fish, spiny lobsters, sea urchins, and sponges have taken residence on the wreck. They provide all the entertainment and subject matter an underwater photographer could ask for, a tribute to how beautiful a dive into history can be.

Chapter 8

U.S.S. *San Diego*— Mined or Torpedoed?

Location: 12 miles southeast of Fire Island Inlet, New York
Approximate depth of water: 110 feet
Visibility: poor to good
Current: little, but there is often a strong surge on the wreck
Access: boat

The only major U.S. warship lost in World War I lies inverted, superstructure buried in sand, and keel uppermost, only 12 miles southeast of Fire Island Inlet, New York. *San Diego*, victim of a German U-boat, rests in her humiliating posture, under approximately 110 feet of the Atlantic, with a depth of about 65 feet to the upended keel. It no longer matters whether the armored cruiser was sunk by mine or torpedo; it is generally agreed that she was sent to the bottom by *U-156*, one of Imperial Germany's underwater fleet assigned to maraud the Eastern Seaboard of the United States.

The U-boat crew forever lost their opportunity to celebrate the coup and resolve how it was accomplished when *U-156* disappeared while returning to her home port. It is ironic that she was last reported trying to penetrate a massive mine field that the U.S. Navy had planted in the North Sea.

Conflicting casualty reports circulated immediately after *San Diego* sank. The count was difficult to validate because survivors reached different havens

Armored cruiser California, *later renamed* San Diego. (*Courtesy of the Naval Historical Center.*)

by so many routes. Some were rescued by Navy or Coast Guard vessels, some by merchant ships, and several boat loads reached shore at Fire Island under their own power. The night of the disaster, 30 to 40 of the crew managed to reach the streets of New York City—with no idea of where or to whom they should report. The validation process was further complicated by the availability of only two copies of the ship's official muster roll. One went down with the ship; the other was at the Portsmouth Navy Yard.

The Navy first reported 1,187 survivors, but records indicated only 1,114 assigned to the ship. More up-to-date records increased the number aboard to 1,255; apparently 141 additional crew members were added somewhere along the line. One early Navy report claimed no loss of life, quickly followed by announcement that casualties might total 62. Naval authorities later released the names of three known dead and 47 missing. Within two days, all but eight were accounted for. It was five days after the disaster before the secretary of the navy released an official statement that six enlisted men were lost. That much, at least, is confirmed.

The cause of the sinking is not so certain, although the Navy officially concluded that it was a mine laid by *U-156*. Others, including Captain Christy, *San Diego*'s commander, felt that a torpedo was more likely. The *New York Times* carried an interesting report in the July 21, 1918 edition, under a July 20, dateline:

> In the opinion of Captain H.H. Christy, commander of the armored cruiser *San Diego*, formerly the *California*, which was sunk yesterday ten miles from Fire Island, his ship was torpedoed by a German submarine. He does not make this position positive, however, for reasons telegraphed to the Navy Department.

Any uncertainty the captain may have entertained at that time was reflected later, in his official report of the disaster:

> . . . The cause of the accident was a severe external explosion of a submerged mine or torpedo which occurred well below the water line on the port side at the forward end of the engine room . . .

Further confusion was added by officers of two U-boats, who made conflicting claims to the crews of small Allied vessels. The first captured the schooner *Fornfonstein* in the Bay of Fundy on August 2, and the Canadian crew was informed that the U-boat had sunk *San Diego* with a mine. In mid-August, the commander of another U-boat announced to the crew of the Canadian trawler *Triumph*, that his U-boat had done the job with a torpedo. Today, it doesn't really matter.

The keel of the lost warship was laid May 7, 1902, at the Union Iron Works, San Francisco, California. Five years later, on August 1, 1907, she was commissioned U.S.S. *California* (AC-*6*), Captain C.H. Arnold commanding. Fully loaded, the armored cruiser displaced 15,335 tons; overall length was 503 feet 11 inches; beam 69 feet 6.5 inches; draft at normal displacement 24 feet 1 inch. Her designed complement was 47 officers and 782 enlisted men.

The ship's impressive armament consisted of four 8-inch, fourteen 6-inch, eighteen 3-inch, twelve 3-pounder, two 1-pounder, and four .30-caliber guns, and two submerged 18-inch torpedo tubes.

The principal wartime modification of *San Diego* was a reduction in her armament. The reason was two-fold; to provide guns for auxiliaries and merchant ships, and to improve watertightness of the warship for convoy duty under North Atlantic winter conditions. By 1918, several of the armored cruiser's 6- and 3-guns had been removed and the ports sealed.

Guns bristle from the sides of California *at San Diego, California in 1910. (Photo courtesy of the Naval Historical Center.)*

Engraving of U.S.S. San Diego *issued for the Panama-California Exposition, 1915. (Courtesy of the Naval Historical Center.)*

Power was provided by two sets of four-cylinder, triple-expansion coal-fired engines driving twin screws, with coal capacity of 2,685 tons. Five to six inches of tapered armor plate protected the hull above and below the water line against enemy firing or ramming. During her trials, the new armored cruiser generated 29,381 hp at 22.20 knots.

Until Congress passed legislation reserving the names of states for battleships, the armored cruiser served as U.S.S. *California*. She lost that identity on September 1, 1914 when she was renamed U.S.S. *San Diego* to serve another four years, throughout most of World War I. She was in constant demand for convoy service because of her heavy armament and the outstanding reputation of her gun crews. Thousands of Allied seamen and troops, terrified by the threat of Germany's U-boats, were reassured by her impressive presence as their escort on hazardous trans-Atlantic crossings.

An incident on January 21, 1915 suggested the ultimate fate of the cruiser; nine crew members perished in a prophetic boiler room blast. Another boiler room explosion destroyed the vessel 3 1/2 years later. *San Diego* now rests under 110 feet of ocean off the coast of Long Island, New York. The formidable warship has become an artificial reef, abounding in marine life

Admiral Thomas B. Howard, commander-in-chief of the Pacific Fleet, center, standing before a San Diego *8-inch gun turret with members of his staff in 1917. (Photo courtesy of the Naval Historical Center.)*

and artifacts of another age. But the wreckage still carries potential destruction in the tremendous amounts of live ammunition still housed in her hull. Not only did the original U.S.S. *California* achieve a new identity during her life, but a new image after her death.

The Sinking

It was the morning of July 19, 1918—only four months before the Armistice that ended World War I. *San Diego*, by then commanded by Captain H. H. Christy, was underway to New York City from Portsmouth, New Hampshire. At about 10 a.m., a look-out alerted the bridge to a small object moving on the surface. Its speed was faster than the prevailing current, leading to speculation that it might be a German U-boat.

The threat of U-boat action galvanized *San Diego*'s gun crews into action. After several rounds were fired, the unidentified target disappeared—further supporting the belief that it was a U-boat. Lookouts were even more alert. Yet, less than an hour later, the zig zagging cruiser shuddered from an external explosion that shattered her portside hull and two massive internal blasts that erupted in the boiler room. Her gun crews again sprang into action, firing at every real or imagined object within range—but too late to avert disaster. The port engine was destroyed by the initial explosion. Full speed ahead on the starboard engine was ordered in an effort to beach the warship before she sank. That only hastened the inevitable, as tons of seawater, driven into the ruptured hull by the vessel's forward speed, drowned the remaining engine.

San Diego wallowed at the mercy of the Atlantic as Captain Christy ordered "Abandon Ship." Hundreds of seamen leaped into the ocean, huddled in lifeboats, clung to rafts or treaded water. They watched the warship list until the forward turret, with its two 8-inch guns, broke free and slipped beneath the surface as if on well-greased launching rails. The big cruiser capsized and slowly disappeared underwater within 30 minutes of the first blast. Her emotional crew choked on the National Anthem in a farewell salute while they struggled for their own survival.

C.E. Sims, an engineer from Islip, Long Island, an 18-year-old seaman at the time of the sinking, recalled forty-one years later:

> I was on the bridge and had just rung 6 bells (11 a.m.). I was looking through a telescope when I heard the explosion. It was on the port side, near the engine room. I looked aft and saw a huge column of smoke about 100 feet high. The general alarm went off almost immediately. . . . We were all told to go aft. There was no panic. They gave everyone life jackets and canteens of fresh water. There was an officer who stood on the ladder with his hand on his holster. I remember he said, "If any one jumps before Abandon Ship is given, I'll shoot him." It was calm as a lake on the ocean. It took twenty minutes before the ship started to go down.

The cruiser had not radioed for help because the first explosion destroyed all communication equipment. However, Navy aircraft in the vicinity reported the explosions and the gun crews' firing. Alerted authorities immediately flooded the air waves with distress signals. All ships in the area converged on the site in an intensive search for survivors.

Captain James F. Brewer, commanding one of the rescue ships, observed:

> Just before rescuing the men, my vessel passed a school of perhaps twenty sharks, which were feeding on the body of a small whale. The sight gave me a scare, for I was afraid they were also after the men in the water, but I was told that no sharks had been seen by them.

Proximity to shore, quick response by rescue vessels, calm seas, and no interference from predator or enemy assured a high rate of survival. Only six lives were lost; three were caused by the initial explosion, one by a collapsing funnel, one by a falling lifeboat, and a lookout was trapped inside the cage mast. Some of the crew actually rescued themselves, rowing to shore at nearby Point O' Woods on Fire Island.

The sinking, almost within hailing distance of New York City, was of such concern to the Navy that an immediate ban was imposed on civilian use of communication facilities to ensure that misinformation would not be circulated. All telephone and telegraph wires from Long Island regions where the explosions had been heard were commandeered at once. The explanation was that all communication facilities were reserved for official Navy business during the emergency. "In the interest of security," the survivors were placed in quarantine as soon as they were rounded up, although some information did leak out from those who had rowed to shore at Point O' Woods and others wandering around New York City.

By 6 p.m. on the day of the sinking, lookouts on submarine chasers that were patrolling the area reported air bubbles breaking the surface. Depth charges were dropped, on what was thought to be a U-boat, but the target proved to be the remains of *San Diego*. The additional damage inflicted by her own navy added insult to injury.

U.S. Navy divers visited the wreck to determine the feasibility of salvage. They found *San Diego* bottom up, her keel at the bow only 36 feet underwater. A commercial salvage company, contracted to conduct a more extensive survey, found that the bridgeworks had collapsed and the top of the remaining turret was touching the sand. In addition, thousands of rivets had shaken loose, opening seams in the hull. Even if the gaping hole in the engine room could be patched, the wreck could never be made watertight. To further complicate any salvage attempt, unexploded depth charges lay on and around the hull.

The underwater survey report convinced the Navy that salvage efforts would be fruitless. *San Diego* was struck from the Naval Vessel Register in August, 1918, the month following her sinking.

Mine or Torpedo?

Authorities were concerned that the disaster might signal the beginning of an all-out German Admiralty campaign to disrupt Allied troop transport by using long-range U-boats along the American coast. Such a suggestion might have created panic in shipping circles that would damage the war effort. A *New York Times* editorial in the July 21, 1918 edition was characteristic of the type of rumor the Navy was anxious to discourage:

. . . but the sinking of the *San Diego* must not be regarded lightly as the fortune of war. A serious condition exists when an American armored cruiser is torpedoed on this side of the Atlantic and not far from a port which convoyed vessels are constantly leaving for France.

The significant difference between a torpedo and a mine is that a torpedo can be directed against a specific target—a troop-laden transport, for example. The success of a mine is left to chance. Captain Christy's initial assessment was that his ship had been sunk by a torpedo because it was struck aft of the beam, an unlikely point of contact between a speeding vessel and a floating mine. However, the Navy publicly announced that a mine was responsible. Reinforcing that conclusion, naval forces located six contact mines in the area the day after the disaster.

A merchant captain who had lost three steamships to U-boat torpedos agreed with the Navy's conclusion. He was convinced that the cruiser had struck a mine, because the destructive force of a mine is far more damaging than a torpedo, and *San Diego* would have stayed afloat longer if she had been hit by a single torpedo.

It was noted that not one of the ships that stood by to pick up survivors had been attacked—nor had naval air or surface craft detected any sign of a submarine. The chief of staff, U.S. Naval Cruiser Force, asserted in an official statement that there was no evidence of a U-boat in the vicinity, nor had any of the *San Diego* crew positively identified one. Some naval officers believed that a cargo ship under a neutral flag might be responsible; ships flying Swedish and Norwegian flags had been captured in Europe with mines hidden in their holds.

As previously mentioned, the crew of the captured and burned Canadian schooner *Fornfonstein*, reported that the commander of *U-156* claimed credit for sinking *San Diego* with a mine. However, 18 days later, another U-boat commander boasted to two American crew members of the captured Canadian fishing trawler, *Triumph*, that he had sunk the cruiser with a torpedo. That was only one of the contradictions to support Captain Christy's immediate judgment that his ship had been struck aft of the beam by a torpedo.

The presence of U-boats in the area was discounted by the Naval Cruiser chief of staff—but submarines had been reported on the northerly steamship routes for several days before the sinking. Ship captains had been warned to set courses as close to shore as possible. Only three days before *San Diego* sank, the Norwegian bark *Marosa* was torpedoed and sunk close enough to shore for survivors to reach Nova Scotia the following day. Two days after the cruiser went down, several barges were shelled by a U-boat off Cape Cod. U-boats were certainly operating along the Atlantic coast.

The argument that only a mine could have dealt such a devastating blow to the armored cruiser and caused her to sink so quickly was countered by equally persuasive reasoning. One of the two internal explosions could have been a powder magazine to add to the torpedo damage—or a second torpedo could have multiplied the explosive effect of a single torpedo. The quick sinking was accounted for by the fact that the ship was steaming full speed ahead on her remaining engine, scooping sea-water into the gaping hull at an extremely high rate.

A court of inquiry appointed by the Navy Department to investigate the sinking absolved Captain Christy, his officers, and men of responsibility for the loss. It also commended them for their bravery and discipline that contributed to the minimal loss of lives. The court agreed that the ship had been sunk by a mine laid by *U-156*.

Whether by mine or torpedo, the armored cruiser fell victim to a U-boat in home waters after not sighting an enemy submarine on seven round-trips to France.

Six U-boats raided the American coast during the First World War, sinking 91 vessels for a total of 166,907 tons of shipping. *U-156*, the only German naval vessel to sink a U.S. capital ship during the war, was the only German raider that did not reach home.

Ironically, the U-boat that had generated so much mine vs. torpedo controversy was sunk by a mine laid by the U.S. Navy. This was a new type of mine, more deadly than previous types, known as Mark H2. It was a copy of the basic German mine such as the one that the U.S. Navy credited

The silhouette of U-156, *credited with sinking the armored cruiser* San Diego *with a mine in 1918. In a twist of irony, the U-boat was sunk by an American mine while she was trying to return to Germany. (Photo courtesy of WZ-Bilddienst, Wilhelmshaven, West Germany.)*

for sinking *San Diego*. *U-156* was lost on her homeward voyage in an attempt to penetrate a U.S.-laid mine field in the North Sea. An immense 240-mile barrage of 70,000 mines was laid between Norway and Scotland. On October 22, five U-boats (*U-100, U-102, U-117, U-140,* and *U-156*) attempted to run that mine field. An Allied prisoner aboard *U-140*, Second Officer Bastin of the tanker *O.B. Jennings*, gave this account:

> We were allowed to go to the conning tower for fresh air, as the air was very bad in the submarine. During the night the air was so bad that everyone had a dry throat and could not speak. We could feel down below that the submarine must be steaming at high speed. When we came up and looked through the hatch we could see the submarines steaming after us. . . . I was up in the conning tower, I suddenly saw a submarine blown up—it was the German *U-156.* She was on our port quarter and steaming in line with the *100*, which was a small sub. She must have struck a mine and was blown 500 feet in the air. A few seconds and everything had disappeared.

The U.S. Navy Historical Center in a letter to William Clark, author of *When the U-boats Came to America*, states of *U-156*:

> . . . she struck a mine and sank in a short time. Twenty-one survivors were landed on the Norwegian coast. . . . The fate of the rest of the crew is unknown but it is probable that they perished with the U-boat.

Liberty Bonds

During the spring of 1917, *San Diego* had been on the West Coast during a Liberty Bond drive. Officers and crew responded by paying for bonds out of their savings. A year later, the bonds were delivered aboard when the cruiser entered New York Harbor to join the convoy services. The subscribers had no alternative but to retain possession of them. They could not be transmitted to relatives by the ship's mail with any assurance of safety because registration of valuable packages was not available. As a consequence, bonds worth $100,000 were lost when the ship sank.

The Treasury Department refused to honor requests from *San Diego* personnel for reimbursement because there was no evidence that the bonds had been destroyed. The Navy Department informed Treasury officials that the ship was underwater to stay; she could not be raised; and no one could ever present the lost bonds for redemption. Even that would not satisfy the Treasury Department, so the Navy took further action. Thirty depth charges were dropped on the wreck. Then, a Navy survey dive team attested that the resulting damage was so extensive that the bonds had certainly been

The wreck of San Diego *lies inverted in about 110 feet of water. Many openings in her hull provide easy access for divers. However, penetration can be dangerous because of sediment and complicated passageways. (Plaque produced by L. Listing from a sketch by G. Gentile and K. Warehouse.)*

destroyed. With that assurance, the Treasury Department relented, and the claimants were reimbursed.

The wreck lay undisturbed for more than three decades—until early in the 1950's, when a Freeport, New York fisherman returning from Montauk observed a large profile on his depth recorder. Following up that chance observation, he noted the Loran numbers and returned the following day. He had rediscovered the lost warship, already a bountiful, artificial reef, ideal for fishing.

Salvage

The Navy sold salvage rights to Maxter Metals Company of New York City. Based on underwater photographs, the salvage operators planned to blow up the vessel's remains for its scrap metal value, at that time $70 a ton. Before the plan could be implemented, three concerned organizations joined forces in opposition and founded the San Diego Fund. The groups were the American Littoral Society, the National Party Boat Owners Association, and the Association of Marine Angling Clubs. Their mutual objective was to preserve wrecks as marine habitats. The destruction of any offshore wreck would defeat that purpose. Their effective lobby convinced the Navy to cancel the Maxter contract and adopt a policy that *San Diego* would remain undisturbed—never again to be offered for salvage.

The starboard propeller was freed from its shaft with explosive charges by a group of unauthorized divers, but the Navy intervened, and it was left

One of San Diego's *props, minus one blade, after salvage. (Photo by Steve Bielenda.)*

Diver inspects one of San Diego's *props while it was still attached to the shaft. He carries a "bang stick" that contains a shotgun shell at its tip to protect against potential shark attack. (Photo by Michael deCamp.)*

lying on the bottom. While the authorities were monitoring the 37,000-pound bronze relic, a group of six divers discovered that the port drive shaft had broken and the propeller was laying in the sand. They made off with it using a 200-foot tanker that had been converted into a salvage vessel. They rigged the propeller under the hull and started towing it toward Staten Island, New York. However, the propeller broke loose and was lost when it dropped to the bottom. Even though official surveillance over the wreck site was probably sporadic, the Navy's reputation for vigilance was not enhanced by the almost successful theft.

After the furor died down, a Long Island diver, operating under a salvage contract from a private group, attempted to raise the remaining propeller. The operation was set up with professional attention to detail, and a barge equipped with an A frame to raise heavy objects. Equipment included underwater cutting gear, burning bars, a 600-cubic-foot-per-minute air compressor, 25 sets of doubles, 60 air storage bottles and oxygen bottles. A shark cage was even included for extended decompression hangs, more for comfort than protection from sharks. Decompressing divers could relax on the bottom of the cage and communicate with those above instead of holding onto the anchor line in solitude.

The divers had lifted a large amount of bronze from the wreck before they rigged the propeller for lifting. It was to be the last item of salvage, a 37,000-pound artifact. As the propeller was being raised, it fouled on a strut. Before the operator could declutch the crane motor, the A frame was overstressed and its starboard leg was forced down four to five inches, opening a leak in the hull of the 700-ton barge, *Lehigh Valley 402*. Despite energetic pumping by the crew, water came in faster than they could pump it out. The 140-foot-long barge, a sizable wreck with a 45-foot beam and a large, 25×20×25-foot deckhouse, with all its expensive equipment, plummeted down to join *San Diego* on the bottom.

The barge, now broken up, still rests where she sank within 100 feet of *San Diego*'s starboard stern, a favored source of over-sized lobsters for "bug-gathering" divers. The elusive propeller was retrieved eventually by others who benefited from having had most of the labor performed for them. Another group of divers retrieved and kept the lost equipment from the sunken barge, including a set of tanks with gold plated valves and the owner's name engraved on the cylinders.

Diving U.S.S. *San Diego*

San Diego lies inverted, in about 110 feet of water, her keel only 65 feet below the surface. In the six decades since her sinking, the hole created by the German mine or torpedo has rusted back until it is now approximately eight feet high and 20 feet long. The huge opening allows easy access to the engine room and its artifacts. The internal explosions that followed the initial blast left another gaping hole that provides easy entry into the boiler room.

Winter storms continue to open new sections of the wreck, providing access to additional areas of the ship's interior each year. She offers a constantly-changing cornucopia of souvenirs for sport divers, and her easy access, close to the shore of Long Island, has made her one of the region's most popular charter boat dive sites. Artifacts abound, but because it is a relatively easy dive with so many attractions to divert the unwary, care and common sense must be exercised. At least three divers have lost their lives inside the wreck—running out of air before they could find their way out.

The interior of *San Diego*, like any shipwreck immersed in seawater for six decades, is no longer recognizable as a ship. Some bulkheads and partitions have collapsed, and in some areas, decks have rusted through. Piles of debris and twisted wires, cables, and conduits are scattered about—like an underwater junkyard. Winter storms continually add to the

A diver inspects the barrel of a 6-inch gun that is encrusted with marine life. (Photo by Michael deCamp.)

shifting layers of silt and sediment that varies in depth from one inch to several feet throughout the wreck. When divers swim through such an interior, their fins stir up that loose material and cloud visibility. All familiar landmarks cease to exist.

Most experienced divers use a reel with several hundred feet of line, tying off the loose end where they enter the wreck. When the penetration is finished, the line is reeled in as they follow it back to the wreck's exterior. It is worthy of note that those divers who lost their lives within *San Diego* did not use penetration lines.

Captain John Lachenmeyer made a rewarding find almost 66 years after the sinking, while he was serving as divemaster aboard Captain Steve Bielenda's 55-foot Dive Boat, R/V *Wahoo*. He secured the anchor line to the wreck for the divers who would follow, then he entered the hull on his own dive. A chunk of encrusted debris, wedged between a beam and the

Speaking tubes for communicating between gun crews and the ship's magazine. They are inverted because of the up-ended position of the wreck. (Photo by Jon Hulburt.)

deck, about 30 feet within the hull, caught his attention in visibility of only five feet. Carefully manipulating his crowbar, an essential tool for artifact recovery, he freed what proved to be a championship trophy cup inscribed with: ". . . presented to the Jackies of the U.S.S. *California* by the City of Vallejo (California), July 4th, 1911." Carefully cleaned of its marine growth, it is one of Lachenmeyer's most prized links to the past.

Dangerous temptations and potential hazards greet divers who enter the ship's magazines to retrieve ordnance that includes live ammunition. Many find powder canisters for the 6-inch cannon, oak cylinders trimmed with copper and brass. Those canisters contain raw silk bags of compressed gun powder pellets. Vast quantities of other live ammunition have also been removed—to adorn walls, mantles, and tables in the homes of divers, friends, or relatives.

In June 1982, the Suffolk County (NY) Police Bomb Squad confiscated a 98-pound piece of ordnance that had been retrieved by a sport diver. The projectile for a 6-inch gun contained 55 pounds of explosive that could have detonated just from drying out, according to Lt. Thomas Compitello,

Closeup of a powder canister. (Photo by H. Keatts.)

Scattered powder canisters for the 6-inch guns in one of the warship's magazines. (Photo by Brad Sheard.)

Above: Divers from the charter boat Wahoo *were able to enter one of the ship's storerooms in 1987. Lanterns, bugles, silverware, dinnerware, and other artifacts were recovered. The divers displaying their find on the stern of the boat are from left to right: Sharon Kissling, Captain Steve Bielenda, Richie Kohler, Ed Murphy, John Lachenmeyer, Dan Berg, Don Schnell, and Richie Gomberg behind the rail. (Photo by H. Keatts.)*

Left: One of the engine room telegraphs. (Recovered by and photo courtesy of Michael deCamp.)

commander of the bomb squad. The object was too large to be handled at the Westhampton Beach Police bomb site and was transferred to the Army Ordnance Division for detonation at Fort Dix, New Jersey. That action aborted the plans of the misguided diver who had intended to sandblast, polish, and place the live projectile next to his fireplace. If it had reached the fireplace, the demolition of his own home and his neighbor's might have followed. The cruiser, *San Diego*, still carries the potential destruction for which she was designed.

This small rectangular compartment with its door hanging open, contained a brass electric lantern. The other end of the compartment was equipped with three glass ports to transmit light into one of the San Diego's *magazines. The ports were tightly sealed to ensure that a spark from the lantern would not ignite the gunpowder. (Photo by Brad Sheard.)*

The Navy reacted to the incident through Lt. Joseph Tenaglia of the Naval Explosive Ordnance Disposal Team from the Earle Naval Ammunition Depot, New Jersey. A cadre of U.S. Navy personnel have received highly specialized training in dealing with unexploded ordnance. Lt. Tenaglia and a team of Navy divers toured *San Diego*'s ammunition room, guided by Stephen Bielenda and Henry Keatts. They concluded that the ordnance rooms should be sealed against further removal of live ammunition to prevent divers from endangering, not only themselves while underwater, but also their families, friends, and neighbors. Eight years later, that action has not been taken; it probably never will be.

Armored cruiser U.S.S. *San Diego*, formerly *California*, lies dormant— but dangerous. She invites examination by the curious, and assesses a terrible penalty on the foolhardy or careless.

Chapter 9

U.S.S. *Wilkes-Barre*— Lethal Lady

Location: 12 miles southeast of Key West, Florida
Approximate depth of water: 250 feet
Visibility: good to excellent
Current: little to strong
Access: boat

World War II introduced a new era of sophisticated naval weapons and delivery systems including powerful torpedoes, depth charges, and ingeniously sensitive mines. All can sink ships, but a ship need not sink to be put out of action. Direct exposure to a near contact explosion can cause hull rupture and immediate flooding. Such an underwater explosion can shake loose vital equipment including propulsion systems; it can produce damaging vibrations in delicate electronic equipment. Also, it can make weapons completely inoperable. A direct hit therefore is not necessary to produce significant damage. For that reason the Navy established the Underwater Explosions Research Division in 1946. The UERD was chartered to develop technology that would allow ship designers to strengthen the hulls of ships and submarines and to improve shipboard installations. Another objective was to provide guidance for improved underwater weapon performance.

Initially, the explosion resistance of existing hull designs was studied by using large-scale models and obsolete submarines. Later, larger ships

Tugs remove Wilkes-Barre *from her anchorage at Philadelphia in preparation for her use in an UERD experiment. (Photo courtesy of UERD and Billy Deans.)*

from the Navy's mothball fleet were subjected to underwater explosions simulating actual weapon attacks. Systems to be evaluated were installed on ships that were then subjected to explosions. The data obtained provided the basis for development of effective structural systems to better protect warships from torpedo attack.

Experiments with a complete ship serve a dual purpose. They provide actual measurements of weapon effects and allow designers to identify weaknesses so that more effective protection can be included in future designs. Shock measuring devices are placed throughout the ship to measure target response. Other measurements are made with velocity meters, string gauges, and accelerometers. All are monitored by high-speed recording equipment on a barge nearby the target. After the targets are instrumented, gauge wires are connected to the recording equipment on the barge.

Research of this nature enables designers to propose equipment that is more shock resistant. It is also invaluable in developing more efficient warheads for underwater weapons. It is of particular value to determine the minimal amount of explosives required and the best location under a hull for detonation. Such a combination can lead to immediate sinking or severe weakening of the hull structure, leaving the warship unable to perform her mission. In 1971, it was decided to use a large warship as a target for UERD researchers. The 10,000-ton light cruiser *Wilkes-Barre* was selected from the mothball fleet and instrumentation was installed throughout the warship. The cruiser sank within minutes after the explosives were detonated, providing valuable information to UERD researchers and establishing a new artificial reef to the benefit of scuba divers and the fishing industry.

The United States was two and a half years into the war with Japan when *Wilkes-Barre* was commissioned. Another five months elapsed in shake-

Wilkes-Barre *settles to the bottom after spewing heavy smoke and breaking in two from explosive charges. The barge on the right was recording the effects of the explosion on various sections of the ship. (Photos courtesy of Billy Deans.)*

Starboard view of the light cruiser Wilkes-Barre's *wartime camouflage. (Photo courtesy of the Naval Historical Center.)*

down, training exercises, and travel before she could join the U.S. Navy's Third Fleet at Ulithi in the Caroline Islands. That left only eight months of combat duty for the new warship to make her mark in World War II. And that she did, with four Battle Stars, seven enemy planes downed, assists on four others, and three air-sea rescues.

The "Lethal Lady" of World War II, never far from the thick of battle, always made her presence felt. She survived the war and 27 years more before she was memorialized, not as a symbol of naval power, but as an artificial reef to serve fishermen of the Florida Keys. Spawned by war and accomplished in spewing death and destruction, *Wilkes-Barre* has found peace in the docile role of habitat for abundant marine life.

The 10,000-ton warship was one of 32 *Cleveland*-class light cruisers ordered in 1940 to cope with the growing threat of war with Germany and Japan. Several were converted into aircraft carriers of the *Independence*-class. The others carried their own complement of aircraft—four Kingfisher seaplanes that were launched by one of the two catapults.

Armament included twelve 6-inch guns, twelve 5-inch guns, and an antiaircraft battery of twenty 40-mm and ten 20-mm guns. Armor measuring 1½ to 5 inches thick protected sides, decks, and gunhouses. *Wilkes-Barre* was 610 feet long; her beam was 66.5 feet; and her draft was 20 feet (mean). She was designed for a speed of 33 knots and carried a crew of 992.

Wilkes-Barre (CL-*103*), was laid down on December 14, 1942 at the Camden, New Jersey yards of the New York Shipbuilding Corporation. She was launched on December 24, 1943, sponsored by Mrs. Grace Shoemaker Miner, the wife of a prominent Wilkes-Barre, Pennsylvania physician. Commissioning followed on July 1, 1944 at the Philadelphia Navy Yard, with Captain Robert L. Porter, Jr. in command.

After fitting-out, followed by a shakedown cruise in Chesapeake Bay and Trinidad, British West Indies, *Wilkes-Barre* returned for her first mission. On October 23, the new warship left Philadelphia for the Pacific via the Panama Canal and San Diego, California. After provisions and ammunition were loaded and exercises were held off San Clemente Island, the cruiser headed for Hawaii on November 10. She arrived at Pearl Harbor on the 17th, two years, eleven months and ten days after the Japanese left it in ruins, launching World War II.

Several exercises were conducted in the Hawaiian Operations area before *Wilkes-Barre* left Oahu on December 14 for Ulithi in the Carolines. She joined Cruiser Division (CruDiv) 17, and sortied on December 30 in support of Vice-Admiral John S. McCain's Task Force (TF) 38. The cruisers were to screen the aircraft carriers of the task force with a ring of antiaircraft fire, protect them from attack by conventional naval forces, and provide the armament for bombarding enemy land targets.

Task force planes first battered objectives on Formosa and the southern Ryukus, then hit Japanese bases in support of landings on Luzon. En route to the South China Sea where the enemy posed a threat to Lingayen Gulf landings, McCain's task force delivered a second strike on Formosa. Three days later Navy planes sank a record 127,000 tons of merchant and naval shipping in the Indo-China area.

Wilkes-Barre, with other ships from CruDiv 17, was detached to deal with enemy warships reported off Camranh Bay, French Indo-China. No trace of the enemy was found, but the task group did do battle with a tropical disturbance that had *Wilkes-Barre* rolling as much as 38 degrees from squalls, heavy seas, and strong winds. When the weather cleared, air strikes by American planes hit Japanese shipping and targets on the China and French Indo-China coasts. Takao, Amoy, and Swatow were hit on January 15; Hainan Island, Indo-China, and Hong Kong were targets for the 16th. The task force returned to Ulithi on January 26 for stores, ammunition, fuel, and repairs. While there, its designation and command were transferred from TF-38, under Vice Admiral McCain, to TF-58, commanded by Vice-Admiral Marc A. Mitscher. Two weeks later, *Wilkes-Barre* was again at sea.

Iwo Jima

The string of islands south of Japan were to serve as stepping stones to the invasion of Japan itself. Iwo Jima, a key stronghold in the chain, was an immediate objective, to be followed by the biggest American amphibious assault of the Pacific war, the invasion of Okinawa. As a diversionary action, U.S. carrier planes struck Tokyo three days before the planned Iwo Jima landing. Air strikes were launched from off the coast of Honshu, Japan with *Wilkes-Barre* one of the CruDiv 17 cruisers screening American carriers. The task group planes pounded Japanese airfields and industrial sites for two days—the first bombing of its kind since Lieutenant Colonel Doolittle's "Tokyo Raiders" strike from the deck of the carrier *Hornet* in April 1942, almost three years earlier.

Its mission accomplished, the task group headed south to Iwo Jima for the invasion. En route, it hit Japanese positions on nearby Chichi Jima and Haha Jima. On February 19, U.S. marines began heading ashore toward the black sand beaches of Iwo Jima.

General Tadamichi Kuribayashi's determined and well-fortified garrison of defenders made it clear that there would be no easy victory for the Americans. *Wilkes-Barre* added her guns to the shore bombardment on February 21 with devastating accuracy. Her fire was directed from above by spotters in her own Kingfishers. On one occasion her prompt and effective response was credited with turning back a fierce counterattack by the Japanese defenders.

Okinawa

By February 25, only six days after the initial assault on Iwo Jima, task group planes were again pounding targets in and near Tokyo—and Okinawa on March 1. Four days later the task group put into Ulithi for supplies and fuel. *Wilkes-Barre* lay at anchor in Ulithi Lagoon for nine days before going out on two days of exercises on March 14 and 15. The carrier task group left on the 16th, to attack the island of Kyushu, east of Okinawa. For the next two days the Japanese island was torn by bombs and rockets, and raked with machine gun fire from the carrier planes.

The damage was extensive, but the raids were by no means one-sided. Two well-placed Japanese bombs turned the carrier *Franklin* into a floating inferno on the 19th, a major disaster for her, and an eventful day for *Wilkes-Barre*; her crew downed their first enemy plane, a Japanese dive-bomber. The task force slowly retired toward its fueling rendezvous, providing protection for disabled vessels, while Japanese aircraft continued their harassment.

Four days later, Admiral Mitscher's carriers again hit Japanese targets in the Okinawa area. The action continued for two days, March 23 and 24. On the 24th, a *Wilkes-Barre* Kingfisher rescued two fliers from the carrier *Bataan* in the seas off Minami Dato Shima. The cruiser returned to the area three days later with a destroyer group and the rest of CruDiv 17 to shell the Minami Dato airfield.

The "softening-up" of Okinawa's defenses by planes of the United States carriers, screened by cruisers and destroyers, continued on the 29th, with dawn searches and strikes against bases along the coasts of Kyushu and the Inland Sea. Again, one of *Wilkes-Barre*'s planes saved two fliers, this time from the carrier *Bunker Hill*, plucking them from the waters off Yaku Shima.

The invasion of Okinawa was launched on Sunday, April 1, 1945 with carrier planes flying cover for the beachhead. Neutralizing raids punished airfields in Kyushi, Shikahaki, and southern Honshu. Shakashima Gunto, in the Nansei Shoto group, proved to be another key base for Japanese planes, and was subjected to heavy air attack. Despite those punishing blows, suicidal Japanese air defenders persisted.

Japan's suicide pilots of World War II flew planes filled with explosives, with orders to crash them into enemy ships, focusing on aircraft carriers. Those suicide planes were called kamikazes, meaning "Divine Wind," referring to a 13th century, vicious typhoon that destroyed a Chinese invasion fleet headed for Japan. Naval historian Samuel Eliot Morison wrote:

> Few missiles or weapons have ever spread such flaming terror, such torturing burns, such searing death, as did the kamikaze in his self-destroying onslaughts.

On April 11 kamikaze planes maintained a continuous attack on the American task force from noon till dark. They swarmed like clouds of angry wasps through the heavy barrages of antiaircraft fire from screening cruisers and destroyers. On that day alone, *Wilkes-Barre* downed a Val dive-bomber and three Mitsubishi "Zeke" fighters, with credit for "assists" on three more.

The heavy concentration of Japanese air strength puzzled the Americans. Surely, the "softening-up" of Okinawa's nearby island bases must have kept hundreds of Japanese aircraft out of the action. It developed that airfields in southern Kyushu, Japan's third largest and southernmost island, were providing many of the planes. The carrier task force headed northward and launched strikes against those bases on the 16th and 17th. Resistance by enemy aircraft was extremely heavy. American combat planes and the antiaircraft fire of *Wilkes-Barre* and the other ships in the carrier screen were kept active throughout the mission.

The now-seasoned cruiser added to her record of kills with the downing of a bomber on the 16th and a Zeke on the 17th. Satisfied that the enemy airfields had been damaged sufficiently, the task force broke off the engagement, and returned to launch strikes against Okinawa from some 60 miles east of the island. That action continued for the rest of April and most of May.

Flames engulf the fleet carrier Bunker Hill *after she was struck by two kamikazes off Okinawa. (Photo courtesy of the Naval Historical Center.)*

On April 26, one of *Wilkes-Barre*'s Kingfisher crews rescued two more Navy flyers, 30 miles east of Okinawa. On May 10, CruDiv 17 was temporarily detached from the task group for a night of shelling Minimi Daito Shima. Japanese Snoopers winging near the carriers, off Okinawa, early the next morning sized up the deployment of the task group and found the opportunity they were seeking. Two kamikazes streaked through the flak like bolts of lightning, and plunged deep into the deck of the fleet carrier *Bunker Hill*. Flames engulfed the flattop's after-deck, trapping many of the crew—dead, dying, injured, and uninjured. *Wilkes-Barre*, back from the shelling of Minimi dato Shima, was ordered to stand by the seriously damaged carrier to help in quenching flames and evacuating crewmen who were trapped by the fire.

Captain Porter maneuvered his light cruiser alongside the carrier at 11:15 a.m., putting his ship's bow hard against the flatttop's starboard quarter. His crew played streams of water on the persistent fires, and supplied fresh water through another hose. Rescue and fire fighting gear were transferred to the carrier as 40 men, trapped astern, scrambled from the stricken ship to safety aboard *Wilkes-Barre*. The cruiser was joined in the battle with the flames by three destroyers: *Stembel* (DD-*644*), *English* (DD-*696*), and *Charles S. Sperry* (DD-*697*). Then, with the cruiser standing 50 feet abeam to starboard, two breeches buoys were rigged to receive 61 injured men, 12 of them dead or dying upon arrival on board.

Bunker Hill had been hit by two of the 150 kamikazes hurled at the American fleet off Okinawa on May 10 and 11. Two huge craters in her flight deck and the flames that engulfed the after-half of the carrier testified to the tremendous impact. Traces of propellers and heaps of ashes were all that remained of 30 planes, fully armed and laden with 12,000 gallons of aviation fuel, that had been lined up on the flight deck. On the hangar deck

Wilkes-Barre *fighting fires on* Bunker Hill *(above). Below, water streams from the flight deck of the stricken carrier. Men can be seen ministering to the wounded on the hangar deck. (Photos courtesy of the Naval Historical Center.)*

below, 48 planes that were being fueled and armed were also destroyed. The motor from one kamikaze was blown into the flag office located in the carrier's superstructure. Fourteen of Admiral Mitscher's staff perished in the disaster. In a ready room below decks, 30 pilots suffocated in the outside passageway trying to escape.

The flames were finally brought under control by the combined efforts of the cruiser, the three destroyers, and the crew of *Bunker Hill*. *Wilkes-Barre* cleared the blackened flattop at 3:34 p.m., after almost four hours and 20 minutes of firefighting and rescue. At 5:00 p.m., she returned to send back 38 uninjured men who had been driven off by the fire and to receive a few additional injured.

Burial services were held aboard *Wilkes-Barre* on May 12, for 13 men from *Bunker Hill*. The wounded who survived were transferred to the hospital ship *Bountiful* (AH-*9*).

Bunker Hill survived and limped to Seattle, Washington for extensive repairs. *Time* magazine reported that the carrier "ranked next to the *Franklin* as the most cruelly ravaged ship ever to reach port under her own power."

Bunker Hill's captain, George A. Seitz, later offered words of praise for the heroic performance of the cruiser and the three destroyers:

> They came alongside, not knowing whether we were likely to have explosions aboard. The *Wilkes-Barre* evacuated our seriously wounded, and with their able assistance we got through.

The task force quickly resumed action. On May 13, it struck the network of airfields that covered Kyushu, Japan's third largest and southernmost island. It was midnight before the Japanese air arm responded, and dawn before *Wilkes-Barre*'s group came under attack. During the enemy action, falling shell fragments (possibly from "friendly" guns) hit the cruiser, wounding nine men on the aft signal bridge. That morning her gun crews shot down an enemy airplane.

A carrier pilot waits on Wilkes-Barre *while the fires are being fought. (Photo courtesy of the Naval Historical Center.)*

Japanese kamikaze being fired on by Wilkes-Barre *gun crews as it dives out of the clouds off Okinawa.*

The enemy plane in a dive after being hit by the light cruiser's fire.

The kamikaze splashes into the sea within yards of Wilkes-Barre. *(Photos taken from the U.S.S.* North Dakota, *courtesy of the Naval Historical Center.)*

On May 28, fleet command was transferred from Vice-Admiral Mitscher to Vice-Admiral John S. McCain. The following day, *Wilkes-Barre* was ordered to the Philippines for repairs and replenishment of supplies. She lay at anchor in San Pedro Bay for the month of June except for four days of gunnery and tactical exercises off Samar.

The cruiser got back into action on July 1, with TF-38. For the first week, the ships engaged in intensive aircraft patrol and firing practice, preparing for an attack on Japan's northernmost home islands. The two largest, Hokkaido and Honshu, were hit on July 10; four days later *Wilkes-Barre* was detached from the task group to engage in antishipping sweeps off northern Honshu.

The Tokyo plains on Honshu were seared by the rockets and incendiaries of American planes on the 17th. One week later *Wilkes-Barre* added her guns to a fierce naval barrage of the Kushimoto seaplane base and the Shionomisaki landing field on the south coast of Honshu.

Navy planes launched strikes at Kure and Kobe between July 24 and 27, ferreting out merchant shipping hidden in the Inland Sea. American planes gutted the busy manufacturing centers of Tokyo and Nagoya on the 30th. Japan was absorbing awesome punishment, but it was only a prelude to air strikes that were to follow. The course of world history would be changed with the atomic bombing of Hiroshima and Nagasaki.

Typhoons accomplished what the Japanese military failed to do. They kept American planes out of the skies for almost the entire first week of

August. It was August 7 before the ships turned north to loose further strikes on the Honshu-Hokkaido area. Persistent foul weather prevented attacks on the 8th, but two days of favorable conditions followed and air strikes again hammered the islands of Japan. Meanwhile, atomic bombing of the Japanese homeland, Russia's entry into the Far Eastern War, and the almost incessant pressure of ships and planes massed off her shores combined to force Japan's unconditional surrender.

American forces were ordered on August 15 to cease offensive operations—the war was over. CruDiv 17 was detached from TG 38.3 on August 23 and after 59 days at sea her ships, *Wilkes-Barre* included, triumphantly entered Sagami Wan, the entrance to Tokyo Bay, with the rest of the Third Fleet.

The cruiser's 6-inch guns were used to cover American occupation of the Yokosuka Naval Base. On September 3, the day after the official surrender, *Wilkes-Barre* moved into Tokyo Bay proper, only 14 months after her commissioning, but with more than 103,000 miles under her hull.

Wilkes-Barre was designated as flagship for TU 35.7.2, a demilitarization group that left Tokyo on September 9 for Tateyama Wan. She covered the seizure of that base for midget submarines and suicide boats, then returned to Tokyo Bay. The cruiser anchored off Koajiro Ko, Sagami Wan from September 12 to 14, to demilitarize the Abursatsubo and Kurihama midget submarine bases. With that accomplished, she returned to Tokyo Bay for refueling and provisions before moving on to Onagawa Wan, then to Katsuura Wan to cover the occupation with her guns.

Wilkes-Barre enjoyed a respite, beginning September 24, laying at anchor within sight of Fujiyama, Japan's sacred mountain, awaiting orders. Gunnery and tactical exercises filled the void until November 5. She left for Jinsen, Korea (now Inchon) on the 9th, and arrived there four days later. That and other occupation duties in company with destroyers *Hart* (DD-*594*) and *Bell* (DD-*587*) took her to Tsingtao, Taku, and Chinwangtao, all in China, where she spent the remainder of 1945.

Five months after the end of hostlities, *Wilkes-Barre* was ordered home, replaced on station by *Columbus* (CA-*74*). She headed for the United States on January 13, 1946. A 400-foot homeward-bound banner left no doubt about her orders as she steamed into Pearl Harbor on the way. On January 31, the triumphant crew enjoyed the welcome sight of San Pedro, California, their home until March 4, when the cruiser headed for the East Coast by way of the Panama Canal.

Wilkes-Barre put into Philadelphia on March 18, and remained there for seven months before sailing to New Orleans for October 27 Navy Day celebrations. Goodwill cruises and naval exercises followed in rapid succession through most of 1947—Guantanamo, England, and Norway.

(text continued on page 129)

A diver videotapes the World War II U.S. cruiser Wilkes-Barre, *with a gun turret looming over him. (Photo by H. Keatts.)*

Henry Keatts (co-author) inspects 40-mm antiaircraft guns, on the U.S. cruiser Wilkes-Barre, minus their barrels, which were removed before sinking. (Photo by Brian Skerry.)

▲ Spare 40-mm antiaircraft gun barrels mounted on a bulkhead inside Wilkes-Barre. (Photo by Brad Sheard.)

▲ A radar unit (on the right) inside Wilkes-Barre's aft combat control room. (Photo by Brad Sheard.)

A divemaster keeps a watchful eye on his divers, below, from Wilkes-Bar e*'s smokestack. The buoy line used by his charter divers is attached to the t p of the smokestack, which is about 145 feet below the surface. (Photo by H. K atts.)*

A barracuda swimming over Bibb *shows a proprietary interest in what's going on. (Photo by Brad Sheard.)*

Below: H.M.S. Culloden *32-pounder cannon balls. The two depressions mark the locations of cannon balls that were illegally removed by scuba divers two weeks before the photo was taken. (Photo by H. Keatts.)*

Two Culloden *cannon photographed in 1988. The one in the bottom photograph was covered with sand, and less deterioration has occurred. (Photos by H. Keatts.)*

A diver peering through a porthole opening of Bibb*'s bridge finds an interior 90°
off center because the cutter settled on her starboard side.
(Photo by H. Keatts.)*

A diver prepares to enter one of the Coast Guard cutter Bibb*'s many open hatches. (Photo by Brad Sheard.)*

Marine organisms have taken up residence on the Coast Guard cutter Bibb. *(Photo by Brad Sheard.)*

(text continued from page 120)

That was to be her "last hurrah." She was decommissioned October 9, 1947 and placed in reserve in Sub Group 2 at Philadelphia—never again to be recalled to service.

On January 15, 1971 the last light cruiser on the Navy list, 27-year-old U.S.S. *Wilkes-Barre* (CL-*103*), was struck from the Naval Vessel Register. The "Lethal Lady" of World War II had outlived her worth to the Navy—except perhaps as a target vessel. But she was to provide a more lasting benefit to society. Active environmentalists were applying pressure for the disposal of naval vessels as artificial reefs at strategic coastal locations. One of those was off Key West, Florida. After *Wilkes-Barre* was designated a target for the Underwater Explosions Research Division, cooperation was obtained from interested regulatory agencies, and the cruiser was cleaned to assure that all potential pollutants were removed from her hull.

Wilkes-Barre was moved into position at 24° 28.8″ N, 81° 33.0″ W for sinking. On May 12, 1972, two underwater explosive charges were detonated, and the cruiser broke in two.

Diving U.S.S. *Wilkes-Barre*

The two sections of the cruiser settled on the bottom approximately 85 yards apart in about 250 feet of water. The bow portion is on its starboard side but the stern settled in an upright position on the sandy bottom.

A diver directs his dive light at the barrel of a 5-inch gun. (Photo by Brad Sheard.)

Top left: Inside one of the cruiser's many compartments. (Photo by Brad Sheard.)

Top right: Bait fish swim past a ladder on the cruiser's starboard side. (Photo by Brad Sheard.)

Left: A hatch cover has fallen to the deck. Note the trawler's net, lost by some unlucky fisherman, to the right of the open hatch. (Photo by Brad Sheard.)

Billy Deans of Key West Diver, Inc. runs a dive charter boat to the cruiser, which is about seven miles south of Saddlebunch Key, approximately 12 miles from his dock. He has been diving the wreck since 1980 and has accumulated a vast background of experience on this deep wreck. Captain Deans maintains a submerged buoy and a mooring line attached to a smokestack on the stern. The top of the smokestack is about 145 feet below the surface; the main deck is approximately 210 feet. These dangerous depths expose a diver to nitrogen narcosis, bends and a host of other hazards. Often, the current is extremely strong and Captain Deans, who is very safety conscious, will abort the dive.

Large barracuda, groupers, jacks, and schools of bait fish swim about the wreck. Many compartments in the cruiser's superstructure are open and easy to penetrate. Compartments are exposed in the area where the warship split in two, but tangled cables and other debris threaten to entrap an unwary diver.

Visibility is good, usually 50 to 100 feet. Although the water is warm, most divers prefer dry suits because of the long decompression necessitated by the deep dive. A suit of some type provides essential protection from the sharp steel edges of World War II's "Lethal Lady."

Brad Sheard is framed by a rising cloud of sediment from below and his mass of bubbles above as he prepares to enter a five-inch gun turret. (Photo by H. Keatts.)

DESTROYERS, CUTTERS AND PATROL VESSELS

Chapter 10

U.S.S. *Jacob Jones—* Double Jeopardy

Location: about 22 miles off the coast of Delaware
Approximate depth of water: 125 feet
Visibility: poor to good (15–20 feet)
Current: little to moderate
Access: boat

The circumstances of two naval disasters that occurred more than two decades apart are too similar to ignore. Both ill-fated warships were named to honor the same man, Captain Jacob Jones who distinguished himself in the War of 1812, then served as commander of U.S. Naval Forces in the Pacific:

Incident #1—The U.S.S. *Jacob Jones*, a World War I destroyer, was sunk by a German U-boat on December 6, 1917. There were 44 survivors from a complement of 99.

Captain Jacob Jones U.S.N., who distinguished himself in the War of 1812. From a crayon portrait by Albert Rosenthal. (Photo courtesy of the Naval Historical Center.)

Incident #2—The U.S.S. *Jacob Jones*, a World War II destroyer, was sunk by a German U-boat on February 28, 1942. There were 11 survivors from a complement of 101.

In each instance pre-set depth charges further destroyed the sinking destroyer as her stern reached the level for which they were set. The real tragedy is that survivors who were already free of the sinking warship were blown out of the water by their own weapons doing only what they had been programmed for.

Two warships of the same name sunk 24 years apart, under circumstances that were so similar, is indeed an unusual coincidence. Seasoned seamen might even look on it as a *Jacob Jones* jinx, but the Navy Department was not a bit deterred. The third *Jacob Jones* (DE-*130*) was laid down only four months after the 1942 sinking. She managed to survive the war after 20 Atlantic crossings, providing escort for merchant and troop convoys. She was decommissioned on July 26, 1946 and entered the Atlantic Reserve Fleet at Orange, Texas. So much for the jinx theory.

The first *Jacob Jones* (DD-*61*) was commissioned on February 10, 1916. She had been in U.S. Navy service for only 22 months when Käpitanleutnant Hans Rose, commanding Imperial Germany's *U-53*, sank her off the coast of Europe.

Only ten weeks later, the second *Jacob Jones* (DD-*130*) was laid down, but commissioning was delayed until October 20, 1919, after the war had ended. The four-stacker destroyer carried a complement of 101 men. She was 314 feet 5 inches long, had a beam of 31 feet 8 inches, and displaced 1,090 tons. Her turbines could propel her up to 28 knots. She survived more than 22 years before the same fate that struck her namesake ended her career off the east coast of the United States. She sank soon after the United States entered World War II, a victim of Nazi Germany's *U-578* under Korvettenkäpitan E.A. Rehwinkel.

The lengthy career of the second *Jacob Jones* covered peacetime years of service in the Pacific, the Atlantic, and the Caribbean, with eight years of decommissioned reserve status between 1922 and 1930. When Poland was invaded, she was on duty with Squadron 40-T in the Mediterranean.

Jacob Jones returned to the United States for conversion to escort duty. Her original armament was four 4-inch guns, two 3-inch guns, 12 torpedo tubes (four triples), depth charges, and two 20-mm machine guns. The escort conversion included replacing the destroyer's four 4-inch guns with six 3-inch guns (two of them replacing the two aft triple-torpedo tubes) and adding four 20-mm machine guns. Also, her depth charge firing capability was increased from two to six positions.

During the months before the United States entered the war, the destroyer was assigned to the Neutrality Patrol. The mission of that patrol was to track and report any warlike operations of belligerents in the waters of the Western Hemisphere. Its intent was to reinforce the Monroe Doctrine, by emphasizing the constant readiness of the U.S. Navy to defend the Western Hemisphere against aggression.

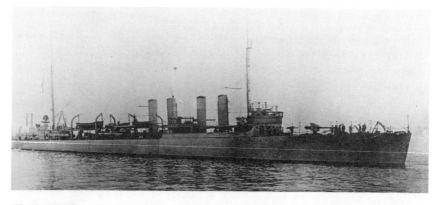

The four-stacker U.S. destroyer Jacob Jones (DD-130) was torpedoed by the German submarine U-578. (Photo courtesy of the National Archives.)

An aerial view of Yorktown *during her commissioning in 1937. The 314-foot destroyer* Jacob Jones *on the opposite side of the pier is dwarfed by the massive aircraft carrier. (Photo courtesy of the National Archives.)*

Jacob Jones' crew had undergone training and exercises but, like most American destroyers, had not yet seen enemy action when the United States entered the war. She had performed escort duty in the North Atlantic, and had even dropped depth charges on two occasions, but without enemy contact.

When the United States became a full combatant, U-boats proceeded to wreak havoc on American coastal shipping. In an effort to stem those losses, Vice-Admiral Adolphus Andrews, Commander of the Eastern Sea Frontier, established a roving ASW (anti-submarine warfare) patrol to cover the area. *Jacob Jones* was assigned to the new duty, and left New York on February 22, 1942 under the command of Lt. Commander Hugh P. Black, Jr. A possible submarine contact was made almost at once in the channel off Ambrose Light Ship. The destroyer struck quickly, dropping 57 depth charges in 12 attack patterns over a 5-hour period. Oil slicks appeared, but no other debris provided evidence of a sunken submarine. With all of her depth charges expended, *Jacob Jones* returned to New York to rearm.

On the morning of February 27, the destroyer departed New York Harbor and steamed southward along the New Jersey coast to patrol the area between Barnegate Light and Five Fathom Bank. She was ordered to concentrate her activity in the waters off Cape May and the Delaware Capes. At 3:30 p.m. she sighted the burning wreckage of the tanker *R. P. Resor*, torpedoed the previous day east of Barnegate Light. *Jacob Jones* circled the ship for two hours searching for survivors before resuming her southward course. She reported her position at 10 p.m., cruising at a steady 15 knots through calm seas, then commenced radio silence. The ship was completely darkened, running without navigation lights, and with good visibility under a full moon. Only her silhouette in the bright moonlight and the foaming wake that trailed her stern gave evidence of the destroyer's location.

Lookouts were on constant watch throughout the night but the destroyer was not zig-zagging. As dawn began to break, two torpedoes literally tore *Jacob Jones* apart. The first struck slightly aft of the bridge, exploding the ship's magazine and shearing off everything forward of the point of impact. The bridge, the chart room, and the officers' and petty officers' quarters were completely destroyed.

The second torpedo struck about 40 feet forward of the fantail, destroying the aft crew's quarters and carrying away part of the ship's aft above the keel plates and shafts. Only the midships section remained intact.

Radioman A. E. Oberg later stated to Navy interrogators that he was off duty, asleep in his quarters in the stern of the ship when the explosions:

> . . . threw him out of his bunk, and that this was the first knowledge he had of the attack; that there were two explosions, one being at the aft bulkhead between the firemen's quarters; that the effect of this explosion was to blow everything completely off the stern; that he left his quarters by climbing over the debris and through a hole in the skin of the ship on the port side and walked forward . . .

All but 25 or 30 of the crew were killed by the explosions. The survivors were hampered in their efforts to launch lifeboats by oily decks, fouled lines, and rigging and twisted wreckage. In the 45 minutes it took for *Jacob Jones* to sink, four or five life rafts cleared the ship and watched her plunge bow first into the sea. As her shattered stern disappeared, the horror continued—her depth charges exploded, killing survivors in the water and on a nearby raft.

An Army observation plane sighted the life rafts at 8:10 a.m., and reported their location to *Eagle 56* of the Inshore Patrol. Of 35 estimated to have originally escaped, 12 were rescued, but one died en route to Cape May. No officers survived the action. The search continued by plane and ship for the next two days, but no others were found.

The torpedoes that tore *Jacob Jones* apart were launched by *U-578*. The German skipper, Korvettenkapitan Rehwinkel, reported in his log that he had identified his target in the early morning haze as a possible cruiser. He was surprised that his U-boat was still undetected when it surfaced and moved in close for the kill. One survivor reported seeing the U-boat through the thick smoke about 100 yards off the port side while rafts were being launched. He stated that the captain was in the conning tower sizing up the damage to the American destroyer; then the submarine swung to her starboard and disappeared into the haze.

The District Intelligence Office of the Fourth Naval District interviewed the 11 survivors at the U.S. Naval Air Station, Cape May, New Jersey. The stories were consistent in reflecting lack of warning, cataclysmic destruction, good discipline without officers, lights that might have been a U-boat off both port and starboard, and the loss of as many as 23 survivors who were victims of the destroyer's exploding depth charges as she sank.

Lt. Commander Hugh D. Black commanded Jacob Jones *when the destroyer was sunk by* U-578. *Black perished with most of his crew. The destroyer* Black *(DD-666) was named in his honor. (Photo courtesy of the Naval Historical Center.)*

A memorial service for the 90 men who lost their lives in the sinking was held on Sunday, March 22, 1942 aboard the U.S.F. *Constitution* at the Boston Navy Yard. It was combined with services for those who perished in the sinking of another U.S. Navy vessel, U.S.S. *Truxton*. The commanding officer of *Jacob Jones*, Lt. Commander H. D. Black Jr., was honored by the naming of another destroyer (DD-666) in his memory.

Within less than six months of sinking the destroyer, U-578 was sunk off Cape Ortegall, Spain, by an Allied bombing attack. The entire crew, including Captain E. A. Rehwinkel, was lost at sea.

Diving U.S.S. *Jacob Jones*

The attack on *Jacob Jones* commenced at 74° 29′W 38° 42′N. Her present site is 74° 29′W 38° 41′N. The bow section, with the heavily damaged bridge, is about a mile away from the rest of the wreck. The scene does not resemble a heroic warship; torpedoes and depth charges exacted their toll many years ago when the forward and aft sections were nearly destroyed.

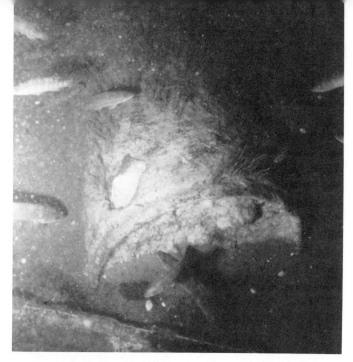

This depth charge, half buried in the sand, was photographed 28 years after the destroyer was torpedoed by a U-boat. (Photo by Michael deCamp.)

The midships is the part of the wreck that is dived most frequently. It is almost upright on the bottom. However, in many areas the deck has collapsed. The engine room and boiler room are the most forward sections of this part of the wreck. Swimming aft from the boilers brings the propeller shafts into view. The propellers were blown off them when the depth charges exploded. Continuing aft, torpedo tubes can be seen on the collapsed deck. Torpedoes are still in their tubes and others are fastened to the deck. Depth charges are fastened to the deck aft of the torpedoes. A 3-inch gun is buried in the sand with only the muzzle protruding, and 3-inch ammunition is scattered about the area.

Scattered wreckage is all that remains of the 314-foot-long, four-stack destroyer. The shambles that was once a U.S. Navy warship is now brass valves, boilers, twisted steel beams and plates, torpedoes, depth charges, and shell casings. The Navy has removed some of the live ordnance, but much remains as a very real threat to the unwary diver.

Charters are operated from Indian River Inlet, Delaware and Cape May, New Jersey for dives on *Jacob Jones* and other wrecks, such as the nearby luxurious ocean liner *Northern Pacific*, which sank in 1922. To an avid wreck diver who is a student of this country's naval history, the marine junkyard that was once *Jacob Jones* is a more exciting and rewarding dive than the intact remains of the magnificent passenger liner.

Chapter 11

U.S.S. *Sturtevant—*
Sunk by a U.S. Mine

Location: 15 miles northwest of Key West, Florida
Approximate depth of water: 90 feet
Visibility: poor
Current: little
Access: boat

Albert D. Sturtevant, a student at Yale University, enlisted in the Naval Reserve Forces in March 1917. He was commissioned an ensign and became a naval aviator.

In February 1918, Sturtevant and another American pilot were flying escort for merchant ships crossing the North Sea. The two Americans were attacked by ten German planes. Sturtevant's companion managed to escape, but he decided to stay and attempt to protect the convoy. He was shot down and posthumously awarded the Navy Cross for his heroic action.

On September 21, 1920 a 1,215-ton, 314-foot destroyer was commissioned at the Philadelphia Navy Yard. DD-*240* was given the name *Sturtevant* in honor of the fallen Navy pilot.

The four-stacker was armed with four 4-inch and one 3-inch guns, 20-mm machine guns, 12 torpedo tubes, and depth charges. The destroyer joined the U.S. Naval Forces, European Waters.

U.S. destroyer Sturtevant, *named after the naval aviator who was posthumously awarded the Navy Cross in World War I. (Photo courtesy of the Naval Historical Center.)*

Between 1921 and 1923, a great famine struck Russia, brought on by a drought and the Russian Civil War. America responded with nearly a million tons of food. *Sturtevant* made many voyages across the Black Sea to numerous Russian ports in conjunction with the massive relief operation that seemed to evoke little appreciation from the new Bolshevik regime.

The destroyer returned to the United States in 1923 to operate along the Eastern Seaboard and in the Caribbean. In 1925, *Sturtevant* transited the Panama Canal and participated in joint Army-Navy maneuvers in which an enemy force was attempting to capture the Hawaiian island Oahu.

From 1926 to 1931, *Sturtevant* was part of the Atlantic fleet. She was placed out of commission, but recommissioned the following year and reported for duty in the Canal Zone. In 1935, the destroyer was reassigned to the Pacific battle force. World War II brought *Sturtevant* back to the Atlantic for escort duties in 1940. The escort conversion included replacement of four 4-inch guns and two aft triple torpedo tubes by five 3-inch guns. Additional 20-mm machine guns and depth charge projectors were added.

On April 26, 1942 *Sturtevant* was escorting a convoy out of Key West, Florida. Two hours out of port, a violent explosion lifted the destroyer's stern out of the water. *Sturtevant*'s captain thought he had been torpedocd and immediately dropped depth charges. A few minutes later, a second detonation rocked the destroyer and she rapidly began to settle on an even keel. Moments later, a third explosion, beneath the aft deckhouse, ripped her keel apart and the midships sank immediately. The stern slowly settled to the bottom, but the bow remained above water for several hours. Fifteen of her 152-man crew went down with the ship.

Sturtevant had strayed into a U.S. Navy minefield laid the day before, about eight miles north of Marquesas Key. The destroyer's captain had not been informed of the mine laying.

Salvage

From August 23–25 and September 1–4, the U.S. Navy conducted diving operations on the wreck to recover wardroom safes, determine presence of depth charges and torpedo warheads and determine the practicality of exploding the warheads in place.

However, salvors had beaten them to the wreck site. U.S. Navy divers made 65 dives on the wreck and submitted the following report:

> The wreck is located . . . about latitude 24–45.9 north, longitude 82–01.1 west . . . lying on a generally southeasterly heading. The forward part of the wreck is relatively intact and lying on its port side. It is severed at about No. 1 fireroom. . . . The midships portion of the wreck is essentially upright and the deck is entirely missing, the sides of the ship being layed over nearly flat. The aft portion has the deck present but appears to be flattened. Fragments of all kinds are scattered over a large area.
>
> Investigation of wardroom area. A large hole was cut in the starboard side plating of the ship (now on top) to permit access to the wardroom and captain's cabin, just forward thereof. Large sections of plating had previously been cut or blown from ship's bottom (now to starboard) in this region. No sign of a safe or anything resembling it was found in either compartment nor in the officer's stateroom forward of the cabin. Drawers and lockers were generally open and empty, indicating the possibility of previous ransacking. Midships' fore-and-aft bulkheads were weak from corrosion and their penetration for access to the port side cabins considered unwise . . .
>
> Both guns were missing from gun mount locations. A bottom search within 100 feet of aft part of wreck yielded many fragments including identifiable portions of four torpedoes. . . . The condition of these fragments . . . gave conclusive evidence of prior demolition probably including detonation of the warheads. The only sign of torpedo tubes was a ruptured four- or five-foot fragment of one tube around the aft end of one torpedo fragment, further indicating that demolition had taken place with the torpedoes in the tubes. Four plaster loaded drill hedgehogs were found. The remains of several unfired three-inch cartridge cases were located, all of which were badly damaged and

distorted apparently by demolition. No projectiles could be found. . . . No evidence of depth charges was seen . . . near the stern of the wreck. The bottom in this area is generally soft mud although in some places made firmer by heavy concentration of coral. It is considered possible that the more dense fragments such as projectiles or depth charges may have sunk out of sight. . . . There is evidence of salvage operations having been conducted in the engineering spaces.

The wreck is in 90 feet of water. Visibility varies with the time of year, but due to the mud bottom is usually not very good, 15 to 20 feet. Many artifacts can be found, including brass shell casings.

Chapter 12

H.M.C.S. *St. Francis*— Lend-Lease Four-Stacker

Location: off Acoaxet, Massachusetts
Approximate depth of water: 60 feet
Visibility: poor
Current: little to none
Access: boat

German troops invaded Poland on the morning of September 1, 1939. Two days later, France and Britain declared war against Germany. World War II had unfolded. Untold millions were to die or be maimed, cities and historic treasures would be obliterated, and atrocities would lay bare the worst side of man's nature.

Many had predicted a second World War. One eminent military authority, Field Marshal Foch of France, had predicted not only a war but, further, "The next war will begin where the last one ended." Allied naval experts on both sides of the Atlantic agreed that submarine warfare and anti-submarine tactics would be a continuation of World War I, during which U-boats finally had been neutralized by the convoy system and depth charges. That conclusion inclined Britain to make light of the U-boat threat. Relatively low shipping losses in the early months of the war supported that complacency. With the fall of France on June 22, 1940, the entire strategic balance changed. Germany had gained ports to base her U-boats in occupied France, with an ocean front of 2,500 miles.

Both sides had entered the conflict unprepared—Germany with too few U-boats and Britain with only 180 destroyers. Germany held the advantage, however; the U-boat's increased operational area made the number of available escort vessels inadequate for the task of protecting Allied convoys. By 1940, Admiral Karl Doenitz, commander-in-chief, U-boats, was so heartened by the increased output of U-boats that he declared, "I will show that the U-boat alone can win this war."

President Franklin Roosevelt was aware of the crisis facing England. Although the United States was neutral, Roosevelt's interpretation of international neutrality was pro-British. He was influenced by the conviction that if Britain were to fall, the United States might be the next object of German attack.

Shortly after the beginning of the war, the United States was supplying arms and ammunition to England. Roosevelt initiated "cash-and-carry." Theoretically, any of the belligerents could procure military supplies from the United States—as long as they paid cash and carried those supplies in their own ships. This was fine with England; she ruled the seas. Germany, however, as had been intended, was unable to take advantage of the offer with her merchant fleet blockaded by British warships. Roosevelt's "cash-and-carry" plan began to break down as England ran short of cash. He circumvented that problem with "lend-lease," lending war materials to England in exchange for leased bases in the Western Hemisphere.

Convoy Escorts

During the summer of 1940, however, German U-boats were close to fulfilling Admiral Doenitz' claim that the U-boat alone could win the war. Britain's trans-Atlantic shipping was suffering terrible losses that threatened to stop the flow of war support from the United States. Britain needed convoy escorts to combat that threat. Roosevelt had already stretched the interpretation of international neutrality laws through "lend-lease." The United States responded to the new conditions by supplying Britain with 50 old four-stacker destroyers. In return, the United States received 99-year leases for bases in the Bahamas, Jamaica, St. Lucia, Trinidad, Antigua, and British Guiana—locations that were crucial for protecting the Panama Canal.

Roosevelt did not consult Congress about his intentions because he anticipated isolationist opposition. The isolationists in Congress and throughout the country denounced his action as dictatorial and a violation of American neutrality that would certainly lead to war. Many others however, supported him, evidencing their willingness to commit the nation to all-out aid to Britain. A debate would have lasted for months.

Roosevelt circumvented Congress by arranging the ships-for-bases deal through executive agreement instead of treaty. Attorney General Jackson found two old laws and a decision by the Supreme Court to uphold the presidential right "to dispose of vessels of the Navy and unneeded naval materials." Also, according to the Attorney General, the transference of the over-age destroyers would be within neutrality limitations because they had not been built specifically for a belligerent nation. Most of the destroyers had been built more than 20 years earlier during World War I to combat a similar U-boat threat.

They may have been obsolete, but Britain desperately needed them to protect the convoys carrying lend-lease war material. British Admiral of the Fleet, Sir James Somerville, wrote in his memoirs:

> Had there been no American four-stacker destroyers available, and, had they not gone into service escorting trade convoys when they did, the outcome of the struggle against the U-boat and the subsequent outcome of the European War itself, might have been vastly different."

The U.S.S. *Bancroft* (DD-*256*) was launched on March 21, 1919, several months after signing of the armistice that ended World War I combat. Her length was 314 feet 4 inches, beam 31 feet 8 inches, with a displacement

U.S.S. Bancroft *was one of the "lend-lease" destroyers assigned in 1940 to the Royal Canadian Navy, and renamed* St. Francis. *(Photo courtesy of the Naval Historical Center.)*

of 1,215 tons. The four-stacker destroyer was part of the Atlantic Fleet until she was placed in reserve in November of the same year. Three years later *Bancroft* was decommissioned and remained in mothballs for 17 years until the threat of war restored her to activity. She was recommissioned in December 1939 and again joined the Atlantic Fleet.

On September 24, 1940, *Bancroft* was again decommissioned from U.S. Navy service. This time, however, for transfer to Great Britain at Halifax, Nova Scotia as one of the 50 lend-lease destroyers. She was assigned to the Royal Canadian Navy and renamed HMCS *St. Francis*.

The old destroyer was modified by the Royal Canadian Navy to fit her for her new role as protector of trans-Atlantic convoys. Asdic, the anti-submarine sounding system that the U.S. Navy called sonar (sound navigation ranging), was installed. One boiler was sacrificed to increase fuel capacity. Her two 4-inch deck guns were replaced with antiaircraft weapons, and "k" and "y" guns (depth charge projectors) replaced her 12 torpedo tubes. Also, the bridge and pilot house were enclosed, improving crew conditions for the cold North Atlantic.

After refitting, *St. Francis* spent the remainder of 1940 based at Halifax; in November she searched for the German pocket battleship *Admiral Scheer*, perpetrator of an attack on convoy HX.84. From January 1941, the destroyer served as one of the much-needed escorts for the North Atlantic convoys and made several attacks upon U-boats.

When newer, faster, and more modern vessels were commissioned, they replaced the old four-stacker convoy escorts. *St. Francis* was converted into a net tender for training exercises at Annapolis Basin, Nova Scotia in February 1944.

On June 11, the *St. Francis* was decommissioned, her armament removed, and she was sold for scrap. She sank about two miles off Acoaxet, Massachusetts, on July 14, 1945 while under tow en route to Baltimore, Maryland. The destroyer was rammed by the collier *Windind Gulf* in dense fog. A large hole was stove in the hull of *St. Francis*. but there was neither loss of life nor injuries.

A thick film of oil from the wreck blanketed a two-mile stretch of Horseneck Beach in Westport, Massachusetts. A 16-foot lifeboat, two life rafts, and several sailors' sea bags were washed up on the oil-soaked shore.

The wreck is often mistakenly referred to as *St. Clair* (U.S.S. *Williams*), a four-stacker that was decommissioned in August 1944. *St. Clair* remained in Halifax as a firefighting and damage control training hulk in Bedford Basin. She was turned over to the Canadian War Assets Corporation late in 1946. The corporation sold the vessel to a Mr. Simon of Halifax, but *St. Clair* was still in Halifax as late as 1950.

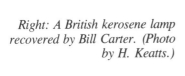

Above: Roger Murphy inspects a depth charge rack amid the scattered wreckage of the destroyer's stern. (Photo by H. Keatts.)

Right: A British kerosene lamp recovered by Bill Carter. (Photo by H. Keatts.)

St. Francis sank in only 60 feet of water and was declared a menace to navigation. The owner of the wreck, Boston Metals Company of Baltimore, wrote the Army Corps of Engineers, ''This company is the sole owner of this vessel and hereby abandons the wreck to the United States, and disclaims any further responsibility in the matter.''

A section of hull plate containing a porthole (center). (Photo by Mike Casalino.)

Diving *St. Francis*

St. Francis was blasted with dynamite, and portions of her wreckage were removed by salvagers. Thirty feet of the bow is intact, sitting upright, pointing toward shore. The rest of the wreck, large plates scattered over the bottom with occasional sandy gaps between them, extends perpendicular to the shore. A stack of tubes is all that remains of the boiler. Porthole rims and other brass artifacts can be found. Visibility ranges from very bad to fairly good, and on a good day *St. Francis* is a very pretty dive.

Chapter 13

U.S.S. *Turner*—
Disarming Error

Location: about four miles from East Rockaway Inlet, New York
Approximate depth of water: 60 feet
Visibility: poor to bad
Current: little
Access: boat

The U.S. Navy destroyer, *Turner* (DD-*648*), swung lazily at anchor three miles from Ambrose Light at the entrance to New York Harbor. It was early morning, January 3, 1944 midway through World War II. The destroyer was waiting for clearance to proceed into the busy harbor after a convoy run from Casablanca.

The warship was named after a naval hero of the War of 1812, Captain Daniel Turner of New York. She was laid down by Federal Shipbuilding & Drydock Company at Kearney, New Jersey on November 15, 1942. Her launching occurred on February 28, and she was commissioned at the New York Navy Yard on April 15, only five months after laying down. The accelerated construction program was dictated by the need to combat the challenge of Nazi Germany's U-boats.

Turner was one of 76 *Bristol*-class destroyers that were built during World War II, each costing $8,814,000. Her length was 348 feet 4 inches, beam 36 feet 1 inch and she had a displacement of 1,630 tons (2,000 tons full load). Armament included four 5-inch guns, several 40-mm and 20-mm anti-aircraft guns, and ten 21-inch torpedo tubes. Her anti-U-boat weapons included depth charges and rocket-propelled projectiles called Hedgehogs. She was equipped with geared turbines, two shafts and four high-pressure watertube boilers that produced a speed of about 36 knots. By contrast, the U.S. Navy's first destroyer, torpedo boat destroyer *Bainbridge* (DD-*1*), commissioned forty years earlier in 1902, was only 250 feet long, displaced 420 tons, and attained a speed of 29 knots.

Convoy Duty

After shakedown in the Portland, Maine area, *Turner* returned to New York early in June for a three-day training cruise with the newly-commissioned carrier, *Bunker Hill*. In late June she joined a screening unit to escort a convoy across the Atlantic. The mission was uneventful, and she returned to New York in August. Later that month *Turner* escorted a convoy to the Caribbean; she returned to New York, then accompanied the British carrier *Victorious* to Norfolk.

On September 24, 1943 the destroyer was assigned to her second trans-Atlantic voyage, part of a screening unit for a convoy to Casablanca. *Turner* made one depth-charge attack on a sonar contact during the 18-day crossing.

The destroyer joined a convoy off Gibraltar on October 19 for the return voyage. Four days later, at about 7:30 p.m., *Turner* was screening ahead of the convoy when her radar crew picked up an unidentified

The destroyer Turner *was named after Captain Daniel Turner, a naval hero of the War of 1812. (Photo courtesy of the National Archives.)*

surface contact. About 14 minutes later the destroyers' lookouts spotted a German U-boat running on the surface with her decks awash. Lt. Commander Henry Wygant, in command of *Turner* since her commissioning, ordered hard to port to close on the U-boat, 500 yards distant with the destroyer's guns blazing. The U-boat's conning tower was damaged by one 5-inch and several 40- and 20-mm hits. The submarine dove before *Turner* could ram her, but the destroyer fired two depth charges from her port K-gun battery, then swung around and dropped a single charge off the stern. The three detonations were followed by a fourth explosion that rocked *Turner* so heavily that she lost power to her sound gear and radar. Power was restored within 15 minutes, and the search for the U-boat was resumed. About 30 minutes later the radar crew relocated the target. It appeared to be sinking by the stern, about 1,500 yards off the port beam. The destroyer broke off the engagement to rejoin the convoy and the remainder of the voyage was uneventful.

Turner departed on her third and final trans-Atlantic voyage late in November, escorting a convoy of 65 ships to Mediterranean ports. She joined a return convoy of 56 ships on December 17, off Casablanca, and returned to the United States without incident.

Disaster

Arriving at Ambrose Light late at night on January 2, *Turner* anchored about six miles northeast of Sandy Hook, New Jersey after having made a suspected U-boat sonar contact during the day. Her Hedgehogs were still armed. Those deadly anti-U-boat weapons were mounted forward to fire a pattern of 24 rocket-launched projectiles from her bow to attack a diving U-boat. Harbor security required that they be disarmed before entering New York Harbor. Early the following morning, a gunner's mate proceeded with the disarming. Something went wrong in the process, and the destroyer erupted in an explosion that was followed by an intense fire.

Turner's engine room quickly filled with smoke, but her six-man engine room crew remained at their stations. They waited in blinding smoke for orders from the bridge, but the officers on watch were already dead, killed by the initial explosion. The engine room crew maintained pressure in the ship's boilers until they were forced to evacuate.

Crewmen lay on deck, bleeding and in shock, some unconscious. Several, wearing rescue-breathing apparatus, rescued some of the injured personnel from the galley passageway and placed them in the electrical workshop and on the fantail. Fire hoses were turned on, and the first streams of water were on the blaze within three or four minutes after the explosion. But it was a futile effort.

Hedgehog projectiles being loaded on spigots. Disarming projectiles like these resulted in the explosion that sank Turner. *(Photo courtesy of the National Archives.)*

The destroyer's mast and radio antennae were destroyed by the explosion, leaving the surviving officers with no means to communicate with other ships or shore-based stations. It was fortunate that several other U.S. warships were in the vicinity. The destroyer escort *Swasey* (DE-*248*), was anchored 3,000 yards from *Turner.* The destroyer escort's "War Diary" reports that two officers on her bridge and several enlisted men on duty topside witnessed a series of shattering explosions on *Turner.* At 6:18 a.m. they heard an explosion and observed

> . . . flames leaping above the *Turner* in a volcanic effect. Three projectiles that resembled rockets appeared above the flames and curved outward in wide arcs. . . .

Swasey was underway at 6:35 a.m. with a fire and rescue team equipped and assembled on her main deck. All of her searchlights were trained upon *Turner.* At 6:45, within 500 yards of the stricken destroyer, a motor whaleboat was lowered with 15 men from the fire and rescue party to board *Turner,* if possible. *Swasey* was then maneuvered to within 20 yards of the blazing destroyer.

All hoses were used that could be brought to bear in vicinity of the fire, but the volume of water we were able to get over was pitifully ineffective for a flame of that magnitude.

Secondary explosions had produced a large triangular hole across *Turner*'s main deck, in the vicinity of number two turret, a tapering "V" shape to the waterline.

Brilliant flames, bright yellowish in color billowed out this hole and through the maindeck and were blown by the wind across the entire bridge superstructure which by this time was also on fire.

Number two turret had been blown into the sea, while number one turret was forced upward and forward. Survivors later reported they witnessed the number two turret flipping end over end through the air. The same secondary explosion had badly twisted and torn the bridge superstructure.

Swasey's crew discontinued their efforts to quench the flames; instead, searchlights were trained on the water to assist the small boats that were searching for survivors. Several of *Turner*'s crew had been blown into the water, others had leaped in to escape the flames. The plate from the large hole where number two turret used to be, had peeled forward, outward, and downward. A dazed enlisted man with a gaping head wound held himself afloat by the distorted plate until he was rescued by one of the small boats. Throughout the rescue, small explosions erupted forward in the destroyer.

The U.S. Coast Guard played a major role in the rescue of survivors who were still aboard the destroyer. One cutter came alongside the stern and took off survivors. Another Coast Guard vessel rescued 34 men from the forecastle. The cutter had just pulled away when a violent explosion, just forward of amidships, showered *Swasey* with flaming debris. It was probably the destroyer's magazine. The explosion blew *Turner*'s entire forward housing over the starboard side. The concussion blew men off their feet on nearby craft and some even lost their coats as the rush of air passed. *Turner* took a sharp list to starboard, spewing fuel oil into the sea. The fuel ignited and wind fanned the flames aft. Paint caught fire, and flames ran across the decks and up her aft deck housing. Five depth charges in the port side K-gun racks began to burn, but fortunately did not explode. However, numerous explosions, probably 5-inch, 40-mm, and 20-mm ammunition, continued to punish the flaming warship.

At 7:50 a.m. a terrific explosion occurred aft of number two smokestack. *Turner* capsized to starboard and her stern sank to the bottom in 60 feet of water leaving about three feet above the surface. About 50 feet from the stem a mass of twisted steel approximately five feet in diameter had been forced through the destroyer's bottom, extending three feet beyond the hull

Rescued Turner *survivors demonstrate their enthusiasm at Staten Island base. (Photo courtesy of the National Archives.)*

plating. The explosion was heard 30 miles away. It shattered more than 200 windows and shook houses along the Long Island and New Jersey shores.

At 8:27 a.m. *Turner* sank from sight. *Swasey* dropped a marker buoy over the destroyer's grave, and at 2:40 p.m. a tender placed a buoy 50 yards from the wreck.

One hundred and thirty-eight men died in the disaster, including 15 of the destroyer's 17 officers; only two ensigns were among the 163 survivors. About 60 would be hospitalized for months having their wounds and burns treated. The loss of life would have been even higher except that many of the crew had left the forward mess area minutes before the initial explosion. The destroyer's crew displayed calm discipline throughout the disaster. Robert L. Freear, a machinist mate, wrote:

> Except for the men who were trapped below burning to death, there was no panic. Even though the ship was hopelessly disabled and shrapnel was rattling over the deck, the men waited in line to be taken off by the Coast Guard. Minutes after the rescue was completed, the ship blew to pieces.

Turner's survivors were taken to the hospital at Sandy Hook. Lt. Commander Frank A. Erickson, USCG, in a Sikorsky HNS-1 helicopter, flew two cases of blood plasma from New York to Sandy Hook. The Coast Guard had acquired the new machine early in the war, but this was the first

Turner *survivor Fireman First-Class S. J. Mickiewicz unpacks his Red Cross survivor's kit. (Photo courtesy of the National Archives.)*

U.S.S. Craneship, *formerly the battleship* Kearsarge, *preparing to remove the bow and superstructure of* Turner. *The bow view of* Craneship *shows the pronounced torpedo "blisters" that were designed to absorb the impact of a torpedo hit. They also contributed unusual stability to the old battleship. (Photo courtesy of the National Archives.)*

use of a helicopter in a life-saving role. The plasma, lashed to the floats of the helicopter, saved the lives of many of the destroyer's injured crewmen.

Turner sank in approximately 60 feet of water about 4.1 nautical miles from Long Island's Rockaway Inlet, a site of heavy shipping traffic. That prompted the U.S. Navy to demolish the wreck during the summer of 1944. U.S.S. *Craneship* (AB-*1*), used Navy divers to remove large pieces of *Turner*'s bow section and superstructure. *Craneship* was the old battleship *Kearsarge*, stripped of her guns and equipped with a large crane mounted amidships.

Four years later U.S.S. *Windlass* (ARSD-*4*) sent navy divers down to determine the wreck's condition. The divers found it to be:

> 120 feet long with a highest point of about 12 feet above the ocean's bottom, which decreases to about five feet toward the stern. It seems to be about eight to ten feet in the sand. There is no superstructure. The wreck is on an even keel. The main deck forward is a mass of holes and is badly distorted. The deck aft is a mass of wreckage. There are numerous holes in the shell plating along both sides.

After the examination it was determined the most economical and expeditious way to dispose of the wreck was to blast it down to the sand level. The commander of the Third Naval District discussed the matter with

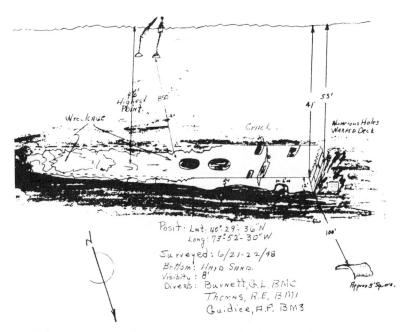

U.S. Navy divers drew this diagram after surveying the wreck in 1948. (Courtesy of the Naval Historical Center.)

Turner *slides down the launching ways in February 1943. Her short career ended less than one year later, when she was demolished by accidental explosion. (Photo courtesy of the National Archives.)*

the Coast Guard and U.S. Army Engineers and all agreed that blasting would be satisfactory although the wreckage would still remain a hazard to ships ground tackle anchoring in the vicinity of the wreck. *Windlass*'s crew was then directed to proceed with demolition of the wreck.

In 1976, the fully-loaded supertanker *Aeolis*, drawing 48 feet of water, hit the only high point that was left on *Turner* and ripped a hole in her bottom. The tanker sank in 60 feet of water, but even at that depth the mammoth vessel still had about 8 feet of freeboard.

The U.S. Coast Guard Pollution Control Department sent its Atlantic Strike Team to raise the tanker before her cargo could escape to foul New York and New Jersey beaches. Under the guidance of Lt. Commander Chambers, Strike Team divers patched the hull and pumped out enough water to raise her four or five feet off the bottom. The tanker was towed into deeper water where the patch was reset and her cargo of fuel was off-loaded. *Aeolis* was taken to a Newport News, Virginia shipyard where her hull was repaired. The supertanker was restored to service and still enters New York's lower bay to make her deliveries.

The wreck of the destroyer lies only 60 feet underwater, slightly more than 4 miles off the shore of Long Island, New York. That should provide an appealing setting for sport divers. However, heavy shipping traffic and usually low visibility prevail. *Turner*'s remains, strewn over the bottom, more resemble an underwater scrap pile than the final resting place of a sleek warship that once served in the U.S. Navy.

Chapter 14

Revenue Cutter *Mohawk*— Cadet at Fault

Location: 10 miles south of East Rockaway Inlet, New York
Approximate depth of water: 105 feet
Visibility: poor
Current: little
Access: boat

The 980-ton, 205-foot revenue cutter *Mohawk*, named after a tribe of American Indians, was commissioned in May 1904. She was based at New York and cruised the waters between Martha's Vineyard, Massachusetts and the Delaware breakwater. Like other vessels of the Revenue Cutter Service, she was to assist vessels in distress and enforce navigational laws.

By Act of Congress on January 30, 1915, the Revenue Cutter Service and the Life-Saving Service became known as the Coast Guard Service, later the U.S. Coast Guard.

Collision

When the U.S. entered World War I, *Mohawk* and other Coast Guard vessels were temporarily transferred to the U.S. Navy. One of the duties assigned to *Mohawk* was to patrol the approaches to New York Harbor while

Revenue cutter Mohawk *was lost in a World War I collision during antisubmarine patrol off Long Island, New York. (Photo courtesy of the U.S. Coast Guard.)*

convoys formed before crossing the Atlantic. The cutter was performing that duty on October 1, 1917, when she was run down by the British steamer *Vennachar*. On that ill-fated morning, a cadet from the Coast Guard Academy was standing watch. *Mohawk*'s commander, First Lieutenant Iben Barker, later reported:

> As Headquarters had authorized Cadet Mandeville to stand a regular watch, and as the weather was clear and fine, and all conditions favorable, the other officers went to breakfast.

Conditions may have been favorable, but Cadet Mandeville who had the watch apparently wasn't watching. The cadet had relieved the officer of the deck at 8 a.m. Lieutenant Barker later reported:

> About 8:20 I came on deck and saw a vessel of the convoy a short distance away on our starboard bow, headed at right angles to our course. I knew that a collision would take place unless action was taken. . . . asked the officer of the deck (Cadet Mandeville) if he had blown any signals, he replied in the negative, and then blew several short blasts. The two vessels were then very close together. I at once rang for full speed ahead and ordered the helm hard starboard, in hopes of getting the blow as far aft as possible.

Vennachar struck *Mohawk* amidships, abreast the engine room. General alarm was sounded and the cutter's pumps were started. After inspecting the engine room, Barker realized his vessel could not be saved and ordered "abandon ship." The order was executed without confusion and *Mohawk* began settling by the stern. An escort vessel, U.S.S. *Bridge*, ran an 8-inch line to the cutter and secured it to the forward bitts. A code message was sent to the Convoy Commander, "Request permission to salve *Mohawk* and join convoy later." *Bridge* had the cutter in tow and her engines running at one-third speed when they received an answer to their request to tow. It was disapproved. *Bridge*'s captain ordered a second request be sent, but before it could be completely transmitted it was noticed that*Mohawk* had begun to sink rapidly and list heavily to port. The tow line was cut.

With her bow high in the air, the cutter settled slowly to the bottom at 40° 25′N, 73° 47′W in about 105 feet of water. Only her mast heads remained above water.

It was 9:35 a.m. when she went under. Only 20 minutes after Cadet Mandeville had gone on watch *Mohawk* was rammed. One hour and 15 minutes later she was on the bottom. Surprisingly, the accident did not hinder the career of Cadet Mandeville, who made ensign five days after the cutter sank. Eventually, he attained the rank of Lt. Commander and retired from the service in 1930 with a physical disability.

There were no casualties and the 77 men of the cutter's crew were rescued by other naval vessels. Confidential papers, signal books, log books for July and August were saved. Only the ship's log for September went down with the cutter.

Mohawk was not salvaged by the Navy because the water was deemed "too deep to warrant such operations." On February 7, 1921, the wreck was sold to H.L. Gotham Corporation, New York, for $111.

Surprisingly, the wreck was not blown apart with explosives, the fate of most shipwrecks. Usually the wrecks, even at 100-foot depth, are considered navigational hazards (their superstructure and masts extend up a great distance) and are demolished.

The wreck site is an area often referred to by environmental groups as the "Dead Sea." For more than five decades over five million cubic yards of sewage sludge per year have been dumped in the area. The sludge, from the Metropolitan New York area, contains high concentrations of organic material, bacteria, and viruses. Also, industrial wastes were dumped in the area, which is less than a dozen miles south of Rockaway Inlet. Petroleum products and heavy metals, such as cadmium, lead, chromium, zinc, copper, nickel, and cobalt were added to the human wastes. Divers usually visit the wreck during the late fall and early spring when the colder water might inhibit bacterial growth. Very few living marine organisms are encountered on the wreck. However, many remains of fish and crabs can be seen.

Biologists who studied the effects of the sludge and industrial wastes on marine life at the dump site were aghast. They applied pressure to close the site. In response the federal Environmental Protection Agency ordered that the dumping cease by January 1, 1982. However, the order was challenged in court by New York City's Environmental Protection Agency, one of several misnamed municipal sewage authorities that dumped on the site. The court ruled that the dumping be continued until 1991, giving time to find land-based sites.

Environmental groups were outraged by the decision and through their efforts the site eventually was shut down in 1986. The new site is on the 1,000 fathom curve, but the annual amount allowed to be dumped was increased about 35 times.

Diving *Mohawk*

Most divers, understandably, did not want to dive *Mohawk* and risk the unhealthy environment. However, since dumping has ceased, the revenue cutter is slowly being scoured by currents and most of the sludge has gone. The bottom, previously covered with several feet of sludge, has cleared to the point where the sand can be seen. Visibility, once very bad, has improved appreciably.

Approximately 25 feet of the cutter's bow is intact and sitting upright. The wreck is broken up in the midships area and the engine and four boilers can be seen amidst the debris. The deck collapsed just forward

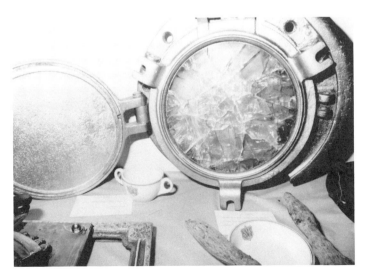

Porthole and other artifacts recovered from Mohawk. *(Photo by Michael deCamp.)*

Mohawk's bell and telegraph. The ship's bell bears the ship's name and year of launching. (Photo by Michael deCamp.)

Artifacts recovered from Mohawk. (Photo by Michael deCamp.)

of the boilers. The stern is lying on its starboard side. Many steel plates have corroded away exposing underlying ribs. A gun mount can be seen, but the gun is no longer there.

Divers have recovered various artifacts, including portholes, bottles, and china dinner plates with USRCS (United States Revenue Cutter Service) embossed on them. Many of the plates have been recovered by digging under the decking.

Chapter 15

U.S.C.G. Cutters *Duane* and *Bibb*—An Honorable Artificial Reef

Location: off Key Largo, Florida
Approximate depth of water: *Duane* 120 feet, *Bibb* 135 feet
Visibility: excellent
Current: little to strong
Access: boat

The Continental Navy that had served to win freedom for the American colonists was disbanded for lack of funds once that freedom was gained. Economic hardship continued to plague the fledgling republic to the extent that the First Congress of the United States was compelled to impose a tax on imports. Enterprising tax evaders did their utmost to avoid payment of those tariffs by smuggling goods into the country. Beginning in 1790, Secretary of the Treasury Alexander Hamilton accepted the challenge; he introduced armed revenue ships called cutters to patrol the coast and intercept the illegal traffic.

In the absence of a U.S. Navy, the Treasury Department's revenue cutters were the only American naval force available to the new country. An Act of Congress on March 2, 1799, provided that the cutters:

. . . shall, whenever the President of the United States shall so direct, cooperate with the Navy of the United States, during which time they shall be under the direction of the Secretary of the Navy.

Officers were granted military rank, and during wartime they and their vessels operated with the Navy. It was a cutter that captured the first enemy vessel during the War of 1812. Another cutter, *Surveyor*, was captured by the British frigate *Narcissus* in one of the most hotly contested engagements of the war. The English captain was so impressed by his opponents' bravery that he returned the American captain's sword during the surrender ceremony accompanied by a letter that stated:

Your gallant and desperate attempt to defend your vessel against more than double your number excited such admiration on the part of your opponents as I have seldom witnessed, and induced me to return you the sword you had so ably used in testimony of mine. . . . I . . . admire . . . the determined manner in which her deck was disputed inch-by-inch.

Revenue cutters worked with the U.S. Navy during the suppression of piracy in southern waters. In 1819, two of them, *Louisiana* and *Alabama* were attacked off the southern coast of Florida by the pirate ship *Bravo*. The buccaneer captain, Jean La Farge, was a bold lieutenant of the notorious Jean La Fitte. The action continued until men from the cutter's boats boarded the pirate ship and captured the decks in hand-to-hand fighting.

In 1837, Congress directed that cutters were to make seasonal cruises along the coast to provide relief for mariners in distress, as required. When war with Mexico erupted, the shallow-draft vessels were used primarily for blockading enemy coasts and for amphibious landings.

The first naval shot of the Civil War was fired by the cutter *Harriet Lane*, a shot across the bow of the steamer *Nashville* while it was attempting to enter Charleston harbor without displaying the flag of the United States. Later in the war "the system of cutters" received its first official name, the Revenue Service, which eventually became the Revenue Cutter Service.

During the Spanish American War, eight cutters participated in the Havana blockade, the Battle of Cardenas, and the Battle of Manila Bay.

The Coast Guard Service came into being by an Act of Congress on January 30, 1915, which combined the Revenue Cutter Service and the Life-Saving Service into a single unit that later became the U.S. Coast Guard.

When the United States entered World War I, the Coast Guard augmented the Navy with 223 commissioned officers, about 4,500 enlisted men, and 47 vessels. One of those warships, the cutter *Tampa*, was on convoy duty in European waters when she was torpedoed and sunk by Germany's *U-53*.

The loss of her 115-man Coast Guard crew was the largest loss of life incurred by any U.S. naval unit during the war.

In 1935, keels were laid for a new class of cutters. The design was based on U.S. Navy Erie-class gunboats; the machinery plant and hull below the waterline were identical. Although that standardization reduced construction expense, the program was criticized for its $2.5 million cost per vessel, nearly double any previous cutter.

The new 327-foot cutters were named for former U.S. Treasury secretaries. All were accomplished politicians, but only one, Alexander Hamilton, was a memorable secretary of the treasury. The others were William J. Duane, who had been fired for refusing to carry out a presidential order; his replacement, Roger B. Taney, whose nomination was rejected by Congress some months later; George Campbell, who served for only seven months; George M. Bibb, who was secretary for only one year; John Spencer, who opposed the annexation of Texas, and resigned after 13 months; and Samuel Ingham, who resigned, apparently over a social dispute with the wife of the secretary of war. Though six of the seven were not outstanding as secretary of the treasury, the cutters named for them would have illustrious careers, and six would serve from World War II to Vietnam.

William J. Duane (WPG-*33*) was commissioned August 1, 1936, and *George M. Bibb* (WPG-*31*) on March 10, 1937. The cutters were 327 feet in length, with a beam of 41 feet 2 inches, and displaced 2,750 tons. Two

Coast Guard cutter Bibb *passes through the Cape Cod Canal. (Photo by William P. Quinn.)*

Coast Guard cutter Duane *coming into Support Center, Boston after seizing the drug-laden* Biscayne Breeze. *(U.S. Coast Guard photo.)*

double-reduction geared turbines and twin propellers produced a top speed of 19.5 knots. Their wartime complement was 24 officers, two warrants, and 226 men. Their original armament was two 5-inch guns, two 6-pounders, and one 1-pounder. By the end of World War II, *Duane*'s armament was three 5-inch and three 3-inch guns, fourteen 40-mm (two quad and three twin) and eight 20-mm (single) guns, depth charge tracks, and one Y-gun for depth charges. *Bibb* was armed with one 5-inch and one 3-inch gun, six 40-mm (twin) and four 20-mm (single) guns, and a Hedgehog on her bow. Both cutters carried aircraft, considered essential for high-seas search and rescue. In June 1937, the cutters' names were shortened to surnames only.

World War II

Coast Guard vessels were assigned to the Navy beginning in September 1939, when World War II threatened to involve the United States. *Duane* and *Bibb* were among the first to join Destroyer Division 18 as part of the Grand Banks Patrol. Both operated in 1940 as weather stations east of Bermuda. *Duane* left her station in August so her aircraft could survey Greenland's west coast. In June 1941, she rescued 46 survivors from the torpedoed steamer

Tresillian. Both cutters were transferred to the Navy on September 11, 1941; they were assigned to escort duty in the North Atlantic.

During the next two years, *Bibb* rescued 301 survivors from six torpedoed ships. On April 17, 1943, *Duane* assisted her sister cutter *Spencer* in sinking *U-175* while they were in the vanguard of convoy HX233, 600 miles west of England. The convoy consisted of 19 tankers and 38 freighters, in addition to the escorts. The captain of *U-175* sighted the convoy, but before he could get his U-boat into position for attack, it was spotted by *Spencer's* lookouts. The U-boat submerged, but the cutter's sonar locked into the enemy submarine. Eleven depth charges were dropped on *Spencer's* first pass followed by 11 more on her second run. *U-175's* air compressors and diving controls were so severely damaged, her captain ordered the U-boat to the surface. *Duane* and *Spencer* were waiting when she broke through and opened fire immediately. The Germans poured out of the U-boat's hatches and raced for their guns, a fusillade killed the German captain and six of his crew. The deck of the U-boat was quickly reduced to a shambles that discouraged resistance. The Germans scuttled their vessel and jumped into the ocean. *Duane* rescued 22 German sailors and *Spencer* saved 19 as *U-175* sank.

In August 1944, *Duane* served as flagship for the commander of the 8th Amphibious Force for the invasion of southern France. During the 1945

Duane *on convoy escort duty during World War II. (Photo courtesy of the National Archives.)*

A depth charge explosion off the stern creates a monstrous geyser as the Coast Guard cutter Spencer *attacks U-175 in April 1943. The escorted convoy can be seen in the distance. (Photo courtesy of the National Archives.)*

Depth charge attacks forced U-175 to the surface; there the U-boat was greeted by heavy gun fire from Spencer *and* Duane. *(Photo courtesy of the National Archives.)*

invasion of Okinawa, *Bibb* served as the flagship for the commander of Mine Craft, Pacific Fleet.

The 327's (as the class was called) sank four U-boats during World War II; all other Coast Guard vessels combined sank seven more enemy submarines. The only toll exacted on U.S. cutters was the torpedoing of *Hamilton* 17 miles off Iceland by *U-132*. One American officer and 19 enlisted men were killed; six later died of burns.

The 327's were excellent convoy escorts and Captain A. G. Shepard, USN, stated:

> They are considerably more roomy, so that they can carry a large number of survivors. They are better sea boats than destroyers, and lend themselves better to boat operations and rescues. In connection with picking up people, their hospital accommodations are superior to those of destroyers.

German sailors attempting to fight back were dissuaded by accurate gunfire from the two cutters, which reduced the U-boat's deck to a mass of twisted steel. One of the German crew is seeking shelter behind the severely damaged conning tower. He disappeared a moment later, and it is not known if he was among the survivors. (Photo courtesy of the National Archives.)

Coastguardsmen rescuing survivors from the scuttled U-boat as it sinks by the stern. (Photo courtesy of the National Archives.)

The number of Coast Guard vessels serving in World War II was small compared to the total U.S. Navy, but it was larger than either the Russian or French navies. Over 230,000 men and 10,000 women served in the Coast Guard during the war. More than 600 lost their lives in military action. Almost 2,000 were awarded decorations. One received the Congressional Medal of Honor and six the Navy Cross. When hostilities ended, the Coast Guard returned to the Treasury Department.

Top: A German submariner, one of 41 survivors, calls for rescue. (Photo courtesy of the National Archives.)

Bottom: A survivor of U-175 *climbs aboard* Spencer, *nearly an hour after abandoning the submarine. (Photo courtesy of the National Archives.)*

Right: Two coastguardsmen march a U-175 survivor along the deck. Note the German survival gear, including underwater breathing apparatus and inflatable life preserver. (Photo courtesy of the National Archives.)

Below: U-175 *survivors are marched away by British marines after being landed at Gowrock, Scotland.* Duane *and* Spencer *are in the background, to the left of two British destroyers. (Photo courtesy of the National Archives.)*

Both *Duane* and *Bibb* served in Vietnam as part of the Coastal Surveillance Force, and *Duane* assisted in escorting boats to the Florida coast during the 1980 boatlift of refugees from Cuba. Both proved to be effective deterrents to the illegal drug trade. *Bibb* was responsible for the seizure of 113 tons of marijuana during her career.

In 1985, after almost 50 years of service, both cutters were decommissioned and turned over to the U.S. Maritime Administration for disposal. Excessive repair costs and unavailable spare parts had terminated their long careers of valiant performance.

Artificial Reef

The Key Largo (Florida) National Marine Sanctuary and the adjacent John Pennekamp Coral Reef State Park have long been noted for their protected coral reefs, abundant marine life, and interesting historical shipwrecks. However, the Key Largo diving community wanted something more as an attraction to stimulate business while diverting divers from the fragile reefs to reduce ecological damage. They wanted an artificial reef, " . . . but not just any derelict freighter," specified Stephen Frink, president of Keys Association of Dive Operators. They wanted one with a sense of history—a warship. Two years of organizing,

The two cutters were white-washed to cover their red stripes and insignia before being sunk. (Photo by Geo Toth.)

$160,000 of fund raising, and interfacing with several government agencies bore fruit; they received what they had asked for, doubled— *Duane* and *Bibb*. The two 327's more than satisfied the criteria from the perspective of historical significance.

The two cutters were stripped of their armament and sent from Boston to Bayonne, New Jersey where fuel oil and other potential contaminants were removed and fuel tanks were steam-cleaned. They were made safe for diving by the removal of superstructure hatch doors for easy penetration and to prevent their closing behind a diver, trapping him inside. The main masts (each weighed almost four tons) were removed to ensure that the top of the wreck

Hatches were torched off to provide for easy and safe access to interior compartments. (Photo by Geo Toth.)

would be more than 50 feet from the surface, to satisfy navigation requirements. Hatches were welded to restrict divers to the superstructure, reserving the below-deck areas for marine life.

The cutters were towed to Key Largo where they were scuttled in November 1987 at an Army Corps of Engineers approved artificial reef site, about seven miles offshore, just outside the marine sanctuary. *Duane* was sunk in darkness, but *Bibb* went under in a cacophony of bells and whistles from the boats of a host of spectators who had assembled for the occasion. A handful of former crew members also witnessed the sinking. One of *Bibb*'s World War II veterans observed:

> I'm a sailor and I don't like to see any ship sink, but this is a distinguished and useful way for both cutters to be retired. . . . It is much better than cutting up the ships for scrap.

The U.S. Navy Experimental Dive Unit, under Commander John Devlin, coordinated the sinking of the cutters. Both vessels were carefully flooded, with the hope that they would settle upright on the sand bottom. *Duane* did land on her keel, but *Bibb* disappointed the Navy divers by rolling onto her starboard side. The Navy Experimental Diving Unit is considering an attempt to right her.

The cutter Bibb *slowly settles into about 135 feet of water. (Photos by Geo Toth.)*

Diving *Duane* and *Bibb*

Duane sits upright with a very slight list to starboard in about 120 feet of water. The main deck is at approximately 100 feet, the large bridge wing about 70 feet and the crow's nest within 50 feet of the surface. The crow's nest is a good spot for divers to stop on their descent and orient themselves before continuing.

Bibb is in about 135 feet of water. The port side hull, however, is encountered at approximately 90 feet and a controlled dive to 120 feet will present most of the interesting aspects of the cutter.

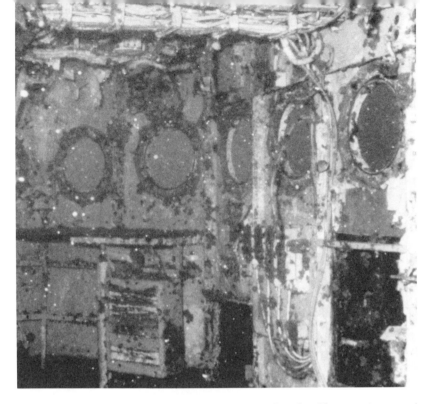

Inside Duane's *bridge. The portholes were removed and sold at auction to raise money to prepare the ship for sinking. (Photo by Mel Brenner.)*

Subsurface mooring buoys have been installed on both cutters to facilitate boat anchoring and diver descent.

Within months of their sinking, algae began to accumulate on the cutters. Schools of baitfish followed. They, in turn, attracted predators such as amberjacks and barracudas—to the delight of underwater photographers.

Both cutters have much to see, photograph, and explore. Many hatchways lead to stairways, companionways, and compartments. Crew's quarters contain bunks, stoves are in the galley, furniture is in the commanding officer's cabin and there is a teletype in the radio room.

The clear blue water of the Gulf Stream provides excellent visibility, usually more than 100 feet. The current, however, can be a problem to an inexperienced or out-of-condition diver.

The fondest dreams of the Keys Association of Dive Operators have been fulfilled. The two Coast Guard cutters, especially *Duane* in shallower water, have lured many divers to the area. Many local dive shops and related services are available to serve them. The two historic vessels are now at rest after brilliant careers in this country's oldest naval service, first revenue cutters of the secretary of the treasury, then Revenue Service, succeeded by the Coast Guard, and finally the United States Coast Guard.

Chapter 16

U.S.S. *Moonstone*— Luxurious Sub-Chaser

Location: about 27 miles off the coast of Delaware
Approximate depth of water: 125 feet
Visibility: bad to excellent
Current: little
Access: boat

"Live aboard a luxury yacht while you serve your country in the United States Navy." That prospect would swamp recruitment offices with volunteers willing and anxious to trade a few years of civilian life for duty to their country. But veterans of the service will attest that life aboard a U.S. Navy warship was never meant to be a luxury cruise. That explains why U.S.S. *Moonstone*'s 50-man crew was denied the privileges enjoyed by the rich and famous occupants of the vessel when she was listed as the privately-owned luxury yacht *Lone Star.*

The sleek pleasure craft was built in 1929 by Germania Werft at Kiel, Germany with all the appointments to satisfy a wealthy owner. She was 170 feet long, with a 26-foot 9-inch beam and 9-foot 5-inch draft. Two Krupp-Diesel engines provided a top speed of 13 knots and a cruising range of 4,400 to 5,000 miles at 10½ knots. The Navy purchased *Lone Star* from Frederick H. Prince of Aiken, South Carolina for $80,000 on February 10, 1941 for conversion into a Navy patrol boat to protect

176

The privately-owned luxury yacht Lone Star *owned by Frederick H. Prince. (Photo courtesy of the National Archives.)*

against German U-boats, although the United States was not yet a full combatant in World War II.

The Gibbs Gas Engine Company modified the yacht for her new use at Jacksonville, Florida where she was commissioned April 10, 1941. Her primary purpose was to drop depth charges on U-boats from two depth charge tracks installed on the stern. In addition, the new U.S.S. *Moonstone* (PYc-9) was armed with a 3-inch deck gun and two .30 caliber machine guns.

The converted yacht sailed on May 5, 1941, for patrol duty in South American waters with the Panamanian Sea Frontier. She was engaged in no enemy action and sighted no U-boats for the next year and a half. On January 2, 1943, *Moonstone* sailed for Ecuador to assist in training that country's naval forces.

The U.S. Navy decided to transfer *Moonstone* to Ecuador, with a target date of August 9, 1943 for delivery. She sailed to Charleston, South Carolina in March to prepare for the transfer, and in July returned to Balboa, Panama for the transfer. There, cracks were discovered in the cylinder blocks of her engines. She was ordered north for repairs after it was estimated that it would take six months to obtain and install new cylinder castings. On September 3, the order for *Moonstone*'s transfer was rescinded and she reported on August 30, for temporary patrol duty on the Atlantic coast as replacement for U.S.S. *Alabaster*.

October 15, while on U-boat patrol, *Moonstone*, under the command of Lieutenant W.R.S. Curtis, entered the south entrance channel off the Delaware Capes in low and variable visibility. Her course lay directly across

The sleek pleasure craft was converted to antisubmarine patrol by the U.S. Navy, and renamed Moonstone. *Note the 3-inch gun just forward of the bridge and the two depth charge racks hanging over the stern. (Photo courtesy of the National Archives.)*

the bow of the U.S. destroyer *Greer*. Two years earlier, on September 4, 1941 *Greer* had become the first American warship to be attacked by a German submarine. That event prompted President Franklin Roosevelt to issue orders for the Navy to shoot on sight any hostile craft attacking American ships or any ships under American escort.

Greer tracked *Moonstone* by radar for 11 minutes before visual contact was made. Two minutes later, at 11:20 p.m., the destroyer's bow crumpled as it plowed into *Moonstone*'s port side under the bridge. The one-time luxury yacht sank immediately at latitude 38° 32′30″N, longitude 74° 34′30″W. The entire crew was recovered, but one steward's mate was found dead from drowning. The survivors were taken to Brooklyn, New York aboard *Greer*, whose badly damaged bow limited her speed to seven knots. U.S.S. *Moonstone* was stricken from the Navy Register on October 26, 1943, two and a half years after her commissioning.

Diving U.S.S. *Moonstone*

The wreck sits upright in about 125 feet of water, 27 miles off the coast of Delaware. Several dive shops and dive boats along the Delaware and Maryland coasts take divers to the site, generally from spring until late fall,

Assortment of Moonstone *artifacts on display. The ship's bell carries the vessel's original name,* Lone Star. *(Photo by Michael deCamp.)*

depending on weather conditions. Advanced certification or proof of equivalent experience are required by most charter operators because of the depth and distance from shore. Visibility varies considerably, from 80 feet to extremely poor. *Moonstone*'s hull is intact and there are several open areas that allow safe penetration.

In 1985, a team of sport divers, led by NAUI Dive Instructors Scott Jenkins and Ken Smith with charter boat captain Larry Keen, salvaged the 427-pound captain's safe. Jenkins had conducted extensive research and discussion with Lieutenant W. Robert Scott Curtis, who commanded *Moonstone* when she sank. Curtis described the safe's location in detail, but the complexities of bringing it to the surface took two years. Inside the safe was a gold watch and the captain's personal coin collection, which included four Spanish reales dating from 1789. The safe and many other artifacts are on display at Poseidon Adventures dive shop in Wilmington, Delaware. Other artifacts that have been recovered from the wreck include coins (U.S. and Ecuadorian), a wallet, a gold ring, the ship's horn, silver service, a telescope, china service, and the spanner wrench that was used to disarm the depth charges that were aboard when the ship was sunk.

The three-inch deck gun is still mounted on the bow, a fitting landmark at the bottom of the sea to link the luxury yacht *Lone Star* to the World War II warship U.S.S. *Moonstone*.

THE DISCOVERED
AND UNDISCOVERED

Chapter 17

A Summary of
Warship Wrecks

Sailing Vessels

H.M.S. *Winchester*

The 60-gun ship-of-the-line H.M.S. *Winchester* was lost off Key Largo, Florida on September 24, 1695. She was on convoy duty en route from Jamaica to England with Captain John Soule in command. The 933-ton warship struck Carysfort Reef in what is now the northern part of John Pennekamp Coral Reef State Park. Two hundred and forty-three years later her coral-encrusted cannons were sighted in 25 feet of water. Cannon, cannonballs, musketballs, and silver and brass coins were among the many artifacts recovered. The British Admiralty identified the wreck from markings on the recovered cannon. During the salvage operation the salvors broke apart two crossed cannon which had been cemented together by coral growth. Surprisingly, a sailor's prayer book was found crushed between the symbols of war and destruction. Some pages were perfectly preserved from the press of the huge cannon and the subsequent coral encrustations.

H.M. Frigate *Feversham* and *Ferret*

The 36-gun British frigate *Feversham* was lost in October 1711. The 372-ton warship struck the rocky shore at Howe Point, Scatarie Island, Nova Scotia. Cannon, cannonballs, timbers, and fastenings can be seen scattered about a large submerged rock at the southern tip of Howe Point. A few coins have been recovered. Water depth ranges from about 18 feet to over 70 feet. Wind, heavy seas, and strong currents can make this a hazardous dive. The wreckage is reported to be mixed with that of the British warship *Ferret*, which was lost in September 1757.

Le Chameau

In 1725, the French warship *Le Chameau* was wrecked by an east-southeast gale near Louisbourg, Nova Scotia, on a reef less than a mile off Cape Breton Island. There were no survivors of the 100-man crew and 216 passengers. All 316 bodies washed ashore. The ship, carrying supplies and pay (80,000 livres in gold and silver coins) for the French forces at Louisbourg, had broken up on a rock that was covered by only a few feet of water at low tide. All but the after part of the ship washed ashore. An unsuccessful attempt was made to salvage the guns and treasure.

After years of research Alex Storm and other local divers found the warship in the mid 1960's and formed a salvage company. They recovered most of the gold and silver and found many historical artifacts. Storm operates a personal museum in Louisbourg, where some of the artifacts are exhibited. The salvage company has now opened the wreck site to sport divers.

H.M.S. *Astrea*

In 1743, several men died when the British warship *Astrea* accidentally caught fire near the mouth of the Piscataqua River at Portsmouth, New Hampshire. Captain Robert Swanton survived but his ship was lost. Today a bridge passes over the wreck site, but little wreckage can be found.

Celebre, Entreprenant, and *Capricieux*

The British laid siege to the important French fortress at Louisbourg Harbor, Cape Breton Island, Nova Scotia in 1758. On June 28 and 29 four French warships, *Apollon*—50 guns, *Fidele*—26 guns, *Chevre*—16 guns, and *Ville de Saint Malo* were sunk to block entry to the harbor. The following day *Biche*—16 guns, was scuttled.

The crew and soldiers of five other French warships in the harbor, a total of 1,490 men, were landed to man the siege defenses. In the early afternoon of July 21, a shot from a British siege gun struck the 64-gun *Celebre*, setting fire to a powder magazine. The fire spread to the mizzen mast and the few men left on board were unable to control the blaze. As the warship swung at anchor, wind carried sparks to the 74-gun *Entreprenant*. The under-manned crew could not check that fire either, and it spread to the 64-gun *Capricieux*. Two other French ships escaped. One was windward, the other managed to avoid the fire by swinging on her cable.

To compound the problem the British siege guns intensified their fire on the burning French ships-of-the-line. The loaded guns aboard the stricken French warships fired when they became hot, adding to the conflagration. Some of the shot hit the other two French ships and town buildings.

The French warships blazed all night and the tide carried them ashore. The following morning they lay with their guns tumbled into their holds. Only 47 cannon were recovered from the hulks.

Celebre is in less than 20 feet of water, a few hundred yards from the old fortress. Cannon are scattered over the ballast pile. Cannon balls, anchors, timbers, and other artifacts can be viewed but not disturbed. The wrecks in Louisbourg Harbor are designated as "protected areas."

Fortress of Louisbourg National Historic Park is Nova Scotia's number one historical preservation project. Three local dive-charter boat operators are permitted to take divers on underwater tours of the historic wrecks. These diving tours follow guidelines developed by the park. The tour operators are Aqua Tours Ltd., P.O. Box 124, Louisbourg, N.S., B0A 1M0; Gustavo Ruan, 90 Upper Warren St. (Louisbourg); and Sea-Quatic Ventures, 2275 Shore Road, Point Edward, R.R. #1, North Sydney, N.S., B2A 3L7.

H.M.S. *Augusta* and *Merlin*

British land forces under General Sir William Howe captured Phila-delphia in September 1777. The loss of America's largest city, and national capital, was a great blow to the Colonists. However, General Washington's forces still encircled the city, cutting off land supply routes. If Philadelphia was to be held for the Crown, the Delaware River had to be opened from the city to the Atlantic.

Washington wrote that General Howe's situation:

> . . . would not be the most agreeable: for if his supplies can be stopped by water . . . . the acquisition of Philadelphia may, instead of his good fortune, prove his ruin.

The American defenses on the Delaware River consisted of obstructions, forts, and a squadron of small warships. The first barrier to the British were the obstructions at Billingsport on the New Jersey shore. Box-like structures of heavy timbers filled with stones were sunk in two rows across the channel. Wooden stakes, tipped with iron points and slanting downstream, were set in these foundations. A small, unfinished fort was part of that first line of defense. As British forces, which had been landed below the fort, attacked from the rear, the garrison spiked their cannon and retired hastily. The obstructions were removed and the British fleet, under Admiral Lord Richard Howe, sailed through.

A little further upstream the British naval forces faced a more formidable defense. There were several more rows of obstructions, but this time guarded by two forts—Fort Mercer, an earthworks with ditch, abatis, and 14 guns on the New Jersey shore, and Fort Mifflin on Fort Island in the river. Behind the barriers lay the American warships.

On October 22, a force of 1,200 Hessians under Colonel von Donop, supported by artillery, attacked Fort Mercer. The garrison of 400 Rhode Islander's and grapeshot from several galleys in the river drove von Donop's grenadiers back. British casualties were 377 men, including von Donop, one of the most distinguished officers among the Hessian mercenaries. Colonel Greene, of the Continental force, reported only 35 casualties.

American warships (center background) exchange fire with H.M.S. Augusta, Roebuck, *and* Merlin *near Fort Mercer on the Delaware River October 22, 1777. (Photo courtesy of the Naval Historical Center.)*

In support of the ill-fated attack, Admiral Lord Richard Howe, General Sir William Howe's brother, ordered six warships to attack the fort and the American galleys. The largest British ship was the 64-gun ship-of-the-line *Augusta*, the smallest *Cornwallis*, a galley. The naval action lasted from 5 p.m. to shortly after 8 p.m. As the British squadron attempted to withdraw downstream, *Augusta*, under the command of Captain Francis Reynolds, ran aground. The large warship, within range of guns from both forts and the enemy warships, was holding her own when the 18-gun sloop-of-war *Merlin*, with a shallow draft, came in to support her. However, *Merlin* also grounded.

Every effort was made during the night to refloat the warship, but unsuccessfully. At 6 a.m. a British frigate, using a cable, attempted to pull *Augusta* off the shoal. That effort alerted the Colonial forces to the plight of the British warships. Relentless cannon fire forced the British frigate to release the cable and escape. She had been hit several times and reported six killed and ten wounded.

The Colonists then sent four fire ships (the brigs *Comet, Hellcat, Volcano,* and the sloop *Aetna*) downstream in an unsuccessful attempt to set fire to the stranded British warships. However, the cannonade continued until around 10:45 a.m., when the Colonials observed *Augusta* to be on fire.

According to Lord Howe's report to the British Admiralty, hot cotton wadding from *Augusta*'s own guns started a fire in a gunpowder bucket. When the fire spread to her timbers, Captain Reynolds ordered more fires set and the crew to abandon ship. Captain Samuel Reeve of *Merlin* followed suit. When the fires reached the magazines both ships exploded. The concussion from the explosion of *Augusta*'s magazines was felt for miles around Philadelphia. *Augusta* was the largest warship destroyed in action with American forces in either the Revolution or the War of 1812.

Augusta carried twenty-six 24-pounder cannon on the lower deck, twenty-six 18-pounders on the upper deck, ten 9-pounders on the quarter deck, and two nine-pounders on the forecastle. Most were salvaged by Colonial forces. Even though the two warships exploded, many articles were recovered including one hundred and fifty-four 24-pound shot, uniforms, shoes, hats, flags, doctors' instruments, and 24 shillings. When the warship was raised and dragged ashore in 1876, at Gloucester, it was reported only a few 24-pounders were found.

In late November the British forces attacked again, this time with success. They took the forts, and had the satisfaction of forcing the Americans to destroy their ships to prevent capture. Among those destroyed were the 8-gun galleys *Fly* and *Wasp*, the 10-gun sloops *Racehorse* and *Hornet*, and the 14-gun brig *Andrea Doria*.

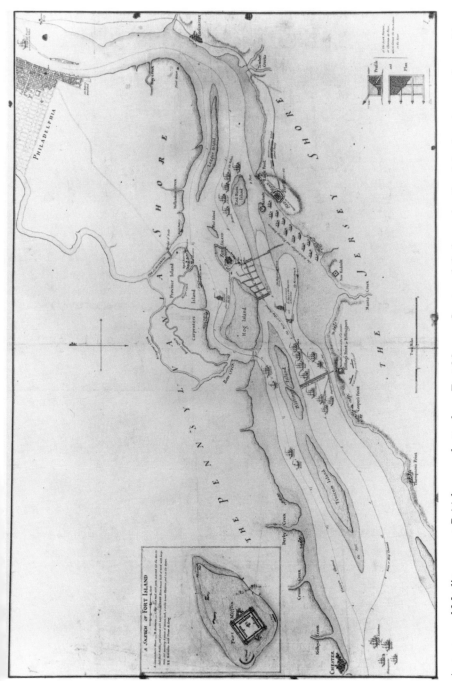

Augusta and Merlin support British ground attack on Fort Mercer. Inset on left shows details of the fort that was located in the center of the Delaware River. Lower right insert shows the type of obstructions that the American defenders placed in the river. (Photo courtesy of the Naval Historical Center.)

Stranded Augusta's *magazine, exploding in an accident on October 23, 1777. (Photo courtesy of the Naval Historical Center.)*

Remains of the 64-gun British Augusta *in 1937. (Photo courtesy of the Naval Historical Center.)*

Many artifacts that were recovered from *Augusta* in 1937 are now displayed by the Philadelphia Maritime Museum.

H.M. Frigate *Tribune*

The projection of land at the head of Herring Cove, Halifax, Nova Scotia is named Tribune Head for the site of a major marine disaster. On November 16, 1797 the 44-gun British frigate *Tribune* (ex-French warship

La Tribune) grounded on Thrumcap Shoals while entering Halifax Harbor. To refloat his vessel, Captain Scory Barker ordered the crew to jettison all cannon on the exposed upper deck. That accomplished his purpose, but a raging storm blew the 916-ton warship across the harbor to the headland at Herring Cove, where she broke up. Only 9 of more than 200 men on board survived the disaster.

Wreckage is scattered in 30 to 90 feet of water, where it can be found under gravel and sediment in rocky crevices. Cannon, cannonballs, grapeshot, brass fastenings, sheathing and other artifacts are occasionally recovered from a kelp covered area. Strong currents are frequent on this wreck.

H.M. Brig *DeBraak*

The 16-gun British brig-of-war *DeBraak*,, commanded by Captain James Drew, capsized and sank in 1798, two miles off Lewis, Delaware, with a loss of 35 men. Reportedly she carried 70 tons of copper ingots, gold and silver specie and bullion. The British warship had captured one French vessel and two Spanish ships in the Caribbean. Her hold supposedly carried treasure from the successes. The war prize *San Francisco de Xavier* was in tow when *DeBraak* foundered, and in all likelihood contributed to the sinking.

The wreck was discovered in 1984, and is being salvaged under license by the state. The treasure on board the British warship is valued by the salvage

Cannon and other artifacts from the British 16-gun DeBraak. *(Photo courtesy of Peter Hess.)*

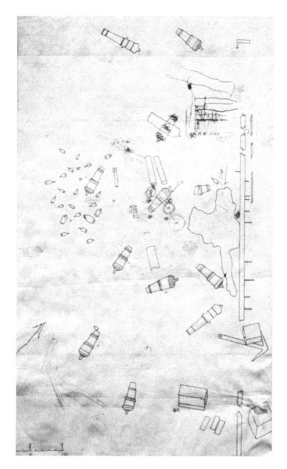

Map showing where artifacts were recovered from DeBraak. *(Photo courtesy of Peter Hess.)*

company to be between $5 million and $500 million. However, only a few silver and gold coins have been recovered, Spanish doubloons, British guineas, and French specie among them. Also, a gold ring bearing the inscription, "In memory of a belov'd brother, Capt. John Drew, drown'd 11 Jan 1798, aged 47," identified the wreck. The ring belonged to *DeBraak*'s captain, who was lost in the disaster. His twin brother John was captain of the British frigate *Cerberus* when his launch capsized and he drowned off Cornwall, England, only about five months before his brother James.

Most of the ship's hull was recovered and placed in a holding tank, awaiting preservation. What little of the ship's structure remains, is scattered in about 85 feet of water, with poor visibility and is constantly swept by strong currents.

In addition to a small amount of treasure, divers have recovered bottles, pewter and silver eating utensils and plates, deadeyes, hundreds of copper spikes embossed with the King's broad arrow, cartographers' tools, a brass telescope, well preserved muskets, a set of matched dueling pistols, a French-inscribed ships' bell bearing the name "Le Petrocle" (probably removed from the captured French ship), cannon, cannonballs, and other assorted artifacts. Over 26,000 artifacts have been recovered and Delaware state officials are considering a museum to house them after preservation. Under its lease arrangement, the salvage company is only required to turn over to the state 25 percent of the net value of what is recovered after expenses, or a representative sample. However, the principal investor is considering donating all of the artifacts to the state.

General Arnold

On Christmas morning 1778, two American privateers set sail in a snow storm from Boston Harbor for South Carolina. One was *Revenge*, the other the 20-gun brig *General Arnold*, named after Continental Army Brigadier General Benedict Arnold who later betrayed his trust and joined the British.

The privateers carried a detachment of marines and a cargo of military supplies for American troops. As the vessels crossed Massachusetts Bay, the snow storm developed into a blizzard. Captain Barrows of the *Revenge* made the correct decision to ride out the storm off Cape Cod. Captain James Magee of *General Arnold* decided to weather the storm in Plymouth Harbor. However, after reaching apparent safety the privateer's anchor would not hold against the raging wind. The anchor line parted and the ship was driven onto a shallow water sand flat about a mile from shore, not far from Plymouth Rock.

As the privateer settled into the sand, waves washed over her main deck. The crew sought safety on the quarter-deck, but Captain Magee later reported:

> . . . within a few hours presented a scene that would shock the least delicate humanity. Some of my people were stifled to death with the snow; others perished with the extremity of the cold, and a few were washed off the deck and drowned.

Clothing, soaked by icy salt spray, froze to the bodies of the crew. A number of the men wrapped themselves in the brig's sails to survive. By the following morning 30 of the original 105 sailors and marines had frozen to death.

The blizzard continued, exposing the men to more nights in sub-freezing temperatures before the people of Plymouth could rescue them. Eighty-one died; all of the 24 survivors, except Captain Magee, were crippled for life by intense cold and frostbite.

Captain Magee died in 1801 at 51 years of age. At his request he was buried with the *General Arnold*'s crew at Burial Hill, Plymouth.

In 1976, a 75-foot section of a wooden ship suddenly appeared above the sand at low tide on White Flat in Plymouth Harbor. The Pilgrim Society of Plymouth, Plymouth's International Military Museum, and Barry Clifford each filed claim to the wreck with the Massachusetts Board of Underwater Archaeological Resources. The Pilgrim Society, the first to present a request in writing, was granted title to the wreck. However, they later withdrew their claim stating:

> We do not believe this wreck is that of the *General Arnold,* and further research into the subject reveals that the *Arnold* was repaired and later sailed for Europe.

Charles Sanderson III, director of Plymouth's International Military Museum, was then given title to the wreck. By 1982, he had recovered many artifacts clearly identifying the wreck as the privateer.

H.M. Sloop *Zebra*

A British fleet that was anchored in the Mullica River, New Jersey was ordered to sail for New York without delay. To facilitate its departure, two boats were moored to mark the North and South Breakers. At 8 a.m. on October 19, 1778, *Nautilus*, the leading ship, grounded on a sandbar. The 16-gun sloop-of-war *Zebra* was forced to take avoiding action and also stranded close to the lead warship. *Nautilus* was able to get underway, but *Zebra* had hit hard and was driven to leeward and out of the channel. An attempt was made to warp her off, but without success and water was pouring into her hull. The following day her stores were removed and the sloop was burned to prevent her capture.

The wreck, under New Jersey state jurisdiction, is in the Mullica River on the ocean side of the Garden State Parkway bridge. It is reported that visibility is zero, making it a hazardous dive, but divers who have entered the hull found ballast stones, and recovered a small cannon.

Warren and *Defence*

In 1779, the third year of the American Revolution, the British were building a fort on Penobscot Bay at the site of present day Castine, Maine. The new colony would be called New Ireland. An American naval squadron of 20 warships, bristling with more than 350 cannon, and 25 supply and transport vessels carrying about 1,200 sailors, marines, and militia were sent to capture the British position. It was the largest naval force assembled by the Colonists during the war.

When the American force arrived in July, the British earthen fort was only one-fourth complete and manned by 750 soldiers. Only three British sloops-of-war with a total of 56 cannon, lay offshore. However, the diminutive British naval force would prove to be all that was needed until reinforcements arrived to inflict on the Colonists America's greatest naval disaster until Pearl Harbor.

Brigadier General Soloman Lovell, commander of the American land forces, assessed the capabilities of the partially completed British fortifications and naval force and concluded that he had an easy victory in hand. However, Commodore Dudley Saltonstall, commanding the naval force, was reluctant to attack the three British warships within the confines of the bay. Lieutenant David Porter of the 20-gun *General Putnam* and 30 other naval officers presented Commodore Saltonstall with a petition that read in part:

> We think that delays in the present case are extremely dangerous, as our enemies are daily fortifying and strengthening themselves, and are stimulated . . . in daily expectation of a reinforcement. We don't mean to advise or censure your past conduct, but intend only to express our desire . . . to go immediately into the harbour and attack the enemy ships.

The commodore's reply: "I'll not take my ships into that damned hell hole." He continued to find excuses to delay attack on the three British warships guarding the fort. He was always backed by a minority of naval officers and Lt. Colonel Paul Revere (who would go to his grave bemoaning his participation), in command of the field artillery.

On August 11, more than two weeks after the American arrival, General Lovell wrote the following to Saltonstall:

> The destruction of the enemy's ships must be effected at any rate, although it might cost us half our own . . . . any further delay must be infamous. And, I have it at this moment, by a deserter from one of their ships, that the moment you enter the harbor, they will destroy themselves . . . with the enemy's ships safe, the operations of the Army cannot possibly be extended an inch beyond the present limits. . . . The information of the British ships at the Hook (New Jersey) which have probably sailed before this, is not to be despised; not a moment is to be lost . . .

Lovell's concern was well founded. British headquarters in New York had received information in regard to the siege in Penobscot Bay.

Saltonstall reluctantly agreed to attack the enemy ships on Friday the 13th. However, he had procrastinated too long. A British relief squadron arrived off Penobscot Bay, and General Lovell ordered his army to retreat.

The following morning, as the British squadron approached, the American troop transports got underway; with their only course up river, the enemy blocked the entrance to the bay. General Lovell, watching from land later reported:

> . . . the transports . . . weighed anchor, and to our great mortification, they were soon followed by our fleet of Men-of-War, pursued by only four of the enemy's ships. The ships-of-war passed the transports, many of which were going aground, and with the British ships coming upon them, the soldiers were obliged to take to the shore and set fire to their vessels. . . . To attempt to give a description of this terrible day is out of my power. . . . To see four ships pursuing seventeen . . . nine of which are stout ships. Transports are on fire, Men-of-War blowing up . . .

Hunter (18 guns) and *Defence* (16 guns) tried to reach the open sea, but failed. *Hunter* ran ashore and was captured by the British. *Defence* was scuttled in the bay, behind Sears Island, to prevent capture.

The commodore's flagship *Warren* (32 guns) sailed 15 miles up the Penobscot River, ran aground off what is now Winterport and burned. The two 20-gun warships *Vengeance* and *General Putnam* were sunk opposite Hampden. *Hector* (20 guns), *Monmouth* (20 guns), *Charming Sally* (20 guns), *Black Prince* (18 guns), *Tyrannicide* (16 guns), *Diligent* (14 guns), *Providence* (12 guns), *Hazard* (10 guns), and several transports were sunk above and below Kenduskeag Stream at Bangor, Maine.

The supply ship *Spring Bird* with a cargo of arms and ammunition was set afire several miles up the river and allowed to drift.

The British captured 11 of the Colonial vessels. Commodore Saltonstall was court martialed and cashiered from the service for his part in the disaster.

In 1953, John Cayford was one of a construction crew working on the General Chamberlain Bridge, across the Penobscot River at Bangor. The workers found four cannon that were identified as Revolutionary War period.

Later it was determined that they were from the 12-gun sloop *Providence*. However, the wreck site was sealed by tons of cement during the construction.

Cayford realized that other Revolutionary War period wrecks must be in the area. Three years and hundreds of diving hours later, he was rewarded with Commodore Saltonstall's flagship, the 32-gun frigate *Warren*, from which he recovered a 6-pound bronze cannon.

During the next seven years Cayford located two more wrecks. In 1972, he informed Massachusetts Institute of Technology's Summer Lab Afloat of his findings. MIT's program uses the facilities of the Maine Maritime Academy (MMA) at Castine, where Cayford felt *Defence* would be found

(text continued on page 201)

Baitfish surround a Schurz *valve handle. (Photo by Chip Cooper.)*

A diver swims over a stack of 5-inch projectiles that replaced the original 4.1-inch armament of the German warship when she was taken over by the U.S. Navy. (Photo by Jon Hulburt.)

Divers search for artifacts amidst the light cruiser Schurz's *scattered wreckage. (Photos by Brad Sheard.)*

Diver sits atop naval converted yacht Moonstone*'s deck gun. (Photo by Jon Hulburt.)*

*Moonstone's telegraph
being recovered in 1970.
(Photo by Michael
deCamp.)*

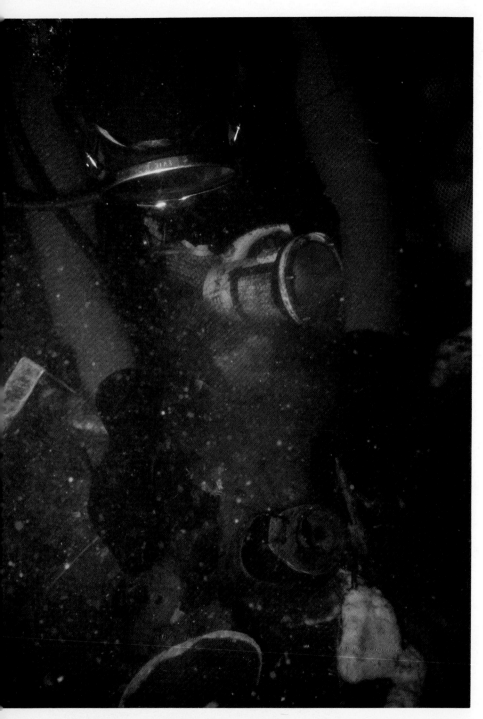

Diver uncovers a compass on Jacob Jones . . .

. . . and swims to the surface with his find. (Photos by Michael deCamp.)

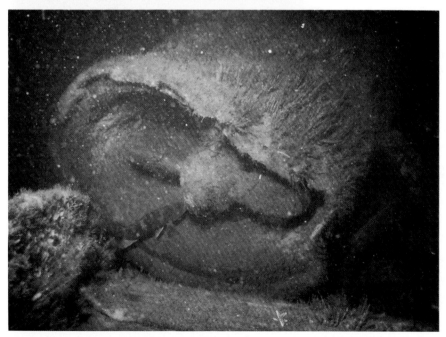

This 1970 photograph shows the propeller of a torpedo that still remained inside a twisted torpedo tube on the U.S. destroyer Jacob Jones. *(Photo by Michael deCamp.)*

The barrel of a 3-inch gun projects out of the U.S. cruiser San Diego's *hull, just above the sand. (Photo by Brad Sheard.)*

Two projectiles for 6-inch guns and clips of 30-06 rifle ammunition inside San Diego. *The steel I-beam rests on the tip of one of the projectiles. (Photo by H. Keatts.)*

Springfield rifles inside San Diego's *armory. They must be excavated with care; some divers have broken them in two while trying to work them free. (Photo by Jon Hulburt.)*

Cases of ammunition for the 3-inch guns inside one of San Diego's *many magazines. (Photo by Jon Hulburt.)*

▲ *A diver peers through an opening in one of* San Diego's *crow's nests that now rest on its side in the sand. (Photo by H. Keatts.)*

◄ *Projectiles for* San Diego's *8-inch guns inside one of the warship's magazines. (Photo by Jon Hulburt.)*

(text continued from page 192)

in Stockton Harbor, across Penobscot Bay. The 170-ton, 16-gun brig was located in 25 feet of water on the first pass of their magnetometer by a team of faculty and students from MIT and MMA.

The state of Maine enacted a statute protecting land and underwater archaeological sites. A task force from the MMA, the Maine State Museum, and the Institute of Nautical Archaeology was granted approval to work the wreck and preserve recovered relics. Many artifacts have been recovered—hand spikes, sail makers' tools, pewter eating utensils, buckles (one, pewter with USA embossed on it), bottles (including cobalt colored ones), grapeshot and grapeshot stands (some packed), barshot, various size cannonballs, and iron cannon.

One of the cannon that was sent to the Naval Research and Development Center for initial preservation was found to be booby trapped. The Naval Ordnance Depot disarmed it and determined that even after 174 years underwater, the charge was still capable of firing.

H.M. Sloop *Amaranth*

On October 25, 1799, the 14-gun British sloop-of-war *Amaranth*, commanded by Captain John Blake, went aground off Pompano Beach, Florida, while on blockade duty in the Straits of Florida. Twenty-two of the 86-man crew perished.

The warship was the former French brig *L'Amaranth* captured by the British vessel *Diamond*, off the Contentin Peninsular, France, on December 31, 1796.

The wreck lies approximately one mile north of the Hillsboro Inlet. It is referred to as the "Old Silver Wreck" in several treasure hunting books. Reportedly, "silver bars" had been found on the beach in the wreck's vicinity.

In 1959, divers recovered nine or ten cannon, cannon balls, brass uniform buttons, ship fastenings and other artifacts, but no silver.

The main portion of the wreck lies east to west, with the eastern seaward part in 15 to 20 feet of water under about eight feet of sand.

U.S.S. *Huron*

The four-gun U.S. sloop-of-war *Huron* was powered by both sail and steam. She displaced 541 tons and was 175 feet in length. The U.S. Navy warship was commissioned in 1875, but was on a scientific expedition to Cuba when she grounded on November 24, 1877, north of present-day Oregon Inlet, North Carolina.

Winds increased to gale force as huge waves crashed on and over the stranded ship. Only 34 of the 132 on board survived. The sinking of *Huron* was one of the worst disasters at Cape Hatteras, an area often referred to as the "Graveyard of the Atlantic."

The subsequent court of inquiry determined that the sinking occurred because of an error in the compass that was caused by the listing of the ship. However, the warship's captain was found to be primarily responsible because of his failure to perform other navigational procedures that would have determined his correct position.

The wreck site is in 20 feet of water, approximately 200 yards north of Nags Head Pier. All that remains to be seen of the old warship are her engine, boilers, hull ribs and keel. Due to the shallow depth, there is often a strong surge that can be a hazard to divers. It can hurl a diver onto the scattered wreckage, then pull him off and toss him back again.

H.M.S. *Somerset*

Remains of the British 64-gun Somerset *in 1970. (Photo by William P. Quinn.)*

An early November storm in 1778 wrecked the 64-gun British ship-of-the-line *Somerset* on the tip of the Cape Cod peninsula near Provincetown, Massachusetts. Captain George Curry was in command.

The warship was laden with a cargo of war materials, which was heavily salvaged by Colonists. The wreck broke up and over the years was covered by the shifting sand of Cape Cod. Many artifacts were recovered by souvenir hunters when storms uncovered the warship in 1886 and again in 1924. In the 1970's high tides and sand action again exposed *Somerset*. All that surfaced were jagged pieces of worn timber. However, much more must still be covered by sand. The wreck is now under the protection of the Cape Cod National Seashore Rangers to prevent further removal of artifacts.

H.M.S. *Phoenix*

The three-masted, sail and steam powered British warship *Phoenix* was en route from Quebec to Halifax, Nova Scotia on September 12, 1882. A raging gale forced her onto East Point Reef, a submerged reef off East Point, Prince Edward Island, where she was lost.

Salvors have worked the 1,137-ton warship, but much wreckage is scattered about the reef and in adjacent coves. Water depth varies from just beneath the surface to about 40 feet. Diving should be attempted only at slack tide to avoid the extremely strong currents that prevail.

Battleships

U.S.S. *Texas*

The first U.S. Navy ship named *Texas* was a 6,315-ton, 309-foot battleship launched in June 1892.

In 1898, conditions in Cuba and the destruction of the U.S. battleship *Maine*, precipitated war between the United States and Spain. *Texas* was ordered to Cuba as part of a "Flying Squadron" for blockade duty. In June

Battleship Texas, *prior to the Spanish-American War. (Photo courtesy of the Naval Historical Center.)*

of the same year the battleship and another warship bombarded the Spanish fort on Cayo de Tore in Guantanamo Bay. Their combined fire reduced the fort to impotency.

On July 3 the Spanish fleet under Admiral Cervera made an attempt to escape from Santiago de Cuba. *Texas* attacked four of the fleeing enemy warships. Her main battery of two 12-inch guns pounded the cruisers *Vizcaya* and *Cristobal Colon*, her secondary battery of six 6-inch guns, aided by the battleship *Massachusetts* and one other U.S. warship, battered two destroyers. The heavily damaged destroyers quickly broke out of the action and beached. One of the larger enemy warships met the same fate. The *Colon* was forced to retire into the safety of the inner harbor. *Texas* and the other ships of the Flying Squadron had annihilated the small Spanish fleet.

In the early 1900's *Texas* served as flagship for the Coast Squadron. By 1908, she had become station ship at Charleston, South Carolina. On February 15, 1911 her name was changed to *San Marcos* to allow the name Texas to be assigned to a new battleship (which has been restored and is now on display just outside of Houston). In 1911, her name was struck from the Navy list and she was subsequently sunk as a target in Tangier Sound in Chesapeake Bay. All parts of the wreck projecting above the water were destroyed in 1944. Several vessels have struck the hulk and sunk.

The old battleship San Marcos *(ex-Texas) in March 1911 at Chesapeake Bay ordnance tests, before being fired on as a target. The canvas screens were rigged to increase her target area. (Photo courtesy of the Naval Historical Center.)*

Battleship New Hampshire *(BB-25) firing on the target ship* San Marcos *in March 1911. (Photo courtesy of the Naval Historical Center.)*

San Marcos *resting on the bottom after destructive salvos from* New Hampshire. *Shell holes pockmark the old battleship, which subsequently sank. Photo courtesy of the Naval Historical Center.*

Battleship Alabama *(BB-8) hit by a white phosphorus bomb from U.S. Army plane at San Marcos Proving area in 1921. At left are wrecks of the battleships* San Marcos *and* Indiana *(BB-1), both expended in earlier ordnance tests.* Alabama *and* Indiana *were later removed from Chesapeake Bay, but* San Marcos *remains. (Photo courtesy of the Naval Historical Center.)*

The wreck is seven miles SSW from the lower tip of Tangier Island. The old battleship was for many years, and may still be, marked by a red nun buoy and a black can buoy. Wreckage is scattered in about 25 feet of water and visibility is usually poor, five to 15 feet. The large caliber shells and bombs used on her when she served as a target left large pieces of jagged steel that can be a hazard to divers, especially in the poor visibility. Also, unexploded ordnance is found in the area. Currents are usually moderate, but they fluctuate with the tide.

U.S.S. *Massachusetts*

The 10,288-ton battleship *Massachusetts* (BB-2) was launched in June 1893. In May 1897, after an overhaul at the New York Navy Yard, the 351-foot warship steamed for Boston for a celebration in her honor, including the presentation of the Massachusetts Coat of Arms.

At the outbreak of the Spanish American War in 1898, *Massachusetts* joined *Texas* in the Flying Squadron for the blockade of Cuba. On May 31, the two battleships, in company with one other warship, bombarded the forts at the entrance to Santiago de Cuba, and exchanged fire with the Spanish cruiser *Cristobal Colon,* forcing the enemy warship to retire into the safety

Battleship Massachusetts *before the Spanish-American War. She was scuttled off Pensacola, Florida in 1921. (Photo courtesy of the Naval Historical Center.)*

of the inner harbor. On July 6, battleships *Massachusetts* and *Texas* forced the Spanish cruiser *Reina Mercedes* to run aground and surrender.

Massachusetts was decommissioned January 8, 1906. In May 1910, she was placed in reduced commission to serve as a training ship for Naval Academy midshipmen. The battleship entered the Atlantic Reserve fleet in September 1912, but had a brief respite when she steamed to New York in October for the Presidential Fleet Review. *Massachusetts* was decommissioned again in May 1914. However, World War I gave the old battleship new life, when she was recommissioned in June 1917. *Massachusetts* would not see action in that war, but she did serve by training Naval Reserve gun crews in Block Island Sound and Chesapeake Bay (probably using the old battleship *San Marcos* [*Texas*] as a target). The aging warship was decommissioned for the final time on the last day of March 1919. The following year the battleship was struck from the Navy list and loaned to the War Department as a target ship. She was scuttled off Pensacola, Florida on January 6, 1921. Then, for four years she was bombarded by batteries from Fort Pickens. The hulk was returned to the Navy in 1925 to be sold for scrap. However, no acceptable bids were received, and in November 1956 she was declared the property of the state of Florida.

Today, *Massachusetts*, which had served her country in two wars, is a popular dive site only two miles off the rock jetties southwest of the mouth of Pensacola Bay. In only 20 to 30 feet of water, with some of her superstructure exposed, the wreck can easily be located.

Destroyers, Cutters and Assorted Vessels

H.M.C.S. *Assiniboine*

The Canadian destroyer *Assiniboine* was sold for scrap after World War II. While being towed through Northumberland Strait, at the East Point of Prince Edward Island, Canada, she grounded at the east end of South Lake. The warship was heavily salvaged, but wreckage is still scattered over the sandy bottom in six to 24 feet of water.

The 1,330-ton warship had been commissioned into the British Royal Navy in 1931 as H.M.S. *Kempenfelt*. The British rated her as a "leader," a vessel similar to the destroyer design with additional staff accommodations. During World War II, the ship was transferred to Canada for anti-submarine patrol and renamed *Assiniboine*.

Alexander

Although divers on this former destroyer escort refer to her as "The Alexander," her service in the U.S. Navy was under a different name, and research has so far failed to uncover what that might be. It is known that she was scuttled in 1972 or 1973 by a local salvor named Chet Alexander, hence her current identity.

This wreck lies five miles west of the navigational buoy on the Gulf side of Key West, in only 35 feet of water. It is broken in half, with the stern about 150 yards from the bow section. After sixteen years underwater the scattered wreckage has accumulated a luxurious growth of soft corals and sponges. Yellowtail snappers, Atlantic spadefish, porkfish, and groupers abound.

Albert Gallatin

During a violent gale, the revenue cutter *Albert Gallatin* proved that a rocky ledge off Manchester, Massachusetts was appropriately named Boo Hoo Ledge.

The 250-ton, 142-foot, iron-hulled *Gallatin* was built during 1870 and 1871 at Buffalo, New York. The cutter proved unsatisfactory during her trials, and alterations had to be made by the builder. She was finally accepted into service in October 1874 and ordered to Boston. She continued on the Boston station as a revenue cutter, cruising the Massachusetts and New Hampshire coasts for almost 20 years. The only interruption occurred in 1887, when the two-masted steamer was ordered to New York for several months to receive a new boiler.

Gallatin carried two brass cannon and some small arms. She was square-rigged for the summer and schooner-rigged for winter. Her complement was 7 officers and 30 men. In November-December 1891, the cutter underwent a $100,000 overhaul.

On the morning of January 7, 1892, *Gallatin* left Portsmouth, New Hampshire for Provincetown, Massachusetts. The east-southeast wind was blowing fresh, and rising. Within three hours the winds had reached gale force and were accompanied by a blinding snow storm. The cutter's captain decided to run for Gloucester Harbor under reduced steam.

When land was sighted, the cutter's pilot thought it was Kettle Island. He headed *Gallatin* to what he thought was Eastern Point, for protection from the mounting seas. Within minutes the cutter struck Boo Hoo Ledge and water rushed into the ship.

The captain ordered "abandon ship," with seas breaking over his vessel and water pouring into the hull. While the first lifeboat was being lowered, the cutter lurched to port, tearing off the main top mast and smokestack. The ship's carpenter was struck in the head by the falling stack and was instantly killed. His body fell overboard and was lost.

The lifeboats were launched with great difficulty because of the raging sea. They reached Singing Beach at Manchester, Massachusetts. Three boats were destroyed by heavy rollers while landing, but no lives were lost.

Revenue cutter Albert Gallatin *was lost on Boo Hoo Ledge off Manchester, Massachusetts in 1892. (Photo courtesy of the Peabody Museum of Salem.)*

A piece of anchor chain and a saber recovered from Gallatin *by Bill Carter. (Photo by Bill Carter.)*

This brass letter "G" stands for Gallatin. *(Photo by Dave Clancy.)*

The crew lost all their clothing, money and jewelry, except what they wore. After investigation of the sinking, though they were not found to be at fault, the men were discharged from the service. A board of inquiry found the disaster was the result of an "Error in the Judgement of C.O."

Two months after the sinking, the collector of customs at Boston transferred *Gallatin's* title to three Boston men who intended to salvage the vessel. The cutter had been valued at $50,000 prior to her sinking; the winning bid for her remains was $679.

Today, the hull lies broken and scattered among huge rocks in from 15 to 50 feet of water. The rocks are surprisingly free from kelp. Many sea urchins are in the area, and their spines can easily penetrate wet suits and gloves. Visibility is usually good, 25 to 30 feet.

U.S.S. *Grouse*

The wood-hulled motor minesweepers, given the designation YMS, proved to be one of the U.S. Navy's more durable and versatile warships. They filled a variety of roles for several navies. During World War II, the vessels were used for inshore sweeping prior to amphibious assaults. In 1947, YMS's were reclassified as AMS, given names, and rerated as mine warfare ships. In 1955, they were redesignated as MSC(O), which was changed to MSCO in 1967. These vessels bore much of the mine warfare burden in Korea.

The first YMS was launched in January 1942. The last of her kind was struck from the Navy list in November 1969. The motor minesweepers were 136 feet in length, with a beam of 14.5 feet and fully loaded displaced 320 tons. Armament consisted of one 3-inch gun and two 20-mm machine guns. Their two diesels were designed to produce 12 knots.

YMS-*321* was commissioned on October 25, 1943. She arrived in Pearl Harbor on May 1, 1944. The following month she departed for sweeping, patrol, and escort duties in the Guam-Saipan-Tinian area. After escorting a convoy to Eniwetok in March she bombarded the defenses at Maug Island, Marianas. In April 1945 the wooden minesweeper patrolled around Iwo Jima. She was damaged during a kamikaze raid near Okinawa.

On February 25, 1947, YMS-*321* was reclassified as AMS-*15* and named *Grouse*. For the next ten years she performed a variety of tasks along the Eastern Seaboard. In 1954 and 1955, the warship was attached to the Hydrographic Office for project "Vamp," a coastal survey along the Massachusetts and Virginia shores.

In 1958, *Grouse* was assigned to the 1st Naval District as a reserve training ship based at Portsmouth, New Hampshire.

On September 20, 1963, the warship put to sea, bound for Cape Cod for a week-long training cruise. Early the following morning *Grouse* struck the infamous rock ledges of the Little Salvages off Rockport, Massachusetts. That afternoon three navy tugs and several other rescue vessels tried to pull the grounded vessel off, but were unsuccessful. By evening, strong winds and heavy seas halted salvage operations. The bad weather continued for three days causing further damage to the hull and sealing the fate of the small warship. The damage report stated:

> *Grouse* appears to be breaking up. Generator room open to the sea from the bottom . . . General impression is that the bottom is stove in. Mast is broken. Slight injuries sustained by several (during today's operations). It is considered unsafe to remain aboard except at low water . . . Successful floating of the *Grouse* is extremely doubtful. Intentions are to board at low water and salvage magnetic tail and other valuables. Pull off reef and keep afloat by pumping.

The following day's report sealed the fate of *Grouse:*

> Patching impossible. 5′ × 6′ opening starboard, center of frame 52. Daylight visible from many holes. Have started salvage of valuable materials.

On September 28, 1963, *Grouse* was set on fire and the wooden vessel burned to the waterline. The two diesel engines were blown apart with

Wood-hulled U.S. Navy minesweeper Grouse *aground on the Little Salvages off Rockport, Massachusetts in 1963. (Photo courtesy of Mrs. Paul Sherman.)*

Grouse *could not be refloated from the rocky ledge and was burned to the waterline. All that remained were two diesel engines, other machinery, and part of the wood hull. (Photo by Brad Luther.)*

explosives and the area was cleared of refuse. For weeks local salvors picked over the wreck site. The locals were upset that the Navy did not let them salvage the valuable diesel engines.

The subsequent court of inquiry reported the cause of grounding was a two-degree error in the plotting of the course.

Wreckage is scattered in 10 to 25 feet of water on the west side of the Little Salvages, which are clearly marked on nautical charts. However, heavy kelp growth makes it difficult to find pieces of the wreck. Brass and copper artifacts have been recovered by divers.

U.S.S. *Strength*

The U.S. Navy minesweeper *Strength* was sunk to provide an artificial reef, near Panama City, Florida, in 1987.

Beginning in 1938, more than 200 steel-hulled AM "fleet sweepers" were built. *Strength* (AM-*309*), commissioned in September 1944, was 184 feet 6 inches in length, with a beam of 33 feet and displacement of 850 tons. After shakedown and training exercises she arrived off Iwo Jima on February 16, 1945 and began sweeping operations to clear the waters for the invasion fleet, which arrived on the 19th.

The following month, while sweeping off the Ryukyus, *Strength* was attacked by a partially surfaced Japanese midget submarine. Two torpedoes passed underneath the minesweeper, and two sped by astern. *Strength*'s gun crews, on the secondary batteries, opened fire, driving the submarine off, but with no apparent damage to the enemy vessel.

The minesweeper assisted in clearing the approaches to the beaches off Okinawa. The assault on that island began on April 1. Five days later the Japanese launched their heaviest air attack by kamikaze suicide planes. One chose *Strength* for its target, but her machine guns downed the enemy plane several hundred yards astern. The minesweeper received three battle stars for World War II service.

Strength was placed out of commission, in reserve, on July 19, 1946, and was struck from the Navy list on April 1, 1967.

Today the fully intact minesweeper rests on her starboard side in about 70 feet of water, projecting 32 feet above the bottom.

U.S.S. *Tarantula*

W.K. Vanderbilt of New York City ordered a 129-foot, 160-ton motor yacht to be built at Newponset, Massachusetts by George Lawley and Son Corporation. *Tarantula* was completed in 1912, but Vanderbilt would be able to use the luxuriously appointed yacht for only five years.

On April 25, 1917, the Navy acquired the motor yacht for antisubmarine patrol and armed her with two 6-pounders and two 30-caliber machine guns. Designated SP-*124*, she patrolled the coastal waters of Connecticut, New York, and New Jersey for six months.

On October 28, 1918 *Tarantula* was rammed by the Royal Holland Lloyd Line steamship *Frisia*. The subchaser quickly sank in about 115 feet of water, 20 miles south of Fire Island Inlet. For many years the wreck was referred to as the "Good Gun Boat Wreck" because of her armament. The guns are no longer there, but projectiles for the 6-pounders and clips of rifle ammunition are scattered in the starboard bow area.

When a diver recovered the warship's brass bell, the wreck was identified.

The wreck is on a sand bottom and visibility is usually good, 30–40 feet. Various artifacts and an occasional large lobster are found.

U.S.S. *PC-11* and *-1203*

The steel-hulled anti-submarine patrol craft PC-*11* is in about 100 feet of water near Palm Beach (Florida) Inlet. Three-knot currents occasionally sweep the wreck. The 173-foot subchaser PC-*1203* was lost on Horseshoe Shoal, Nantucket Sound at 41° 30′55″N, 70° 22′20″W. The wreck is about nine miles SSW from the boat ramp at Hyannis, and part of the wreck protrudes above the surface. The subchaser sits on a sand bottom in 5 to 20 feet of water. Usually there is a moderate to strong current over Horseshoe Shoal.

H.M. Trawlers *Senateur Duhamel, Bedfordshire,* and *Pentland Firth*

In the early stages of World War II, Germany's U-boat campaign seemed about to win the war. England did not have enough escort vessels to protect the merchant vessels carrying life-sustaining supplies and war materials to that island nation. Although the United States was neutral, President Roosevelt's interpretation of international neutrality was pro-British. He instituted "lend-lease," lending war materials to England in exchange for leased bases in the Western Hemisphere.

During the summer of 1940, Roosevelt responded to the U-boat menace by supplying Britain with 50 old four-stacker destroyers. When Japan attacked Pearl Harbor on December 7, 1941, U-boat activity shifted to America's Eastern Seaboard. The U.S. Navy did not have adequate escort vessels and the U-boats created havoc. Britain did not return the 50 destroyers, but did send a number of armed trawlers, with experienced Royal Navy crews, to patrol our coast. These ocean-going fishing trawlers were armed with deck guns, machine guns, and depth charges.

Three of these vessels were sunk while in American waters, two off North Carolina and one in New Jersey waters.

The 165-foot, 739-ton *Senateur Duhamel* was rammed and sunk by the U.S. destroyer *Semmes* on May 6, 1942. She sank in 65 feet of water, 6.7

miles southeast of Beaufort Inlet, North Carolina. The wreck site is marked with a buoy with the number 8. The armed trawler was blown apart with explosives and wreckage is scattered over the area.

Five days later the 170-foot, 900-ton *Bedfordshire* was patrolling off Cape Lookout, North Carolina when she was torpedoed by *U-558*. The U-boat commander was Kapitanleutnant Gunther Krech, something of an eccentric. He kept an aquarium, aboard *U-558*, containing fish named after various Allied leaders.

All 37 on board the armed trawler were killed. Four bodies washed ashore and were buried on Ocracoke Island. One was Sub-Lieutenant Thomas Cunningham, who a few weeks before had provided the U.S. Navy with six British flags. Four were to be buried with British seamen recovered from a torpedoed tanker. Ironically, one of the remaining two Union Jacks would drape his own coffin.

The wreck is in about 100 feet of water, approximately 36 miles from Beaufort Inlet. The torpedo's explosive force scattered wreckage over a large area. Visibility is usually excellent, 50 to 100 feet.

The 164-foot, 485-ton *Pentland Firth* was lost off New Jersey on September 19, 1942. While on patrol duty the armed trawler was rammed by the converted minesweeper U.S.S. *Chaffinch*. The wreck was blown apart with explosives and is scattered in 60 feet of water.

U.S.S. *Rankin*

The U.S. Navy experimented with landing craft in the 1930's. By World War II the attack cargo ship (AKA) was a specialized type designed to carry troops, supplies, and landing craft and put them ashore under combat conditions. With their armament of one 5-inch deck gun, eight 40-mm, and sixteen 20-mm machine guns they could shell the beaches before the troops disembarked into the landing craft.

Rankin (AKA-*103*), 459 feet 2 inches in length, with a beam of 63 feet 2 inches and displacing 13,910 tons—was commissioned on February 25, 1945 at the Charleston Navy Yard. The following month she passed through the Panama Canal and joined the Pacific fleet on April 1. In May *Rankin* took on 5,000 tons of ammunition at Honolulu and steamed for Okinawa where the vital cargo was discharged between kamikaze raids.

In June the attack cargo ship transported landing craft to Saipan, then steamed to San Francisco to pick up more landing craft. During loading operations hostilities ended. *Rankin* steamed to the Philippines, then Japan, and returned to San Francisco in November where she was decommissioned in May 1947. She was recommissioned in 1952 and operated out of Norfolk.

In 1958, *Rankin* was part of the amphibious force that landed a peace-keeping force of 5,000 U.S. marines at Beirut, Lebanon.

During the Cuban missile crisis of October and November of 1962, *Rankin* operated in Cuban waters, prepared for any eventuality. She was redesignated amphibious cargo ship LKA-*103* in 1968 and continued operating with the Atlantic fleet until she was decommissioned on May 11, 1971.

In July 1988, *Rankin* was sunk as an artificial reef off Stuart, Florida. She is on her starboard side in 120 feet of water. The superstructure is intact and the wheelhouse and engine room can be easily penetrated. Her 16-foot-long deck gun is a photographer's delight.

Chapter 18

Warships Awaiting Discovery

The exact location of each of the following sunken warships is uncertain. However, a brief description of each is included as a stimulus for further research by readers of this book. Civil War shipwrecks will be addressed in a future volume on such ships.

Canada

- Sir Humphrey Gilbert's flagship H.M.S. *Delight* was lost in August 1583, when she grounded on a shoal near Sable Island, Nova Scotia.

- The 64-gun British ship-of-the-line *Mars* (Captain John Amherst) was wrecked at Halifax, Nova Scotia in June 1755.

- A hurricane, on September 24, 1757, blew the French frigate *l'Abenaquise* up on the beach in Louisbourg Harbor, Cape Breton Island, Nova Scotia. The same storm sank Captain Henry Barnsley's 60-gun British ship-of-the-line *Tilbury*. She struck rocks, near St. Esprit (Nova Scotia), which still bear her name. Gold coins, which have been found in recent years, are believed to be from the warship.

- The 74-gun British ship-of-the-line *Terrible* was wrecked in the St. Lawrence River in 1759.

- The following year two other British warships were wrecked in the St. Lawrence River, Captain Joseph Deane's 28-gun *Lowestaft* and Captain John Elphinstone's 20-gun *Eurus*.

- A British fleet sank 25 French ships in Chaleur Bay, in the Gulf of St. Lawrence, on July 8, 1760. Three of the vessels were warships:

Marquis Marloze (18 guns); *Bienfaisant* (22 guns), and *Marchault* (32 guns).

- In 1761, the 60-gun French ship-of-the-line *Leopard* arrived at Quebec with the plague on board. The vessel had to be burned to keep the disease from spreading.

- On June 26, 1766, the British armed schooner *St. Lawrence* was lying at anchor at Niginish, Cape Breton Island, about 60 miles north of Louisbourg. During a thunderstorm the ship was struck by lightning; the magazine exploded and the ship sank in less than a minute. Surprisingly, of 26 men on board at the time, only three died and six were injured (one would die of his wounds). An attempt was made to salvage the warship, in 36 feet of water. The salvagers managed to raise her a few feet off the bottom before the slings broke. The salvors recovered some anchors, damaged sails, and the three bodies, but nothing else.

- The British sloop-of-war *Savage* (8 guns) was lost in 1775 near Louisbourg, Cape Breton Island, Nova Scotia; Captain Hugh Bromelge was in command.

- The British armed brig *Diligent* was leading a convoy through Seal Island Passage, in the Bay of Fundy, at night on May 16, 1777. She ran onto Gannot Rock Ledge and crushed her hull. The brig was a loss, but her crew warned the other ships before they met the same fate.

- In 1778, heavy seas in the Gulf of St. Lawrence were responsible for the capsizing of the British 14-gun *Dispatch*, under command of Captain J. Botham.

- The British 32-gun *Blonde*, with a captured vessel in tow, struck a rock, now known as Blonde Rock, off Seal Island, Nova Scotia on May 10, 1782.

- On October 11, 1780, the British 16-gun *Viper* (Captain John Augustua) was wrecked in the Gulf of St. Lawrence.

- The British 32-gun *Active* (Captain Edward Gower) was wrecked on July 5, 1796, in the St. Lawrence River.

- The 16-gun British sloop-of-war *Rover* (Captain George Irwin) was wrecked in the Gulf of St. Lawrence on June 23, 1798.

- On September 25, 1798, a gale sank the British warship *Lynx* in Halifax Harbor, Nova Scotia.

- The 12-gun British storeship *William* was wrecked in the Gut of Canso, Nova Scotia, on November 11, 1807.

- The 22-gun British warship *Banterer* was lost in the St. Lawrence River in 1808.
- The British 12-gun *Plumper* (Captain W. Frissel) foundered in the St. Lawrence River in November 1810.
- On August 3, 1812, the British 18-gun *Emulous* (Captain William Mulcaster) was wrecked on Sable Island, Nova Scotia.
- The British 2-gun *Chubb* (Captain Samuel Nisbett) capsized off Halifax, Nova Scotia on August 14, 1812. All hands were lost.
- On September 28, 1812 the British 28-gun *Barbadoes* (Captain Thomas Huskisson) was wrecked on Sable Island, Nova Scotia. She was reportedly carrying more than $500,000 in gold and silver.

In 1969, Chip Cooper was divemaster for the Bob Ellsworth Productions team that spent three weeks filming the island, its seals, flowers, wild horses, and searching for artifacts from shipwrecks. The treacherous shoals of the 25-mile-long, one-mile-wide island has claimed hundreds of ships.

Cooper reported to the authors that the team filming the documentary discovered the remains of several ships that were now inland and mostly covered with sand. One was the British freighter *Skidby*, which

Members of the 1969 expedition to Sable Island working on a wreck believed to be the remains of the British 28-gun Barbadoes. *(Photo courtesy of Chip Cooper.)*

was lost in 1902; another wreck they believe to be *Barbadoes*. After making a "very small" excavation they recovered bronze ship fastenings and solid oak chocks, all marked with the "broad arrow" of British warships. *Barbadoes* is believed to have been lost on the north side of the island in 40 feet of water, but the warship they found in the sand was on the south beach, about a quarter mile inland from the shoreline. However, *Barbadoes* was the only British warship of that era lost on Sable Island.

- On September 27, 1813 the British 12-gun *Bold* (Captain John Skekel) was wrecked on Prince Edward Island, in the Gulf of St. Lawrence.

- The British 18-gun *Atalante* (Captain Frederick Hickey) was wrecked off Halifax, Nova Scotia, on November 10, 1813.

- In 1814, two British 4-gun warships, *Cuttle* and *Herring*, foundered and sank near Halifax, Nova Scotia.

- On June 28, 1814, the 50-gun British frigate *Leopard* (Captain Edward Crofton) was wrecked on Anticosti Island, in the Gulf of St. Lawrence.

- The British 18-gun *Fantome* (Captain Thomas Sykes) was lost near Halifax, Nova Scotia on November 24, 1814.

- In 1822, the French frigate *L'Africaine* sank in 72 feet of water off Sable Island, Nova Scotia.

Maine

- The 14-gun British schooner *Halifax* ran aground on a rocky ledge off Sheep Island, 9 miles (27 miles in another account of the disaster) from Bucks Harbor near Machias on February 15, 1775. The rising tide and heavy seas pushed the wreck off the ledge until only her masts extended above the water. Only some provisions had been salvaged from the warship.

- On August 14, 1779, 11 American warships were destroyed by fire or scuttled in the Penobscot River to prevent capture by the British. For more information regarding that naval action see *Defence*, under sailing vessels in Chapter 19.

- World War II in Europe was almost over. Only about two weeks remained when the 200-foot, 615-ton *Eagle Boat 56* (PE-56) was destroyed by an explosion off Portland. A more detailed description of Eagle Boats can be found in the brief coverage of *Eagle Boat 17* on page 225. PE-56 was on anti- submarine patrol off Cape Elizabeth. It was the lunch hour and many of the crew were resting below deck after eating. An explosion broke the ship in two and she sank within minutes.

Only 13 of the 62-man crew survived, all below deck when the explosion occurred. The 49 who were lost constituted the U.S. Navy's greatest loss of life in New England waters during World War II. The lightship off Portland Harbor was only two miles from the scene and quickly went to the aid of the survivors.

Earlier on the morning of the explosion the Eagle Boat had dropped depth charges on what they initially believed was a U-boat. However, they were uncertain whether the contact was a U-boat or a wreck.

Lieutenant Scagnelli, a survivor who was taking a nap when the explosion occurred, later reported that as he made his way to the main deck he noticed that the ship's magazine was intact. Therefore, it was not an accident in the magazine that caused the explosion. It is now known that the German submarine *U-853* was patrolling that general area at the time. It is very likely that *Eagle Boat 56* was sunk by *U-853*, a possibility that will never be confirmed because the U-boat was sunk early the following month off Block Island, Rhode Island.

Massachusetts

- The 32-gun British frigate *Solebay* was lost with all hands at Boston Neck on Christmas Day 1709.

- The British sloop-of-war *Hazard*, carrying a cargo of munitions, was lost with all hands in 1714 in Green Bay, about 30 miles from Boston.

- Near the end of May 1775, Colonial troops raided the British-held Noddle's Island, Boston Harbor, by wading across at low tide. The British armed schooner *Diana* ran aground while trying to repel them. The warship was abandoned by her crew and the rebels salvaged 16 small cannon before destroying the British warship by fire.

- In 1782 the 32-gun British frigate *Blonde* (Captain Edward Thornborough) struck a rock on Nantucket Shoals. Several of her crew were lost.

- Two Spanish warships, *Magnifico* and *Cibila*, were sunk in Boston Harbor sometime before 1799.

Rhode Island

- In June 1772, the British armed schooner *Gaspee* was aground on a sandbar in Warwick, then named Namquit Point, now Gaspee Point.

The British had sent the schooner to the Colonies to stop smuggling. Rhode Islanders had threatened to burn Royal Navy vessels performing the same function. *Gaspee* grounded while giving chase to the Colonial packet *Hannah*. The British had no choice but to wait for a change in tide, at 3 a.m. the following morning, to set her free. Just past midnight a sentinel saw eight boats approaching from shore. He hailed but received no response. He then made seven or eight attempts to fire his musket, but it would not fire. He summoned Lieutenant Duddingston, the warship's commanding officer. Duddingston reached the deck in his nightshirt, to be greeted from one of the approaching boats with "God damn your blood, we have you now." The boats, carrying the attacking force, came alongside to board the schooner. Duddingston called first for matches for the cannon, and then small arms to repel the attack. The matches could not be found, and the arms chest was locked. As the boarders swarmed over the ship, Duddingston and several of his crew were severely wounded. The Americans removed *Gaspee*'s crew to Pawtuxent, about two miles away, and burned the captured British warship. The following day the British salvaged the schooner's guns and a few stores and sent them to Halifax.

The rebellious act of the Colonists took place more than a year before the Boston Tea Party. Some consider it to be the first blow for freedom in the American Revolution. Although there are annual celebrations in Rhode Island commemorating the burning of *Gaspee*, the wreck site has yet to be found.

- In February 1777, the British armed schooner *Tryal*, en route to the northern end of Prudence Island to protect the cutter of H.M.S. *Diamond*, was blown on shore by a rising gale. An American sloop with 12 guns arrived from Providence and promptly attacked the stranded schooner. The Americans mounted a cannon on nearby Warwick Point for more punishing firepower. The British commanding officer, Lieutenant J. Brown, ordered his crew to burn the ship to avoid capture. At the subsequent court martial, Brown was dismissed from the service for that action.

- The British 28-gun *Syren*, through the "gross ignorance and neglect" of her pilot, ran onto Point Judith on November 6, 1777. She was "within a pistol's shot of the shore." The frigates *Flora* and *Lark* arrived the following day to help refloat the grounded warship. However, heavy seas prevented salvage attempts. The following morning the seas were breaking over the wreck, which had received further damage from several shots fired from shore by the Americans. *Syren*'s guns were spiked and the wreck abandoned.

- The 16-gun British sloop *Kingfisher* was at anchor in the Seaconnet Passage on July 30, 1778 when two French frigates were sighted. The sloop sailed into Fogland and unloaded her stores. When the French approached, the sloop's guns were spiked and she was set on fire and sank in three fathoms of water. See Chapter 1.

- *Spitfire*, a British galley of eight guns, was anchored off Fogland Ferry with *Kingfisher*. When the French frigates approached, she was run ashore on the northern sandy shore and burned.

- The British galley *Alarm*, also in the area, was run into shallow water and set on fire.

- The 32-gun British frigate *Juno* was anchored close to shore in Coddington Cove, north of Newport, where her guns and stores had been landed to strengthen the shore defenses. When French warships approached on August 5, 1778, she was burned to avoid capture.

- Also, on the same day, the British galley *Pigot* (Lieutenant H. E. Stanhope) was run ashore north of Newport and burned along with the British frigate *Lark*. *Lark* was run ashore between Arnold's Point and Coggershell Point. See Chapter 1.

- The 12-gun British schooner *Redbridge* (Captain Edward Burt) was wrecked near Providence on November 4, 1806.

New York

- In 1777, the British 28-gun *Liverpool* (Captain Henry Bellow) was lost on the south shore of Long Island.

- The 28-gun American warship *Congress* was burned on the Hudson River in 1777 to prevent her being seized by the British.

- The same year, the 24-gun American warship *Montgomery*, also on the Hudson River, was captured and blown up by British forces.

- On Christmas Eve 1777, the British 24-gun *Mercury* was proceeding down the North River (New York City) when she struck the wreck of the *Cheveaux de Frize*. Mercury was three or four miles from Spekendevil Creek, off Fort Knyphausen. Within ten minutes the hold was flooded with seven feet of water and she was run ashore above Blowmandoe, where she sank. Her captain and pilot were acquitted at the subsequent court martial, because it was believed that the wreck of the *Cheveaux de Frize* had shifted from its previously charted position.

- On February 11, 1778 the British 28-gun *Liverpool*, in dense fog, grounded on Long Island in Jamaica Bay. The lighthouse, bearing SW half W, was approximately four leagues away. The warship lay almost entirely out of the water at low tide.

- In 1799, a 12-gun Spanish privateer, with a crew of 133, was sunk off the east end of Long Island during a battle with a New York privateer. Ninety-one of the Spanish crew perished.

- In 1780, the 32-gun British frigate *Hussar* (Captain Charles Pole) struck Pott Rock in an area of the East River, New York City, known as Hell Gate. *Hussar* suffered a huge hole in her hull, and an attempt was made to ground her at Stony Island, now Port Morris in the Bronx. Within less than 100 yards of shore, she sank suddenly, sitting upright in about 75 feet of water, leaving only her topmasts in view. Reportedly, she sank with about 50 American prisoners shackled below deck and a large amount of gold and silver specie aboard.

- The American privateer, *Patience* (Captain Chase) was wrecked on Long Island in 1780.

- On March 6, 1811 the British 10-gun *Thistle* (Captain George McPherson) was lost on Long Island. Six out of a crew of 50 perished.

- In one of Long Island's worst maritime disasters, the 18-gun British warship *Sylph* went ashore January 17, 1815 west of Southampton, on Shinnecock Bar, about opposite Sugar Loaf, the highest Shinnecock hill. The five-year-old sloop-of-war had a crew of 121 and only six survived. Her captain, George Dickens, was a casualty.

- In 1863, during the Civil War, the privately owned 187-ton steamship *Addison F. Andrews* was built in Brooklyn. On December 5 of the same year she was purchased by the Revenue Cutter Service for $42,000. The revenue cutter was renamed *Bronx* on January 13, 1864, and became the workhorse of New York Harbor, constantly in demand for towing the Revenue Service's sailing cutters from place to place. In 1871, the cutter was lost when she struck rocks in Long Island Sound.

- In 1916, before the United States became embroiled in World War I, two German submarines visited the East Coast. One, *Deutschland*, was a cargo-carrying U-boat on a mercantile voyage. The other was on a war patrol. Shortly after a brief port call, without fueling or provisioning, which would have violated neutrality laws, *U-53* sank five ships near the Nantucket Lightship, just outside U.S. territorial waters. That blatant action stimulated the U.S. Navy to acquire small vessels for antisubmarine patrol if the country should enter the war.

Other ship designs were placing heavy demands on industry for steel and the principal shipbuilding yards were fully occupied. These considerations led to the decision to build small, wooden subchasers that could be accommodated by small yards. The result was an 85-ton, 110-foot vessel, designated as SC for subchaser, with three 660-hp gasoline engines, and three props that could produce 18 knots.

- SC-*209* was built at Mathis Yacht Building Co., New Jersey and commissioned in March 1918. At 2:30 a.m. on August 27, 1918, the subchaser was on patrol 20 miles south of Fire Island Light, at 40° 08'N, 73° 18'W. In the darkness the armed freighter *Felix Tausig* mistook the low-lying vessel for a U-boat. The freighter fired five rounds from her two deck guns before the subchaser could identify herself. The accuracy of the freighter's gun crews demolished the subchaser's small superstructure. SC-*209* sank and 18 of her 26-man crew, including her two officers, died in the tragic accident.

- During World War I, the Navy recognized the need for steel ships smaller than destroyers for antisubmarine patrol duty. President

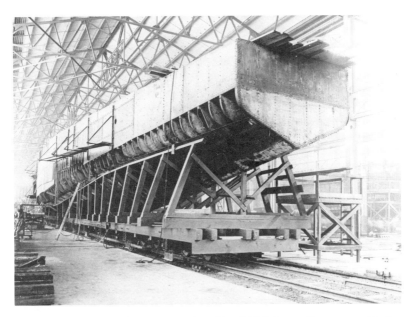

An "Eagle Boat" under construction. The 1,700-foot railway assembly line was similar to that used by Henry Ford in building his automobiles. This marked the first application of the assembly line to marine construction. (Photo courtesy of the National Archives.)

Woodrow Wilson appointed auto-builder Henry Ford to the U.S. Shipping Board. Wilson wanted Ford to use his knowledge of mass production techniques to produce a large number of those patrol craft, quickly.

Ford built a new plant on the Rouge River, outside Detroit, which included an assembly line similar to one used for automobile production.

The first keel was laid in May 1918 and seven 200-foot patrol craft were completed by December 1. However, the armistice ending World War I had been signed in November. The original contract was for 100, then increased to 112, but after the armistice the number was reduced to 60.

The 60 patrol craft were called "Eagle Boats" by the U.S. Navy. The term stemmed from a wartime *Washington Post* editorial that called for ". . . an eagle to scour the seas and pounce upon and destroy every German submarine." Some civilians referred to the patrol crafts as "tin Lizzies of the sea," a reference to Ford's automobiles.

The Eagle Boats never saw service in the First World War, but seven did serve during World War II.

Eagle 17 *was lost on the eastern end of Long Island in 1922. (Photo courtesy of the Naval Historical Center.)*

The 18-knot vessels were armed with one 4-inch gun, one 3-inch deck gun, two machine guns and 12 depth charges. The normal complement was 61.

On May 22, 1922 *Eagle Boat 17* (PE-*17*) en route from Norfolk, Virginia to New London, Connecticut, ran aground on Long Island at Egypt Beach, between East Hampton and Amagansett. A breeches buoy removed the crew safely. The following day the captain's personal automobile was brought ashore by sliding it down two skids extending from the deck to the shore. Two days later a storm pushed the 615-ton vessel onto shore until she was high and dry. It was estimated that 3,500 Long Islanders viewed the stranded patrol craft on one day.

All movable materials were removed to lighten the vessel. Salvage tugs pulled the warship several feet offshore, but she turned onto her starboard side, her masts pointing to sea. The *East Hampton Star* reported that ". . . the two guns were still aboard and are now under water. . . ." The patrol craft was declared a total loss and stricken from the Navy list.

Later, *Eagle Boat 17* was heavily salvaged and a lot of material removed, including large steel plates. By January 1923, storms had moved the wreck several hundred yards to the west of its original site.

New Jersey

- In 1704, an 18-gun British privateer *Castle del Ray* was struck by a gale and stranded on a shoal near Sandy Hook. The 130-ton ship quickly went to pieces and 132 of a crew of 145 perished.

- In November 1777, British naval forces reached Philadelphia too late to prevent the Colonists from sinking the Continental frigates *Washington* and *Effingham*, in nearby Bordentown, New Jersey, to keep them out of British hands. The two frigates were later raised to serve as barracks for nearly 400 officers and men of the Continental Navy.

  In May 1778, British General Sir William Howe organized a joint army and naval expedition to destroy American shipping at Bordentown, on the Delaware River. The British force left Philadelphia and sailed up the Delaware to Whitehill, about two miles below Bordentown. The two raised frigates were stationed in Bordentown with a brig and a sloop. The Americans destroyed the four warships by fire to avoid capture by the British; *Washington* and *Effingham* sunk for the second time in six months for the same reason.

- Two men were lost when the 110-foot, wooden, American subchaser SC-*60* was rammed and sunk at 40° 22′26″ N, 73° 56′34″ W. It was

October 1, 1918, only one month and 10 days before the end of World War I. The subchaser was patrolling without lights, about five miles south of the Ambrose Channel lightship, when she was run down by the tanker *Fred W. Weller.* The wreck should be in about 45 feet of water. For more information on SC designated subchasers look under "New York Wrecks."

- During World War II, a number of diesel-powered private yachts were converted into antisubmarine patrol warships for the U.S. Navy. In May 1942, YP-*387,* a converted yacht with light armament and depth charges, was ordered to meet a convoy out of New York. En route to that port, she was run down by the collier *Jason* at 39° 01′N, 74° 39′W off southern New Jersey.

  Fifteen men survived, but six of the crew were never found. The small navy vessel sank in about 14 feet of water with the end of her mast sticking out of the water. The boat's ensign and the American flag were still flying two days later.

Delaware

- The British sank five American warships in Delaware Bay in 1777: *Mosquito* (4 guns); *Wasp* (8 guns); *Independence* (10 guns); *Dolphin* (10 guns); and *Sachem* (10 guns). Also, *Andrea Doria,* an American warship of 14 guns, was burned during the same battle to prevent her capture.

Maryland

- In 1781, three British ships were scuttled in the northern part of Chesapeake Bay to prevent them from being captured by enemy forces—the 8-gun fire ship *Vulcan* (Captain George Palmer); the 28-gun *Guadeloupe* (Captain Hugh Robinson); and the 44-gun frigate *Charon* (Captain Thomas Symonds).

Virginia

- The 10-gun British sloop-of-war *Deptford* (Captain Thomas Barry) was lost without loss of life on August 26, 1689, near Cedar Island.
- The naval battle off the Virginia Capes on September 5, 1781 was more a skirmish than a battle. However, Michael Lewis in *The History of the British Navy* wrote:

The Battle of Chesapeake was one of the decisive battles of the world. Before it, the creation of the United States was possible; after it, it was certain.

British General Lord Cornwallis had invaded Virginia from North Carolina in May 1781, and by late August was deeply entrenched and strongly fortified at Yorktown on the York River. He was waiting for arrival of the British fleet with crucial reinforcements and supplies. Cornwallis never entertained the thought that the Royal Navy would be forced to abandon him.

Admiral Comte de Grasse with a French fleet of 28 ships-of-the-line arrived in Chesapeake Bay on August 30. The English fleet of 19 ships-of-the-line under Rear Admiral Sir Thomas Graves arrived at the mouth of the Cheasapeake about mid-morning September 5. It was about 4 p.m. before the French could recall seamen who were ashore, and clear the bay.

Admiral Graves' signals to his captains were so confusing that his formation scattered. When firing commenced only a few ships from each side could engage. Darkness ended the fight with neither side losing a ship. However, the British 74-gun *Terrible* was so severely damaged that Graves ordered her to be burned.

The British returned to New York, and Cornwallis surrendered his 7,000 men on October 19, 1781. For practical purposes, the War of Revolution was over. Independence was won. General Washington gratefully wrote to Admiral deGrasse and thanked him ''in the name of America.''

- On December 27, 1797, the 18-gun British warship *Hunter*, Captain Tudor Tucker, was wrecked on Hog Island. All but five of her 80-man crew perished.

- In 1806, near Cape Henry, two British frigates forced ashore and then destroyed the 74-gun French ship-of-the-line *Impetueux*.

- On April 16, 1811 an American warship captured the French privateer *Revanche du Cerf*. The French vessel was stripped and burned at Norfolk.

- Two American frigates, *Guerriere* and *Congress*, were sunk in Norfolk Harbor by a hurricane on September 3, 1821.

- By the end of the nineteenth century, ramming, as a technique of naval warfare, had been in practice for many centuries. The advent of gunpowder and cannon made ram warfare a hazardous technique. The first ironclad, the French *Glorie* in 1859, in turn made smooth-bore cannon obsolete because of her armor.

The only ship designed as a ram by the U.S. Navy, Katahdin, *was commissioned in 1896. By then, ramming had been outmoded by the use of large caliber guns. The obsolete warship was sunk as a target in 1909. (Photo courtesy of the Naval Historical Center.)*

Even though ramming was considered obsolete by the Civil War, the Confederacy built the ironclad *Virginia* (*Merrimac*) with a ram added to her bow. Most Union ships were not ironclad. The Union's wooden warship *Cumberland* was sunk by *Virginia* in 1862 with a combination of gunfire and ram. Then, as her victim sank, she attacked *Congress* (50 guns). *Virginia*'s guns were ineffective, but when the U.S. warship tried to escape the ram, she ran aground. From then on, all Confederate ironclads carried rams.

After the Civil War Rear Admiral Daniel Ammen, Chief of the Bureau of Navigation, lobbied for rams for the U.S. Navy. However, it was 1891 before the Bath Iron Works in Maine received the first contract for one ram; two years later U.S.S. *Katahdin* was launched and she was commissioned in 1896. The bow of the 2,115-ton vessel was designed to be awash at high speed. Often, the ocean swept most of her deck. Unfortunately, ramming as a technique of naval warfare was displaced by the development of large-caliber guns. On July 9, 1909 *Katahdin* was stricken from the Navy list, and redesignated *Ballistic Experimental Target A*. Off Rappahanock Spit, the Navy's only ram was sunk by naval vessels during target practice.

North Carolina

- On November 29, 1710, the British warship *Garland* grounded on a sandbar a short distance south of Currituck Inlet. Fifteen perished and the wreck sanded over before it could be salvaged.
- American gunboat *#140* was wrecked on Ocracoke Island on September 23, 1814.
- Brigadier General William "Billy" Mitchell sank two old battleships off Cape Hatteras on September 5, 1923, to illustrate their vulnerability to airpower.

The 14,980-ton battleship, 441-foot long, *Virginia* (BB-*13*) and her sistership *New Jersey* (BB-*16*) were launched in 1904. Three years later, they were part of President Theodore Roosevelt's "Great White Fleet," and later participated in an unprecedented round-the-world cruise. Nowhere during the cruise did the U.S. sailors meet with more expression of friendship than in Japan. The Japanese had recently emerged on the world scene with their victory in the Russo-Japanese War. President Roosevelt observed: "The most noteworthy incident of the cruise was the reception given to our fleet in Japan." Roosevelt reviewed the fleet on its return on February 22, 1909, over 14 months after it had set sail on the cruise.

Virginia and *New Jersey* did not see action in World War I, but they did participate in the massive troop-lift, that brought American "doughboys" back from "over there." The two warships carried more than 11,000 members of the AEF back home.

Both battleships were struck from the Navy list in July 1922 and transferred to the War Department on August 6, 1923 for use as targets for General Mitchell's bombers.

They anchored three miles off the Diamond Shoals lightship, off Cape Hatteras, on September 5, 1923.

Seven Army bombers, flying at 3,000 feet made three attacks. Each plane dropped two 1,100-pound bombs on the targets. Only one bomb

The 441-foot long battleship New Jersey *at Boston in 1919. (Photo courtesy of the Naval Historical Center.)*

The 19,980-ton battleship Virginia *(above), one of President Theodore Roosevelt's "Great White Fleet."* Virginia *(below) was expended as a target by U.S. Army bombers in a dramatic demonstration of air power. (Photos courtesy of the National Archives.)*

struck *Virginia*. However, that single hit was enough. An observer later wrote that:

> It completely demolished the ship as such. Both masts, the bridge, all three smokestacks, and the upperworks disappeared with the explosion and there remained, after the smoke cleared away, nothing but the bare hull, decks blown off, and covered with a mass of tangled debris from stem to stern consisting of stacks, ventilators, cage masts, and bridges.

Virginia's battered hulk sank within 30 minutes. *New Jersey* followed her to the bottom shortly after.

The dramatic demonstration of air power convinced far-sighted naval officers of the urgent need for developing naval aviation.

South Carolina

- On September 15, 1752, three British warships in Charleston Harbor were sunk by a hurricane.
- In 1776, the British 28-gun *Acteon*, Christopher Atkins in command, was set on fire in Charleston Harbor to prevent her capture by American forces.
- The following year the 8-gun British sloop-of-war *Cruiser* was burned off Charleston for the same reason.
- In 1780, a British fleet under the command of Vice-Admiral Arbuthnot sank three American warships off Charleston: *Notre Dame* (16 guns), *General Moultrie* (20 guns), and *Bricole* (44 guns).
- The 20-gun British privateer *Vigilant* (Captain Thomas Goldesbrough) was burned at Beaufort in 1780 to prevent her capture by enemy forces.
- A hurricane on August 9, 1781 sank two British warships, *Thetis* and *London*, at the Charleston docks.
- The 18-gun British warship *Peacock* (Captain Richard Coote) was lost with her entire crew when she foundered off Charleston in 1814.

Georgia

- In 1779, the 20-gun British warship *Rose* was scuttled at the entrance to Savannah Harbor to prevent entry of a French fleet.

- On February 18, 1780, the 64-gun British ship-of-the-line *Defiance* (Captain Maximillian Jacobs) wrecked on the sandbar outside Savannah Harbor.
- The 16-gun British warship *Hope*, Captain William Thomas, was lost off Savannah in 1781.

Florida

- Sometime before 1570 a richly laden Spanish privateer *El Mulato* was wrecked near Fort Pierce Inlet. A large amount of her treasure was recovered by Indians.
- The Spanish frigate *Nuestra Señora de Concepción y San Josefe* was lost at Key Largo in 1689.
- A Spanish frigate was lost at Cayo de Lobos in 1741.
- In March 1741, the 14-gun British sloop-of-war *Wolf* was wrecked on the east coast of Florida.
- The British warship *Tyger* was lost in the Florida Keys in 1742. Survivors built a small fort, using timbers from the wreck. A Spanish admiral, Torres, ordered their capture, but the English beat off the attacking Spaniards. Torres then sent the 60-gun galleon *Fuerte*, with a large number of troops. However, the galleon was wrecked very near the same spot that had claimed *Tyger*.
- The small, two-decker, 20-gun British warship *Fowey*, and a Spanish prize, reportedly carrying a treasure in coins, were lost in 1748. There were no casualties, and the cargo from the Spanish ship, *Judan* was transferred to a British sloop. The reef, south of Miami, is now known as Fowey Rocks.
- The British 26-gun *Earl of Bute* (Captain B. Hill) foundered in the Gulf of Florida in 1777.
- In 1778, the 10-gun British warship *Otter* was wrecked off the east coast of Florida.
- The 20-gun British warship *Mentor* (Captain Robert Deans) was burned at Pensacola in 1781 to prevent her capture by enemy forces.
- In 1793, the 28-gun British frigate *Carysford* (Captain Francis Laforey) was lost at a site now known as Carysfort Reef. The reef, at the northern end of John Pennekamp Coral Reef State Park, Key Largo, is easily identified by a 112-foot steel lighthouse tower.
- The British warship *Fly*, Captain Powoll Pellew, was wrecked on Carysfort Reef in 1805. The entire crew was rescued.

- In 1806, the 10-gun British schooner *Zenobia* was wrecked on the coast of Florida. There were no survivors.
- On January 8, 1815, the 6-gun Spanish ship *Empecinada* (Captain Juan Villacencio) stranded on Amelia Island while trying to enter the harbor. The crew and cargo were saved, but the ship was a total loss.
- The 10-gun Spanish warship *Volador* (Captain Joaquin Veal) carrying a cargo of rifles and assorted goods, grounded after entering Pensacola Bay on March 25, 1815. The ship broke up. Two seamen and her entire cargo were lost.

BIBLIOGRAPHY

Academic American Encyclopedia. Grolier, Inc., 1985.

Allen, Gardner W. *Our Navy and the West Indian Pirates.* Essex Institute, 1929.

"Arms Hidden On the Geir." *New York Times,* February 13, 1917.

Barck, Jr., Oscar, Theodore, and Blake, Nelson. *Since 1900: A History of the United States in Our Times.* The Macmillan Co., 1959.

Barron, David N. *Atlantic Diver Guide.* Atlantic Diver, 1988.

Bayreuther III, William A. "The 1981 Defence Field Season: An Overview." *Underwater Archaeology: The Proceedings of the 13th Conference on Underwater Archaeology.* Fathom Eight, 1984.

Bear, J. "Life and Death of the *Culloden.*" *Weekender,* September 1, 1983.

Beach, Edward L. *The United States Navy—200 years.* Henry Holt & Co., 1986.

Bekker, Cajus. *Hitler's Naval War.* Doubleday & Co., Inc., 1974.

Bell, Mary E. "Wreck of the *Culloden.*" *Long Island Forum,* February 1942.

Botting, Douglas and the editors of Time-Life Books. *The Seafarers: The Pirates.* Time-Life Books, 1978.

Boyd, Ellsworth. "The Sad Saga of the *Jacob Jones.*" *Skin Diver,* October 1982.

"Broken Back. Fate of the *Gallatin* on Boo-Hoo Ledge." *Boston Daily Globe,* January 7, 1892.

"Cadets Dive on *Culloden* Wreck." *East Hampton Star,* October 3, 1974.

Cahill, Robert Ellis. *Finding New England's Shipwrecks and Treasures.* Chandler Smith Publishing House, 1984.

Calkins, Captain. "The Repression of Piracy in the West Indies, 1814-1825." *U.S. Naval Institute Proceedings,* December 1911.

Casey, William J. *Where and How the War Was Fought: An Armchair Tour of the American Revolution.* William Morrow & Co., Inc., 1976.

Cayford, John E. "The Ill-Fated Penobscot Expedition." *Sea Classics,* March/April 1986.

"The Brig Defence: An Underwater Time Capsule of Major Importance." *Skin Diver,* October 1981.

Chapelle, Howard I. *The History of The American Sailing Navy.* Bonanza Books, 1959.

Chevlowe, Susan. "History's Their Hobby." *East Hampton Star*, August 27, 1981.

Coggins, Jack. *Ships and Seamen of the American Revolution.* Stackpole Books, 1969.

Colledge, J. J. *Ships of the Royal Navy.* A.M. Kelley, 1969.

"Cooke Tells Story of 37 Hours in S-5." *New York Times*, September 5, 1920.

Cowburn, Philip. *The Warship in History.* The Macmillan Co., 1965.

"*Culloden* Cannon Returns." *East Hampton Star*, November 14, 1974.

"*Culloden* Dive Fails." *East Hampton Star*, September 11, 1975.

Cush, Cathie. "Historic Shipwreck Project May Be Up A N.J. Creek." *Underwater USA*, November 1986.

"The Wreck Of the *Moonstone* Lures Artifact Divers." *Underwater USA*, April 1987.

Dean, Love. *Reef Lights: Seaswept Lighthouses of the Florida Keys.* The Historic Key West Preservation Board, 1982.

"Decide Mine Sank Cruiser *San Diego*." *New York Times*, August 6, 1918.

Dulin, Jr., Robert O. and Garzke, Jr., William H. *Battleships.* Naval Institute Press, 1976.

Encyclopedia Americana. Grolier Inc., 1988.

Farb, Roderick M. *Shipwrecks: Diving the Graveyard of the Atlantic.* Menosha Ridge Press, 1985.

"Former Local Man Part Of Movie Crew to 'Shipwreck Island.' " *The Glastonbury Citizen*, September 18, 1969.

"49 Lost Off Maine In Navy Ship Blast." *New York Times*, May 9, 1945.

Friedman, Norman. *U.S. Cruisers: An Illustrated Design History.* Naval Institute Press, 1984.

Frink, Stephen. "*Bibb* and *Duane*: Key Largo's Exciting New Wreck Dives." *Skin Diver*, April 1988.

Furneaux, Rupert. *The Pictorial History of the American Revolution.* J.G. Ferguson Publishing Co., 1973.

Gentile, Gary. *Shipwrecks of New Jersey.* Sea Sports Publications, 1988.

Gentile, Gary. *U.S.S. San Diego: The Last Armored Cruiser.* Gary Gentile Productions, 1990.

Gibbons, Tony. *The Complete Encyclopedia of Battleships.* Crescent Books, 1983.

Goodrich, Rear Admiral Caspar F. "Our Navy and West Indian Pirates." *U.S. Naval Institute Proceedings*, July/August 1916 to August 1917.

Gould, R. F. *The Life of Gould, an Ex-Man-Of-War's-Man, with Incidents On Sea And Shore: Including the Three-Year's Cruise of the Line of*

Battleship Ohio, *on the Mediterranean Station, under the Veteran Commodore Hull.* Claremont Manufacturing Co., 1867.

Graves, Jack. "*Culloden* Cannon Recovered." *East Hampton Star,* October 4, 1973.

Gruppe, Henry E., and the editors of Time-Life Books. *The Seafarers: The Frigates.* Time-Life Books, 1979.

"Gunboat Engines Wrecked." *New York Times,* February 6, 1917.

Hanks, Carlos C. "The German Gunboat That Became A Yankee." *U.S. Naval Institute Proceedings,* September 1934.

Haviland, Jean. "The Lady Loves Wrecks." *Atlantic Coastal Diver,* December 1980.

Hess, Peter. "A Legend Found: The Salvage of H.M.S. *DeBraak.*" *Seafarers: Journal of Maritime Heritage,* 1987.

Hoehling, A. A. *The Great War at Sea: A History of Naval Action 1914-18.* Galahad Books, 1965.

Hucker, Robert. "Battle of the Lend-Lease Destroyers." *Sea Classics,* May 1986.

"In Collision with a Technicality." *New York Times,* October 25, 1918.

Jackson, John W. *The Pennsylvania Navy, 1775-1781: The Defense of the Delaware.* Rutgers University Press, 1974.

Keatts, Henry. *New England's Legacy of Shipwrecks.* American Merchant Marine Museum Press, 1988.

Kirby, Al. "Wrecks of Nova Scotia." *Diver,* March 1989.

Kitchen, Jr., Ruben P. "The First Destroyer." *Sea Classics,* June 1985.

Laing, Alexander. *Seafaring America.* American Heritage Publishing Co., 1974.

Lancaster, Bruce. *The American Heritage Book of The Revolution.* American Heritage Publishing Co., 1971.

Leckie, Robert. *The Wars of America.* Harper & Row, Publishers, 1981.

"Lost Bonds of the *San Diego*'s Men." *New York Times,* January 14, 1919.

Marx, Robert F. *The Underwater Dig: An Introduction to Marine Archaeology.* Pisces Books/Gulf Publishing Co., 1990.

Marx, Robert F. *Shipwrecks of the Western Hemisphere.* David McKay Co., Inc., 1975.

Mayhew, Dean R. "The *Defense.* Search and Recovery, 1972-73." *Nautical Archaeology,* 1974.

Merkel, Jim. "Officials Sorting Through *DeBraak* Artifacts." *Underwater USA,* March 1988.

McCarthy, Jerry. "100 Years Beneath the Sea." *The Suffolk Times,* July 26, 1984.

McLennan, J. S. *Louisbourg From Its Foundation To Its Fall.* Fortress Press, 1969.

Middlekauff, Robert. *The Glorious Cause: The American Revolution 1763-1789.* Oxford University Press, 1982.

"Mine Sank San Diego, Sec'y Daniels Thinks."*New York Times*, July 21, 1918.

Moeller, Henry W., and Giordano, Steven A. "The Search for the *Culloden.*" *Natural History Magazine*, December, 1976.

Morgan, William James. *Naval Documents of the American Revolution. Volume 9.* Government Printing Office, 1986.

Mulvaney, Jim. "As Souvenirs Go, This Was Dynamite."*Newsday*, June 2, 1982.

Naval History Division. *American Ships Of The Line.* Navy Department, 1969.

Dictionary of American Naval Fighting Ships. Office of the Chief of Naval Operations, 1969.

"*Ohio* Goes Once Again Into Battle." *The Suffolk Times*, December 15, 1977.

Parking, H. Sinclair. "Yankee Destroyers Under the White Ensign."*Sea Classics*, July 1987.

Pratt, Fletcher. *The Compact History of the United States Navy.* Hawthorn Books, Inc., 1967.

Preston, Antony. *Destroyers.* Prentice-Hall, 1977.

Preston, Antony, Lyon, David, and Batchelor, John H. *Navies of the American Revolution.* Prentice-Hall Inc., 1975.

Quinn, William P. *Shipwrecks Around New England.* The Lower Cape Publishing Co., 1979.

Raguso, John. "Atlantic Wreck Series: U.S.S. *Turner.*" *The Fisherman*, June 6th/12th, 1985.

"Raised Wreck Gives View of 1790's Shipboard Life."*Houston Chronicle*, February 21, 1989.

Rattray, Jeannette Edwards. *Ship Ashore!* Yankee Peddler Book Company, 1955.

"*Culloden* Wreck Identity Is Definite." *East Hampton Star*, August 5, 1971.

Reynolds, Clark G. *War of the American Revolution, 1763-1783.* William Morrow & Co., Inc., 1974.

Robbins, William. "18th-Century Wreck Yields Gold Ring and Trove of Coins." *New York Times*, September 18, 1984.

Roscoe, Theodore. *Tin Cans: U.S. Destroyer Operations in WWII.* Bantam Books, 1968.

Saltus, Allen R. "Old Silver Wreck Is Poor in Coins But Rich in History." *Archives and History News*, March/April 1970.

"The *San Diego*, Sunk Off Long Island." *New York Times*, July 20, 1918.

"*San Diego*'s Dead May Number 62." *New York Times*, July 22, 1918.

San Diego's Loss Still Unexplained; 1,183 Reach Port.'' *New York Times,* July 21, 1918.

Scheibel, Bill. "Sub Sinks Destroyer Off New Jersey Coast, Many Lost." *Sealift,* October 1971.

Scheina, Robert L. *U.S. Coast Guard Cutters & Craft of World War II.* Naval Institute Press, 1982.

Schmitt, Frederick P. *Diving For The Shipwreck Of H.M.S.* Culloden *At Montauk.* Club Sous-Marin of Long Island, 1961.

Schmitt, Frederick P., and Schmid, Donald E. *H.M.S. Culloden.* The Marine Historical Association, Inc., 1961.

"*Schurz* Sunk In Collision." *New York Times,* June 22, 1918.

"Ship Sunk Off L.I. in 1918 May Be Salvaged."*New York Herald Tribune,* July 12, 1955.

"Six Lost On The *San Diego.*" *New York Times,* July 25, 1918.

Stember, Sol. *The Bicentennial Guide to the American Revolution, Volume 1.* E.P. Dutton & Co., Inc., 1974.

Sweetman, Jack. *American Naval History.* Naval Institute Press, 1984.

Swesie, Stu, and Davidson, Carlton. *The Second Battle of the* Culloden. Unpublished.

Switzer, David C. "Defence Project Symposium: Introduction."*Underwater Archaeology: The Proceedings of the 13th Conference on Underwater Archaeology.* Fathom Eight, 1984.

"Tells of Raiders Start."*New York Times,* August 30, 1918.

Throckmorton, Peter. *The Sea Remembers: Shipwrecks and Archaeology.* Weidenfeld & Nicolson, 1987.

"To Reissue Bonds Lost on *San Diego.*" *New York Times,* July 17, 1919.

"U-Boats Sink Three American Schooners; Germans Say Mine Sank Cruiser *San Diego.*" *New York Times,* August 5, 1918.

"U-Boat Sinks U.S. Destroyer Off Cape May; All But 11 Lost."*New York Times,* March 4, 1942.

Wheeler, Richard. *In Pirate Waters.* Thomas Y. Crowell Company, 1969.

Whipple, A. B. C., and the editors of Time-Life Books. *The Seafarers: Fighting Sail.* Time-Life Books, 1978.

Wilson, Sandy. "*Duane* and *Bibb* Challenge Divers, Operators." *Underwater USA,* February 1988.

Wood, Dr. Clarence A. "The Story of a Figurehead."*Long Island Forum,* September 1950.

"Wreck of the Revenue Steamer *Albert Gallatin.*" *Gloucester Daily Times,* January 8, 1892.

Wukovits, John F. "Life On A Bull's-Eye." *Military History,* December 1988.

Zimmerman, Gene T. "The Last Ram." *Sea Classics,* September 1971.

INDEX

Abbreviations and Symbols

AC—armored cruiser
AH—hospital ship
AKA—attack cargo ship
AM—steel-hulled mine-
sweeper
AuxCr—auxiliary cruiser
BB—battleship
BB 2/c—second class battle-
ship
Bk—bark
Br—barge
Brig—brigantine
Cl—colonial warship
Cr—cruiser
C.S.S.—Confederate
States Ship
CV—aircraft carrier
CVL—small aircraft carrier
DD—destroyer

DE—destroyer escort
Fr—frigate
Gl—galleon
H.M.—His/Her Majesty's
H.M.C.S.—His/Her
Majesty's Canadian Ship
H.M.S.—His/Her
Majesty's Ship
Irc—ironclad
LC—light cruiser
PE—eagle boat
Pr—privateer
PYc—patrol craft
RC—revenue cutter
Rm—ram
SC—subchaser
ScFr—screw frigate
Sch—schooner
ScSlp—screw sloop

ScStr—screw steamer
SL—ship-of-the-line
Sla—slave ship
Slp—sloop
SP—coastal patrol vessel
SS—submarine; or mer-
chant steamship
Tb—torpedo boat
Tk—tanker
Unk—warship of unknown
rating
U.S.C.G.—United States
Coast Guard
U.S.S.—United States Ship
YMS—wood-hulled mine-
sweeper
YP—converted yacht

Acteon, H.M. frigate, 233
Active, H.M. frigate, 218
Admiral Scheer (BB), 146
Adventure, H.M. brig, 30
Aeolis (Tk), 157
Aircraft carriers, 6, 10, 111–115,
117
Alabama (RC), 164
Alabama (SL), U.S.S., 48, 59, 63,
64. See also U.S.S. *New Hamp-
shire.*
Alarm, H.M. galley, 13, 223
Albermarle (Irc), C.S.S., 8
Albert Gallatin (RC), 208–210
"Alexander," 208
Allen, Lt. William H., 71, 72
Allentown, Florida, 72. See also
Key West, Florida.

Alligator Reef, Florida, 72
Alligator (Sch), U.S.S., 67–73
location, 67, 72, 73
sinking, 72
Amaranth, H.M. sloop, 201
America (SL), 45
America (SL), H.M.S., 29, 30
American Littoral Society, 101
American Revolution, 11, 22, 28,
45, 190
American Ships of the Line, 47
Andrea Doria (Cl), 228
Andrews, Vice-Admiral Adolphus,
135
Aquidneck Island, R.I., 13, 14
Arbuthnot, Admiral Marriot, 27–29,
31, 233
Arnold, Capt. C.H., 93

Asama (AC), 83

Assiniboine (DD), H.M.C.S., 208

Association of Marine Angling
   Clubs, 101

Astrea (Unk), H.M.S., 181

Atalante, H.M. sloop, 220

Augusta (SL), H.M.S., 182–186

Bainbridge (DD-*1*), U.S.S., 9, 150

Balfour, Capt. George, 24, 29–31

Bancroft (DD-*256*), U.S.S., 145, 146

Banterer (Unk), H.M.S., 219

Barbadoes, H.M. frigate, 219

Barker, First Lt. Iben, 159

Bataan (CVL-*29*), U.S.S., 113

Battleships, 4–7, 10, 47, 75, 83,
   203–207, 230–232

Beaufort Inlet, N.C., 81, 88

Bedford (SL), H.M.S., 29, 30

Bedfordshire, H.M. trawler, 214, 215

Bell (DD-*587*), U.S.S., 120

Berg, Dan, 106

Bibb, U.S.C.G. cutter, 163, 165,
   166, 168, 172–174
   location, 163, 173
   sinking, 173

Biddle, Commodore, 70

Bielenda, Capt. Steve, 56, 102, 104,
   106, 107

Bienfaisant (Fr), 218

Bismark (BB), 6

Black (DD-*666*), U.S.S., 137

Black, Jr., Lt. Cmdr. Hugh P., 135,
   137

Blonde, H.M. frigate, 218

Bold (Unk), H.M.S., 220

Boston Navy Yard, 48, 50, 54, 68

Bountiful (AH-*9*), U.S.S., 117

Brenner, Mel, 175

Bricole (Cl), 233

Brigantines, 25, 44, 72, 192, 201,
   218

British Sub Aqua Club, 55, 56

Bronx (RC), 224

Bunker Hill (CV-*17*), U.S.S., 114–
   117, 150 Bushnell, David, 17

Buzzards Bay, Massachusetts, 74,
   78, 79

Byron, Vice Admiral John, 25

California (AC-*6*), U.S.S., 92–95,
   105, 107. See also U.S.S. *San
   Diego.*

Cannon, Lt. John, 29

Cardenas, Battle of, 164

Carpentier, Ralph, 39, 41

Carter, Bill, 66, 80, 147, 210

Carysford, H.M. frigate, 234

Carysford Reef, Florida, 72, 234

Casalino, Mike, 58, 148

Castle del Ray (Pr), 227

Cayo Hueso, Florida, 71. See also
   Key West, Florida.

Cembrola, Bob, 20, 21, 22

Celebre (SL), 181, 182

Centaur (SL), H.M.S., 28

Cerberus, H.M. frigate, 11, 13, 15–
   17, 19, 20
   location, 11, 17, 20
   sinking, 16

Chapelle, Howard I., 46, 47, 50

Charles S. Sperry (DD-*697*),
   U.S.S., 115

Charon, H.M. frigate, 228

Cheveaux de Frize (Unk), 223

Christy, Capt. H.H., 92, 95, 96, 98,
   99

Chubb (Unk), H.M.S., 219

Cibilo, 221

Cienega (Pr), 70

Civil War, 3, 8, 48, 59, 60, 217,
   224, 230

Clancy, Dave, 210

Cleveland (LC), U.S.S., 111

Clancy, Dave, 65

Clinton, Lt. General Sir Henry, 31

Columbus (CA-*74*), U.S.S., 120

Conanicut Island, Rhode Island, 13,
   14, 18

Congress (Cl), 223

Congress (Fr), 229

Constellation (Fr), U.S.S., 46

Constitution (Fr), U.S.S., 46, 64.
   See also "Old Ironsides."

Cook, Capt. James, 39

Cooper, Chip, 193, 219

Cornwallis, General, 12
Coventry, H.M. frigate, 13
Crenshaw, Capt. Arthur, 86
Cruiser, H.M. sloop, 233
Cruisers, 5–8, 75, 81, 91–94, 96, 98–100, 106, 109, 111–115, 117–120, 129–131
C.S.S. *Albermarle* (Irc), 8
C.S.S. *Hunley* (SS), 8
C.S.S. *Merrimac* (Irc), 3, 4, 230
Culloden, Battle of, 23
Culloden, H.M.S., 23–34, 36–38, 40–42
    location, 23, 29, 31, 40
    sinking, 29
Curtis, Lt. W.R.S., 177, 179
Cushing, Lt. William B., 8
Cutters, 153, 163–168, 172–175, 208–210
Cuttle (Unk), H.M.S., 220
Dale, Lt. John M., 72
Daniels, Josephus, (Sec. of the Navy), 62
Daphne (Sla), 70.
Davidson, Carlton, 33, 35–39
Davis, Al, 19, 20, 22
Deans, Billy, 109, 110, 131
DeBraak, H.M. brig, 187
DeCamp, Michael, 102, 104, 106, 138, 161, 162, 179, 195, 197
Defence (Cl), 190, 192, 220
Defiance (SL), H.M.S., 234
Delaware (SL), U.S.S., 48
Delight (Unk), H.M.S., 217
Deptford, H.M. sloop, 228
D'Estaing, Comte, 12, 13, 18
Destroyers, 5–10, 114, 115, 117, 120, 132, 139, 140, 144–146, 149–154, 208
Devlin, Cmdr. John, 173
Diana, H.M. schooner, 221
Diligent, H.M. brig, 218
Dispatch, H.M. sloop, 218
"Divine Wind," 114. See also Kamikazes.
Dixon, Lt. George E., 8
Doenitz, Admiral Karl, 144

Dolphin (Cl), 228
Dolphin (Sch), U.S.S., 68
Doughty, William, 49, 50, 68
Duane, U.S.C.G. cutter, 163, 165–168, 171–175
    location, 163, 173
    sinking, 173
Eagle Boat 17 (PE-*17*), U.S.S., 220, 226, 227
Eagle Boat 56 (PE-*56*), U.S.S., 220, 221
Earl of Bute, H.M. frigate, 234
Eckford, Henry, 49
Effingham (Cl), 227
El Mulato (Pr), 234
El Norte (SS), 75. See also U.S.S. *Yankee*.
Empecinada (Unk), 235
Emulous (Unk), H.M.S., 219
English (DD-*696*), U.S.S., 115
Entreprenant (SL), 181, 182
Eurus, H.M. frigate, 217
Falcon, H.M. sloop, 15, 17
    sinking, 17
Fantasque (SL), 14
Fantome, H.M. sloop, 220
Ferret, H.M. frigate, 181
Feversham, H.M. frigate, 181
Fire Island Inlet, N.Y., 91
First World War, 99. See also World War I and "Great War."
Fisher, Sir John, 5
Flora, H.M. frigate, 15, 17, 19
    location, 17, 19
    sinking, 17, 19
Flore (Pr), 19. See also H.M. frigate *Flora* and *Vestale*.
Florida, 86–88
Florida (Cr), U.S.S., 7
Fly (Unk), H.M.S., 234
Fort Pond Bay, N.Y., 29, 41
Fowey (Unk), H.M.S., 234
Franklin (CV-*13*), U.S.S., 113, 117
French Revolution, 45
Frigates, 6, 12–19, 26, 44–47, 181, 186, 192, 217, 220–224, 227–229, 234

Frink, Stephen, 172
Fubuki (DD), 10
Fuerte (Gl), 234
Galleys, 13–15, 18, 19, 183, 184, 223
Gardiner's Bay, N.Y., 28, 30, 32
Gardiner's Island, N.Y., 28–31
Garland (Unk), H.M.S., 230
Gaspee, H.M. schooner, 221
Geier (LC), 81–83, 85, 86, 88. See also U.S.S. *Schurz*.
General Arnold (Pr), 189, 190
General Moultrie (Cl), 233
Gentile, Gary, 5
Gloire (Irc), 3, 229
Gniesenau (AC), 82
Gniesenau (BB), 6
Goat Island, R.I., 16, 18
Graf Spee (BB), 6
Grampus (Sch), U.S.S., 70
Granite State (SL), U.S.S., 61, 63, 64. See also U.S.S. *New Hampshire*.
    training ship 62
Grasshof, Capt. Karl, 83
Graves, Admiral, 12, 31
Graves Island, Massachusetts, 59, 64, 66
"Great War," 81. See also World War I, and First World War.
Greenport, N.Y., 43, 53–56
Greer (DD), U.S.S., 178
Grey, 4th Lt. Ralph, 29, 30
Grouse (YMS-*321*), U.S.S., 210–213
Guadeloupe, H.M. frigate, 228
Guerriere (Fr), U.S.S., 229
Guipuscoano (SL), 26
Gunboats, 6, 46, 76, 81–83, 85, 86, 88
Gustafson, Christine, 38
Haihachiro, Admiral Togo, 4
Halifax, H.M. schooner, 220
Hamilton, Alexander, 45, 46
Hamilton, U.S.C.G. cutter, 168
Hancock (Fr), U.S.S., 44
Harriet Lane (RC), 164
Hart (DD-*594*), U.S.S., 120

Hay, John, (Sec. of State), 76
Hazard, H.M. sloop, 221
Hegeman, Don, 32
Herring (Unk), H.M.S., 220
Hess, Peter, 187, 188
History of the American Sailing Navy, The, 46, 47, 50
History Under the Sea, 38
Hizen (BB), 83
Hood (BB), H.M.S., 6
Hope (Unk), H.M.S., 234
Hornet (CV-*12*), U.S.S., 113
Housatonic (ScSlp), U.S.S., 8
Howard, Admiral Thomas B., 95
Howe, Admiral Lord Richard, 12, 13, 15, 16, 18, 25
Howell, Lt. Cmdr., Glenn F., 87
Hudson, Capt. Charles, 17
Hulburt, Jon, 104, 193, 195, 199, 200
Hull, Commodore Issac, 52, 69
Hunley (SS), C.S.S., 8
Hunter (Unk), H.M.S., 229
Huron (Slp), U.S.S., 201
Hussar, H.M. frigate, 224
Impetueux (SL), 229
Inconstant (Cr), H.M.S., 7
Independence (Cl), 228
Independence (CV-*22*), U.S.S., 111
Iris, H.M. frigate, 44
Iron Duke (BB), H.M.S., 5
Iwo Jima, 112, 113
Jacob Jones (DD-*61*), U.S.S., 132–133
Jacob Jones (DE-*130*), U.S.S., 132–138
Jane (Sch), 70
Jellicoe, Admiral Sir John, 5
Jenkins, Scott, 179
Jones, Capt. Jacob, 132, 133
Jones, Commodore Thomas Gatsbey, 52, 53
Judan (Gl), 234
Juno, H.M. frigate, 13, 15, 17, 19, 22, 223
    location, 17
    sinking, 17

Jutland, Battle of, 5
K-3 (SS-*34*), U.S.S., 86
K-4 (SS-*35*), U.S.S., 86
K-7 (SS-*38*), U.S.S., 86
K-8 (SS-*39*), U.S.S., 86
Kamikazes, 114, 115, 117–119, 213.
   See also "Divine Wind."
Katahdin (Rm), U.S.S., 230
Kearney, Capt. L., 50
Keatts, Carole, 55
Keen, Capt. Larry, 179
Key West Diver, Inc., 131
Key West, Florida, 72, 76, 86, 108,
   129, 140. See also Cayo Hueso,
   and Allentown.
King Fisher, H.M. sloop, 13–15, 223
Kissling, Sharon, 106
Knight, Paul, 35, 36
Koenigsberg (LC), 82
Kohler, Richie, 106
Kuribayashi, General Tadamichi, 113
Lachenmeyer, Capt. John, 104–106
L'Abenaquise (Fr), 217
L'Africaine (Fr), 220
L'Aimable (Fr), 14
L'Alemene (Fr), 14
Languedoc (SL), 19
Lark, H.M. frigate, 13, 15–17, 19,
   20, 223
   location, 17, 223
   sinking, 17, 223
Le Chameau (Unk), 181
Lehigh Valley 402 (Br), 103
L'Eliza (Sch), 70.
"Lend lease," 144, 145, 214
Leopard, H.M. frigate, 220
Leopard (SL), 218
"Lethal Lady," 108, 111, 129, 131.
   See also U.S.S. *Wilkes-Barre*.
Leyte Gulf, 6
Lightning (Tb), U.S.S., 8
Liverpool, H.M. frigate, 223, 224
London (Unk), H.M.S., 233
Lone Star, 176, 177, 179. See also
   U.S.S. *Moonstone*.
Louisiana (RC), 164
Lowestaft, H.M. frigate, 217

Luce, Commodore Stephen B., 61
Luther, Brad, 212
Lynx (Unk), H.M.S., 218
Magnifico, 221
Mahan, Capt. Alfred, 74
Mahan (DD-*102*), U.S.S., 10
Maine (BB 2/c), U.S.S., 75
Manifest Destiny, 74
Manila Bay, Battle of, 164
Marchault (Fr), 218
Mariano Foliero (Pr), 70
Marianna Flora (Pr), 70
Marosa (Bk), 98
Marquis Marlose (Slp), 218
Mars (SL), H.M.S., 217
Massachusetts (BB-2), U.S.S, 76,
   138, 139
Mathilde (Sla), 70.
McCain, Vice-Admiral John S., 112,
   119
Mentor (Unk), H.M.S., 234
Mercury, H.M. frigate, 223
Merlin, H.M. sloop, 182–185
Merrimac (Irc), C.S.S., 34, 230
Mexican War, 52
Miller, Bob, 33–35, 41
Miranda, H.M. torpedo boat, 8
Mitchell, General William "Billy,"
   5, 6, 230
Mitscher, Vice-Admiral Marc A.,
   112, 113, 117, 119
Moeller, Dr. Henry, 37, 38, 41
Mohawk (RC), 158–160
   location, 158, 160
   sinking, 159, 160
Monitor (Irc), U.S.S., 3, 4
Monroe Doctrine, 134
Montgomery (Cl), 223
Moonstone (PYc-*9*), U.S.S., 176–
   179. See also *Lone Star*.
   location, 176, 178
   sinking, 178
Morison, Eliot, 114
Mosquito (Cl), 228
Murphy, Ed, 106
Murphy, Roger, 147
Mushashi (BB), 6

Narcissus, H.M. frigate, 164
Narragansett Bay, R.I., 11, 13, 16
National Naval Volunteers, 62
National Party Boat Owners Association, 101
Naval Explosive Ordnance Disposal Team, 107
New Hampshire (SL), U.S.S., 48–61, 63–66, 68, 75. See also U.S.S. *Granite State*.
  location, 59, 64–66
  receiving ship, 48, 61
  sinking, 63, 64
  training ship 61
New Jersey (BB-*16*), U.S.S., 231, 233
New London, Connecticut, 17, 31, 61
New York Navy Yard, 48, 75–77
New York State Naval Militia, 61, 62, 75
New York (SL), U.S.S., 48
Newport, R.I., 13–19, 21, 27–29, 61
Norfolk Navy Yard, 48, 76
North Carolina (SL), U.S.S., 48
Northern Pacific (SS), 138
Notre Dame (Cl), 233
Nuestra Senora de Concepcion y San Josefe (Fr), 234
O.B. Jennings (Tk), 100
Ohio (SL), U.S.S., 43, 48–56, 58, 59, 63, 65, 66, 68
  location, 43, 54–57
  receiving ship, 53
  sinking, 54
Okinawa, 112–115, 118
"Old Ironsides" (Fr), 52. See also U.S.S. *Constitution*.
Olish, George, 35
Orpheus, H.M. frigate, 11, 13, 15–17, 19–21
Ostriesland (BB), 5
Otter (Unk), H.M.S., 234
Our Navy at War, 62
Patience (Pr), 224
Patterson, Commodore Daniel C., 68
Paulding (DD-*22*), U.S.S., 9

Pearl Harbor, Hawaii, 3, 6, 83, 86, 112, 120
Peacock (Unk), H.M.S., 233
Peterson, Mendel, 38
PC-11, U.S.S., 214
PC-1203, U.S.S., 214
Pentland Firth, H.M. trawler, 214, 215
Phaeton, H.M.S., 19
Philadelphia Navy Yard, 48, 68, 76, 109, 111, 112, 120, 121
Phoenix (Unk), H.M.S., 203
Pigot, General Sir Robert, 13, 15, 16
Pigot, H.M. galley, 223
Pirates, 46, 67, 68, 70–73, 164
Plumper (Unk), H.M.S., 219
Porpoise (Sch), U.S.S., 68
Porter, Capt. David, 68, 71, 72
Porter, Jr., Capt. Robert L., 111, 115
Porter (DD), U.S.S., 10
Portsmouth Navy Yard, 68, 92, 95
Prince of Wales (BB), H.M.S., 6
Prince William (SL), H.M.S., 26
Privateers, 19, 28, 44, 67, 70, 189, 190, 224, 227, 229, 233, 234
Prudence Island, R.I., 16
Purifoy, George, 88
Quinn, William P. 78, 79, 165, 202
Rainbow, H.M. frigate, 44
Randolph (Fr), U.S.S., 44
Rankin (AKA-*103*), U.S.S., 215, 216
Redbridge, H.M. schooner, 223
Rehwinkel, Korvettenkapitan E.A., 134, 136, 137
Revanche du Cerf (Pr), 229
Rose, Kapitanleutnant Hans, 133
Renown (SL), H.M.S., 19
R.P. Resor (Tk), 136
Report 508, Restoration of Cannon and Other Relics from H.M.B. Endeavor, 39
Repulse (BB), H.M.S., 6
Revere, Paul, 64–66
Rhode Island Naval Militia, 78
Rodney, Admiral George Brydges, 26–29
Rose (Unk), H.M.S., 233

Rover, H.M. sloop, 218
Royal Oak (SL), H.M.S., 29, 30
Russel (SL), H.M.S., 28
Russo–Japanese War, 3
Sachem (Cl), 228
St. Clair (DD), H.M.C.S., 146
St. Francis (DD), H.M.C.S., 143, 145–148
  location, 143, 146
  sinking, 146
St. Lawrence, H.M. schooner, 218
Sagittaire (SL), 14
Sakonnet River, R.I., 14
San Diego (AC-*6*), U.S.S, 91–104, 106, 107. See also U.S.S. *California.*
  location, 91, 103
  sinking, 91–93, 95–100
Sandy, H.M. brig, 25
San Marcos (BB 2/c), U.S.S., 204–207. See also U.S.S. *Texas.*
Saramacca (SS), 87, 88
Savage, H.M. sloop, 218
SC-60, U.S.S., 227
SC-209, U.S.S., 225
Scharnhorst (BB), 6
Scheer, Vice Admiral Rheinhard, 5
Schmid, Donald E., 31–33
Schmitt, Frederick P., 31–33, 34, 37
Schnell, Don, 106
Schooners, 44, 67, 68, 70–73, 218, 220–223
Schurz, Carl, 83
Schurz (LC), U.S.S., 81, 83, 86–89. See also *Geier.*
  location, 81, 88
  sinking, 86–88
Seitz, Capt. George A., 117
Senateur Duhamel, H.M. trawler, 214
Seven Year War, 11
Shark (Sch), U.S.S., 68
Sheard, Brad, 89, 90, 105, 123, 124, 129, 194, 198
Sherman, Mrs. Paul, 212
Ship Ashore, 32

Ships-of-the-line, 3, 6, 12, 16–18, 23, 24, 26, 27, 30, 47–49, 51–54, 58, 59, 62, 63, 75, 180, 182, 202, 217, 218, 229, 234
Shrewsbury (SL), H.M.S., 28
Skerry, Brian, 179
Slavers, 69, 70
Sloops, 13–15, 17, 19, 44, 46, 184, 190, 201, 218, 221, 223, 228, 233, 234 Smith, Capt. Joseph, 50, 52
Smith (DD-*17*), U.S.S., 9
Solebay, H.M. frigate, 221
Somerset (SL), H.M.S., 202
Somerville, Sir James, (British Admiral of the Fleet), 145
Southport (SS), 82, 83
Spanish-American War, 61, 74, 77, 80, 203
Spee, Admiral von, 82
Spencer, U.S.C.G. cutter, 167, 168, 170, 171
Spitfire, H.M. galley, 14, 223
Stanley (Brig), 14
Stembel (DD-*644*), U.S.S., 115
Still, John, 37
Stockton, Lt. Robert F., 69–71
Stoddert, Benjamin, (Sec. of the Navy), 46
Strength (AM-*309*), U.S.S., 213
Stribling, Commodore Cornelius K., 53
Stringham, Capt. Silas H., 52
Sturtevant, Albert D., 139
Sturtevant (DD-*240*), U.S.S., 139–141
  location, 139, 141
  sinking, 140, 141
Submarines 6, 8, 17, 86, 91–96, 98–100, 108, 120, 133–137, 143, 151, 167–170, 213
Sullivan, General John, 13, 18
Surveyor (RC), 164
Sylph, H.M. sloop, 224
Symons, Capt. John, 16, 17
Syren, H.M. frigate, 222
Swasey (DE-*248*), U.S.S., 152–154

Tampa (RC), 164
Tarantula (SP-*124*), U.S.S., 213, 214
Tenaglia, Lt. Joseph, 107
Terrible (SL), H.M.S., 217, 229
Texas (BB 2/c), U.S.S., 5, 203, 204.
   See also U.S.S. *San Marcos*.
Thatcher, Commodore Henry K.,
   59, 61
Thetis (Unk), H.M.S., 233
Thistle (Unk), H.M.S., 224
Tilbury (SL), H.M.S., 217
Tirpitz,D (BB), 6
Torpedo boats, 6, 8, 9, 76
Toth, Geo, 172–174
Treaty of Alliance, The, 12
Treaty of Paris, 11, 12
Tribune, H.M. frigate, 186, 187
Trumbull (Fr), U.S.S., 44
Tryal, H.M. schooner, 222
Turner, Capt. Daniel, 149, 150
Turner (DD-*648*), U.S.S., 149–157
   location, 149, 151, 155, 157
   sinking, 151–155
Turtle (SS), 17
Tyger (Unk), H.M.S., 234
U-53 (SS), 133, 164, 224
U-100 (SS), 100
U-102 (SS), 100
U-117 (SS), 100
U-132 (SS), 168
U-140 (SS), 100
U-156 (SS), 91, 92, 99, 100
U-175 (SS), 167, 168, 170, 171
U-578 (SS), 134, 136, 137
U-853 (SS), 221
Underwater Explosions Research Di-
   vision, 108, 109, 121
Unicorn (Unk), 19
Vermont (SL), U.S.S., 48, 61
   receiving ship, 48
Vestale (Fr), 19
Vigilant (Pr), 233
Viper, H.M. sloop, 218
Virginia (BB-*13*), U.S.S., 231–233
Virginia (SL), U.S.S., 48
   Volador (Unk), 235

Vulcan, H.M. fire ship, 228
Wampanoag (Cr), U.S.S., 7
War of 1812, 46, 50, 52, 132, 133,
   149, 150, 164
Warren (Cl), 190, 192
Warren (Fr), U.S.S., 44
Warsen, David, 33–35, 41
Washington (BB), U.S.S., 5
Washington (Cl), 227
Washington (Pr), 28
Washington, General George, 12,
   13, 28, 31, 39, 45, 46
Washington Naval Conference, 5, 7,
   9
Washington Navy Yard, 49, 68
Wasp (Cl), 228
Wells, Cmdr. W.B., 86, 87
When the U-boats Came to America,
   100
Whitehead, Robert, 8
Wilkes-Barre (CL-*103*), U.S.S., 108–
   124, 129–131
   location, 108, 129, 131
   sinking, 109, 129
William, H.M. storeship, 218
William, H.M. transport, 30
Winchester (SL), H.M.S., 180
Windind Gulf (SS), 146
Wolf, H.M. sloop, 234
World War I, 4, 7, 9, 62, 91, 94,
   95, 132, 145, 158, 164, 207,
   224, 225, 228. See also "Great
   War," and First World War.
"World War I Wreck," 88
World War II, 6, 8, 10, 108, 111,
   112, 114, 129, 131, 133, 134,
   140, 143, 149, 165, 166, 168,
   169, 177, 210, 220, 221, 226,
   228
Wygant, Lt. Cmdr. Henry, 151
Yankee (AuxCr), U.S.S., 74–79. See
   also *El Norte*.
Yarmouth (SL), H.M.S., 44
YP-387, U.S.S., 228
Zebra, H.M. sloop, 190
Zenobia, H.M. schooner, 235